Deep Learning with R Cookbook

Over 45 unique recipes to delve into neural network
techniques using R 3.5.x

Swarna Gupta
Rehan Ali Ansari
Dipayan Sarkar

BIRMINGHAM - MUMBAI

Deep Learning with R Cookbook

Commissioning Editor: Sunith Shetty
Acquisition Editor: Yogesh Deokar
Content Development Editor: Nathanya Dias
Senior Editor: Ayaan Hoda
Technical Editor: Joseph Sunil
Copy Editor: Safis Editing
Project Coordinator: Aishwarya Mohan
Proofreader: Safis Editing
Indexer: Priyanka Dhadke
Production Designer: Jyoti Chauhan

First published: February 2020

Production reference: 1210220

Published by Packt Publishing Ltd.
Livery Place
35 Livery Street
Birmingham
B3 2PB, UK.

ISBN 978-1-78980-567-3

www.packt.com

Packt.com

Subscribe to our online digital library for full access to over 7,000 books and videos, as well as industry-leading tools to help you plan your personal development and advance your career. For more information, please visit our website.

Why subscribe?

- Spend less time learning and more time coding with practical eBooks and Videos from over 4,000 industry professionals

- Improve your learning with Skill Plans built especially for you

- Get a free eBook or video every month

- Fully searchable for easy access to vital information

- Copy and paste, print, and bookmark content

Did you know that Packt offers eBook versions of every book published, with PDF and ePub files available? You can upgrade to the eBook version at www.packt.com and as a print book customer, you are entitled to a discount on the eBook copy. Get in touch with us at customercare@packtpub.com for more details.

At www.packt.com, you can also read a collection of free technical articles, sign up for a range of free newsletters, and receive exclusive discounts and offers on Packt books and eBooks.

Foreword

Data and AI give the best hope to the toughest problems that the world faces today. Am I making a sweeping statement? Not really—it's a modest statement of fact. From robotics to self-driving cars, farming that alleviates world hunger, to finding a solution to early diagnostics to critical illness—deep learning is one of the most enthralling areas of discovery and disruption. It has also fuelled the transformation of numerous businesses such as media and entertainment, insurance, healthcare, retail, education, and information technology.

This book is the perfect material for every data science enthusiast who wants to understand the concepts of deep learning: with R codes explained comprehensibly, it is the best place to start. The authors have maintained a perfect balance between theoretical and practical aspects of deep learning algorithms and applications. It turned out to be a great read—thanks to the easy flow of various sections such as Getting Ready, How to Do it, and How it Works.
After starting with some good insights on how to set up a deep learning environment in a local system, the authors address how the reader can leverage various cloud platforms such as AWS, Microsoft Azure, and Google Cloud to scale deep learning applications. If you are looking for some quick thoughts on any topic, you can read any chapter individually without getting bogged about the sequence.

An interesting fact about this book is that it not only covers the generic topics of deep learning such as CNN, RNN, GAN, Autoencoders but also throws light on specific state-of-the-art techniques such as transfer learning and reinforcement learning. I like the practical examples in the chapters: Working with Convolutional Networks, Deep Generative models, Working with Text and Audio and NLP. They are bound to kindle some thought-starters on what can be done using image and text data. The data sets are very aptly chosen for the examples provided.

Overall, this book is an engaging and inspiring read. I congratulate the writers of the book-Swarna, Rehan, and Dipayan for their contribution to this field of study and I look forward to more such works from them.

Pradeep Jayaraman

Head of Analytics, Adani Ports & SEZ

Contributors

About the authors

Swarna Gupta holds a BE in computer science and has 6 years' experience in data science. She is currently working with Rolls Royce as a data scientist. Her work revolves around leveraging deep learning and machine learning to create value for the business. She has extensively worked on IoT-based projects in the vehicle telematics and solar manufacturing industries. During her current association with Rolls Royce, she implemented various deep learning techniques to build advanced analytics capabilities in the aerospace domain. Swarna also manages to find the time in her busy schedule to be a regular pro-bono contributor to social organizations, helping them to solve specific business problems with the help of data science and machine learning.

Rehan Ali Ansari has a BE in electrical and electronics engineering with 5 years' experience in data science. He is currently associated with digital competency at AP Moller Maersk Group in the capacity of a data scientist. Rehan has a diverse background of working across multiple domains including fashion and retail, IoT, the renewable energy sector, trade finance, and supply chain management. Rehan is a firm believer in the agile method for developing AI products and solutions. He holds a strong insight into the latest technologies in the field of data science. Outside of his busy schedule, Rehan manages to explore new areas in the field of robotics and AI.

Dipayan Sarkar holds an Masters in economics and has over 17 years' experience. He has won international challenges in predictive modeling and takes a keen interest in the mathematics behind machine learning techniques. Before opting to become an independent consultant and mentor in the data science and machine learning space with various organizations and educational institutions, he served as a senior data scientist with Fortune 500 companies in the U.S. and Europe. He is currently associated with the Great Lakes Institute of Management as a visiting faculty (analytics), and BML Munjal University as an adjunct faculty (analytics and machine learning). He has co-authored a book *Ensemble Machine Learning with Python*, available from Packt Publishing.

About the reviewer

Sray Agarwal has been working as a data scientist for the last 12 years and has gained experience in various domains, including BFSI, e-commerce, retail, telecommunications, hospitality, travel, education, real estate, and entertainment, among many other sectors. He is currently working for Publicis Sapient as a data scientist and is based out of London. His expertise lies in predictive modeling, forecasting, and advanced machine learning. He possesses a deep understanding of algorithms and advanced statistics. He has a background in management and economics and has attained an MSc-equivalent qualification in data science and analytics. He is also a SAS-Certified Predictive Modeler. His current area of interest is fair and explainable machine learning.

Packt is searching for authors like you

If you're interested in becoming an author for Packt, please visit `authors.packtpub.com` and apply today. We have worked with thousands of developers and tech professionals, just like you, to help them share their insight with the global tech community. You can make a general application, apply for a specific hot topic that we are recruiting an author for, or submit your own idea.

Table of Contents

Preface

Deep learning has taken a huge step in recent years with developments including generative adversarial networks (GANs), variational autoencoders, and deep reinforcement learning. This book serves as a reference guide in R 3.x that will help you implement deep learning techniques.

This book walks you through various deep learning techniques that you can implement in your applications using R 3.x. A unique set of recipes will help you solve regression, binomial classification, and multinomial classification problems, and explores hyper-parameter optimization in detail. You will also go through recipes that implement **convolutional neural networks (CNNs)**, **recurrent neural networks (RNNs)**, **long short-term memory (LSTM)** networks, sequence-to-sequence models, GANs, and reinforcement learning. You will learn about high-performance computation involving large datasets that utilize GPUs, along with parallel computation capabilities in R, and you will also get familiar with libraries such as MXNet, which is designed for efficient GPU computing and state-of-the-art deep learning. You will also learn how to solve common and not-so-common problems in NLP, such as object detection and action identification, and you will leverage pre-trained models in deep learning applications.

By the end of the book, you will have a logical understanding of deep learning and different deep learning packages and will be able to build the most appropriate solutions to your problems.

Who this book is for

This book is for data scientists, machine learning practitioners, deep learning researchers, and AI enthusiasts who want to learn key tasks in the deep learning domain using a recipe-based approach. You will implement deep learning techniques and algorithms in common and not-so-common challenges faced in research work or projects. A strong understanding of machine learning and a working knowledge of R is mandatory.

What this book covers

Chapter 1, *Understanding Neural Networks and Deep Neural Networks,* will show us how to set up a deep learning environment to train models. The readers are then introduced to neural networks, starting from how neural networks work, what hidden layers are, what backpropagation is, and what activation functions are. This chapter uses the keras library to demonstrate the recipes.

Chapter 2, *Working with Convolutional Neural Networks,* will show us CNNs and will explain how they can be used to train models for image recognition and natural language processing based tasks. This chapter also covers various hyperparameters and optimizers used with CNNs.

Chapter 3, *Recurrent Neural Networks in Action,* will show us the fundamentals of RNNs with real-life implementation examples. We will also introduce LSTMs and gated recurrent units (GRUs), an extension of RNNs, and take a detailed walk-through of LSTM hyper-parameters. In addition to this, readers will learn how to build a bi-directional RNN model using Keras.

Chapter 4, *Implementing Autoencoders with Keras,* will introduce the implementation of various types of autoencoders using the keras library as the backend. Readers will also learn about various applications of autoencoders, such as dimensionality reduction and image coloring.

Chapter 5, *Deep Generative Models,* will show us the architecture of another method of deep neural networks, **generative adversarial networks (GANs)**. We will demonstrate how to train a GAN model comprising of two pitting nets—a generator and a discriminator. This chapter also covers the practical implementation of variational autoencoders and compares them with GANs.

Chapter 6, *Handling Big Data Using Large-Scale Deep Learning,* contains case studies on high-performance computation involving large datasets utilizing GPUs. Readers will also be introduced to the parallel computation capabilities in R and libraries such as MXNet, which is designed for efficient GPU computing and state-of-the-art deep learning.

Chapter 7, *Working with Text and Audio for NLP,* contains case studies on various topics involving sequence data, including natural language processing (NLP) and speech recognition. The readers will implement end-to-end deep learning algorithms using various deep learning libraries.

Chapter 8, *Deep Learning for Computer Vision,* will provide end-to-end case studies on object detection and face identification.

Chapter 9, *Implementing Reinforcement Learning*, will walk us through the concepts of reinforcement learning step by step. Readers will learn about various methods, such as Markov Decision Processes, Q-Learning, and experience replay, and implement these methods in R using examples. Readers will also implement an end-to-end reinforcement learning example using R packages such as MDPtoolbox and Reinforcementlearning.

To get the most out of this book

A good understanding of machine learning and strong knowledge of R is necessary for this book.

Download the example code files

You can download the example code files for this book from your account at www.packt.com. If you purchased this book elsewhere, you can visit www.packtpub.com/support and register to have the files emailed directly to you.

You can download the code files by following these steps:

1. Log in or register at www.packt.com.
2. Select the **Support** tab.
3. Click on **Code Downloads**.
4. Enter the name of the book in the **Search** box and follow the onscreen instructions.

Once the file is downloaded, please make sure that you unzip or extract the folder using the latest version of:

- WinRAR/7-Zip for Windows
- Zipeg/iZip/UnRarX for Mac
- 7-Zip/PeaZip for Linux

The code bundle for the book is also hosted on GitHub at https://github.com/PacktPublishing/Deep-Learning-with-R-Cookbook. In case there's an update to the code, it will be updated on the existing GitHub repository.

We also have other code bundles from our rich catalog of books and videos available at https://github.com/PacktPublishing/. Check them out!

Download the color images

We also provide a PDF file that has color images of the screenshots/diagrams used in this book. You can download it here: `http://www.packtpub.com/sites/default/files/downloads/9781789805673_ColorImages.pdf`.

Conventions used

There are a number of text conventions used throughout this book.

`CodeInText`: Indicates code words in text, database table names, folder names, filenames, file extensions, pathnames, dummy URLs, user input, and Twitter handles. Here is an example: "In step 1, we imported the fashion MNIST data using the `dataset_fashion_mnist()` function and checked the dimensions of its training and testing partitions."

A block of code is set as follows:

```
fashion <- dataset_fashion_mnist()
x_train <- fashion$train$x
y_train <- fashion$train$y
x_test <- fashion$test$x
y_test <- fashion$test$y
```

Bold: Indicates a new term, an important word, or words that you see onscreen. For example, words in menus or dialog boxes appear in the text like this. Here is an example: "Go to **Anaconda Navigator** from the **Start** menu."

 Warnings or important notes appear like this.

 Tips and tricks appear like this.

Sections

In this book, you will find several headings that appear frequently (*Getting ready*, *How to do it...*, *How it works...*, *There's more...*, and *See also*).

To give clear instructions on how to complete a recipe, use these sections as follows:

Getting ready

This section tells you what to expect in the recipe and describes how to set up any software or any preliminary settings required for the recipe.

How to do it...

This section contains the steps required to follow the recipe.

How it works...

This section usually consists of a detailed explanation of what happened in the previous section.

There's more...

This section consists of additional information about the recipe in order to make you more knowledgeable about the recipe.

See also

This section provides helpful links to other useful information for the recipe.

Get in touch

Feedback from our readers is always welcome.

General feedback: If you have questions about any aspect of this book, mention the book title in the subject of your message and email us at customercare@packtpub.com.

Errata: Although we have taken every care to ensure the accuracy of our content, mistakes do happen. If you have found a mistake in this book, we would be grateful if you would report this to us. Please visit www.packtpub.com/support/errata, selecting your book, clicking on the Errata Submission Form link, and entering the details.

Piracy: If you come across any illegal copies of our works in any form on the Internet, we would be grateful if you would provide us with the location address or website name. Please contact us at copyright@packt.com with a link to the material.

If you are interested in becoming an author: If there is a topic that you have expertise in and you are interested in either writing or contributing to a book, please visit authors.packtpub.com.

Reviews

Please leave a review. Once you have read and used this book, why not leave a review on the site that you purchased it from? Potential readers can then see and use your unbiased opinion to make purchase decisions, we at Packt can understand what you think about our products, and our authors can see your feedback on their book. Thank you!

For more information about Packt, please visit packt.com.

1
Understanding Neural Networks and Deep Neural Networks

Deep learning has transformed many traditional businesses, such as web search, advertising, and many more. A major challenge with the traditional machine learning approaches is that we need to spend a considerable amount of time choosing the most appropriate feature selection process before modeling. Besides this, these traditional techniques operate with some level of human intervention and guidance. However, with deep learning algorithms, we can get rid of the overhead of explicit feature selection since it is taken care of by the models themselves. These deep learning algorithms are capable of modeling complex and non-linear relationships within the data. In this book, we'll introduce you to how to set up a deep learning ecosystem in R. Deep neural networks use sophisticated mathematical modeling techniques to process data in complex ways. In this book, we'll showcase the use of various deep learning libraries, such as `keras` and `MXNet`, so that you can utilize their enriched set of functions and capabilities in order to build and execute deep learning models, although we'll primarily focus on working with the `keras` library. These libraries come with CPU and GPU support and are user-friendly so that you can prototype deep learning models quickly.

In this chapter, we will demonstrate how to set up a deep learning environment in R. You will also get familiar with various TensorFlow APIs and how to implement a neural network using them. You will also learn how to tune the various parameters of a neural network and also gain an understanding of various activation functions and their usage for different types of problem statements.

In this chapter, we will cover the following recipes:

- Setting up the environment
- Implementing neural networks with Keras
- TensorFlow Estimator API
- TensorFlow Core API
- Implementing a single-layer neural network
- Training your first deep neural network

Setting up the environment

Before implementing a deep neural network, we need to set up our system and configure it so that we can apply a variety of deep learning techniques. This recipe assumes that you have the Anaconda distribution installed on your system.

Getting ready

Let's configure our system for deep learning. It is recommended that you create a deep learning environment in Anaconda. If you have an older version of R in the conda environment, you need to update your R version to 3.5.x or above.

You also need to install the CUDA and cuDNN libraries for GPU support. You can read more about the prerequisites at `https://tensorflow.rstudio.com/tools/local_gpu.html#prerequisties`.

Please note that if your system does not have NVIDIA graphics support, then GPU processing cannot be done.

How to do it...

Let's create an environment in Anaconda (ensure that you have R and Python installed):

1. Go to **Anaconda Navigator** from the Start menu.
2. Click on **Environments.**
3. Create a new environment and name it. Make sure that both the Python and R options are selected, as shown in the following screenshot:

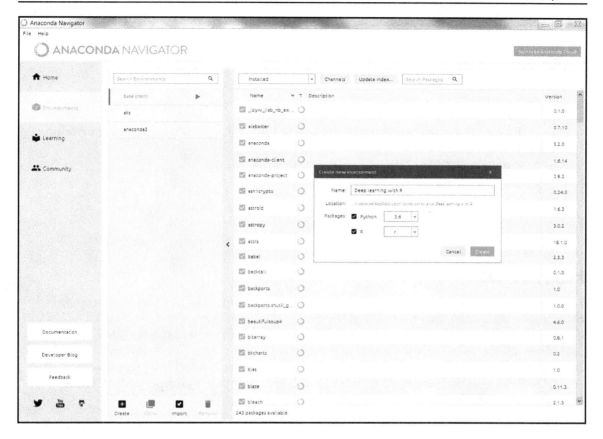

4. Install the `keras` library in R using the following command in RStudio or by using the Terminal of the conda environment created in the previous step:

```
install.packages("keras")
```

5. Install `keras` with the `tensorflow` backend.

The `keras` library supports TensorFlow as the default backend. Theano and CNTK are other alternative backends that can be used instead of TensorFlow.

To install the CPU version, please refer to the following code:

```
install_keras(method = c("auto", "virtualenv", "conda"),  conda =
"auto", version = "default", tensorflow = "default",
extra_packages = c("tensorflow-hub"))
```

For more details about this function, please go to `https://keras.` `rstudio.com/reference/install_keras.html`.

To install the GPU version, please refer to the following steps:

1. Ensure that you have met all the installation prerequisites, including installing the CUDA and cuDNN libraries.
2. Set the `tensorflow` argument's value to `gpu` in the `install_keras()` function:

```
install_keras(tensorflow = "gpu")
```

The preceding command will install the GPU version of `keras` in R.

How it works...

Keras and TensorFlow programs can be executed on both CPUs and GPUs, though these programs usually run faster on GPUs. If your system does not support an NVIDIA GPU, you only need to install the CPU version. However, if your system has an NVIDIA GPU that meets all the prerequisites and you need to run performance-critical applications, you should install the GPU version. To run the GPU version of TensorFlow, we need an NVIDIA GPU, and then we need to install a variety of software components (CUDA Toolkit v9.0, NVIDIA drivers, and cuDNN v7.0) on the system.

In *steps 1* to *3*, we created a new `conda` environment with both the R and Python kernels installed. In *steps 4* and *5*, we installed the `keras` library in the environment we created.

There's more...

The only supported installation method on Windows is `conda`. Therefore, you should install Anaconda 3.x for Windows before installing `keras`. The `keras` package uses the TensorFlow backend by default. If you want to switch to Theano or CNTK, call the `use_backend()` function after loading the `keras` library.

For the Theano backend, use the following command:

```
library(keras)
use_backend("theano")
```

For the CNTK backend, use the following command:

```
library(keras)
use_backend("cntk")
```

Now, your system is ready to train deep learning models.

See also

You can find out more about the GPU version installation of keras and its prerequisites here: https://tensorflow.rstudio.com/tools/local_gpu.html.

Implementing neural networks with Keras

TensorFlow is an open source software library developed by Google for numerical computation using data flow graphs. The R interface for TensorFlow is developed by RStudio, which provides an interface for three TensorFlow APIs:

- Keras
- Estimator
- Core

The keras, tfestimators, and tensorflow packages provide R interfaces to the aforementioned APIs, respectively. Keras and Estimator are high-level APIs, while Core is a low-level API that offers full access to the core of TensorFlow. In this recipe, we will demonstrate how we can build and train deep learning models using Keras.

Keras is a high-level neural network API, written in Python and capable of running on top of TensorFlow, CNTK, or Theano. The R interface for Keras uses TensorFlow as its default backend engine. The keras package provides an R interface for the TensorFlow Keras API. It lets you build deep learning models in two ways, sequential and functional, both of which will be described in the following sections.

Sequential API

Keras's Sequential API is straightforward to understand and implement. It lets us create a neural network linearly; that is, we can build a neural network layer-by-layer where we initialize a sequential model and then stack a series of hidden and output layers on it.

Getting ready

Before creating a neural network using the Sequential API, let's load the `keras` library into our environment and generate some dummy data:

```
library(keras)
```

Now, let's simulate some dummy data for this exercise:

```
x_data <- matrix(rnorm(1000*784), nrow = 1000, ncol = 784)
y_data <- matrix(rnorm(1000), nrow = 1000, ncol = 1)
```

We can check the dimension of the x and y data by executing the following commands:

```
dim(x_data)
dim(y_data)
```

The dimension of the `x_data` data is 1,000×784, whereas the dimension of the `y_data` data is 1,000×1.

How to do it...

Now, we can build our first sequential `keras` model and train it:

1. Let's start by defining a sequential model:

   ```
   model_sequential <- keras_model_sequential()
   ```

2. We need to add layers to the model we defined in the preceding code block:

   ```
   model_sequential %>%
   layer_dense(units = 16,batch_size = ,input_shape = c(784)) %>%
   layer_activation('relu') %>%
   layer_dense(units = 1)
   ```

3. After adding the layers to our model, we need to compile it:

```
model_sequential %>% compile(
  loss = "mse",
  optimizer = optimizer_sgd(),
  metrics = list("mean_absolute_error")
)
```

4. Now, let's visualize the summary of the model we created:

```
model_sequential %>% summary()
```

The summary of the model is as follows:

```
Layer (type)                    Output Shape                 Param #
================================================================
dense_1 (Dense)                 (None, 16)                   12560
_____
activation_1 (Activation)       (None, 16)                   0
_____
dense_2 (Dense)                 (None, 1)                    17
================================================================
Total params: 12,577
Trainable params: 12,577
Non-trainable params: 0
_____
```

5. Now, let's train the model and store the training stats in a variable in order to plot the model's metrics:

```
history <- model_sequential %>% fit(
  x_data,
  y_data,
  epochs = 30,
  batch_size = 128,
  validation_split = 0.2
)

# Plotting model metrics
plot(history)
```

The preceding code generates the following plot:

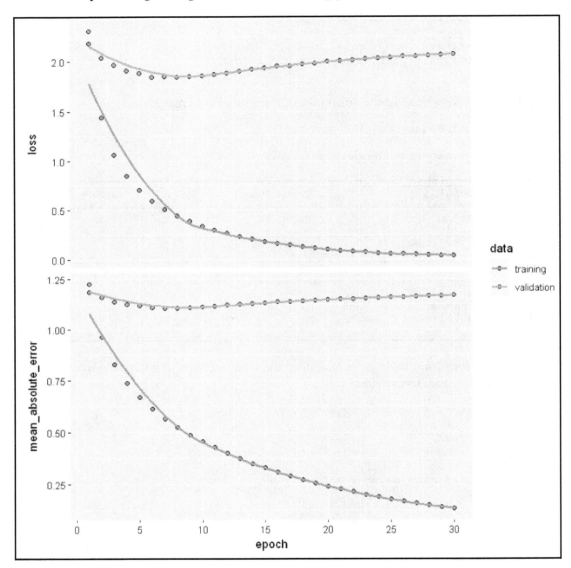

The preceding plot shows the loss and mean absolute error for the training and validation data.

How it works...

In *step 1*, we initialized a sequential model by calling the `keras_model_sequential()` function. In the next step, we stacked hidden and output layers by using a series of layer functions. The `layer_dense()` function adds a densely-connected layer to the defined model. The first layer of the sequential model needs to know what input shape it should expect, so we passed a value to the `input_shape` argument of the first layer. In our case, the input shape was equal to the number of features in the dataset. When we add layers to the `keras` sequential model, the model object is modified in-place, and we do not need to assign the updated object back to the original. The `keras` object's behavior is unlike most R objects (R objects are typically immutable). For our model, we used the `relu` activation function. The `layer_activation()` function creates an activation layer that takes input from the preceding hidden layer and applies activation to the output of our previous hidden layer. We can also use different functions, such as leaky ReLU, softmax, and more (activation functions will be discussed in *Implementing a single-layer neural network* recipe). In the output layer of our model, no activation was applied.

We can also implement various activation functions for each layer by passing a value to the `activation` argument in the `layer_dense()` function instead of adding an activation layer explicitly. It applies the following operation:

$$output=activation(dot(input, kernel)+bias)$$

Here, the *activation* argument refers to the element-wise activation function that's passed, while the *kernel* is a weights matrix that's created by the layer. The *bias* is a bias vector that's produced by the layer.

To train a model, we need to configure the learning process. We did this in *step 3* using the `compile()` function. In our training process, we applied a stochastic gradient descent optimizer to find the weights and biases that minimize our objective loss function; that is, the mean squared error. The `metrics` argument calculates the metric to be evaluated by the model during training and testing.

In *step 4*, we looked at the summary of the model; it showed us information about each layer, such as the shape of the output of each layer and the parameters of each layer.

In the last step, we trained our model for a fixed number of iterations on the dataset. Here, the `epochs` argument defines the number of iterations. The `validation_split` argument can take float values between 0 and 1. It specifies a fraction of the training data to be used as validation data. Finally, `batch_size` defines the number of samples that propagate through the network.

There's more...

Training a deep learning model is a time-consuming task. If training stops unexpectedly, we can lose a lot of our work. The `keras` library in R provides us with the functionality to save a model's progress during and after training. A saved model contains the weight values, the model's configuration, and the optimizer's configuration. If the training process is interrupted somehow, we can pick up training from there.

The following code block shows how we can save the model after training:

```
# Save model
model_sequential %>% save_model_hdf5("my_model.h5")
```

If we want to save the model after each iteration while training, we need to create a checkpoint object. To perform this task, we use the `callback_model_checkpoint()` function. The value of the `filepath` argument defines the name of the model that we want to save at the end of each iteration. For example, if `filepath` is `{epoch:02d}-{val_loss:.2f}.hdf5`, the model will be saved with the epoch number and the validation loss in the filename.

The following code block demonstrates how to save a model after each epoch:

```
checkpoint_dir <- "checkpoints"
dir.create(checkpoint_dir, showWarnings = FALSE)
filepath <- file.path(checkpoint_dir, "{epoch:02d}.hdf5")

# Create checkpoint callback
cp_callback <- callback_model_checkpoint(
 filepath = filepath,
 verbose = 1
)

# Fit model and save model after each check point
model_sequential %>% fit(
 x_data,
 y_data,
 epochs = 30,
 batch_size = 128,
 validation_split = 0.2,
 callbacks = list(cp_callback)
)
```

By doing this, you've learned how to save models with the appropriate checkpoints and callbacks.

See also

- To find out more about writing custom layers in Keras, go to `https://tensorflow.rstudio.com/keras/articles/custom_layers.html`.

Functional API

Keras's functional API gives us more flexibility when it comes to building complex models. We can create non-sequential connections between layers, multiple inputs/outputs models, or models with shared layers or models that reuse layers.

How to do it...

In this section, we will use the same simulated dataset that we created in the previous section of this recipe, *Sequential API*. Here, we will create a multi-output functional model:

1. Let's start by importing the required library and create an input layer:

```
library(keras)

# input layer
inputs <- layer_input(shape = c(784))
```

2. Next, we need to define two outputs:

```
predictions1 <- inputs %>%
  layer_dense(units = 8)%>%
  layer_activation('relu') %>%
  layer_dense(units = 1,name = "pred_1")

predictions2 <- inputs %>%
  layer_dense(units = 16)%>%
  layer_activation('tanh') %>%
  layer_dense(units = 1,name = "pred_2")
```

3. Now, we need to define a functional Keras model:

```
model_functional = keras_model(inputs = inputs,outputs =
c(predictions1,predictions2))
```

Let's look at the summary of the model:

```
summary(model_functional)
```

The following screenshot shows the model's summary:

```
Layer (type)                  Output Shape        Param #  Connected to
===================================================================================
input_1 (InputLayer)          (None, 784)         0
_____
dense_1 (Dense)               (None, 8)           6280     input_1[0][0]
_____
dense_2 (Dense)               (None, 16)          12560    input_1[0][0]
_____
activation_1 (Activation)     (None, 8)           0        dense_1[0][0]
_____
activation_2 (Activation)     (None, 16)          0        dense_2[0][0]
_____
pred_1 (Dense)                (None, 1)           9        activation_1[0][0]
_____
pred_2 (Dense)                (None, 1)           17       activation_2[0][0]
===================================================================================
Total params: 18,866
Trainable params: 18,866
Non-trainable params: 0
```

4. Now, we compile our model:

```
model_functional %>% compile(
  loss = "mse",
  optimizer = optimizer_rmsprop(),
  metrics = list("mean_absolute_error")
)
```

5. Next, we need to train the model and visualize the model's parameters:

```
history_functional <- model_functional %>% fit(
  x_data,
  list(y_data,y_data),
  epochs = 30,
  batch_size = 128,
  validation_split = 0.2
)
```

Now, let's plot the model loss for the training and validation data of prediction 1 and prediction 2:

```
# Plot the model loss of the prediction 1 training data
plot(history_functional$metrics$pred_1_loss, main="Model Loss",
```

```
xlab = "epoch", ylab="loss", col="blue", type="l")

# Plot the model loss of the prediction 1 validation data
lines(history_functional$metrics$val_pred_1_loss, col="green")

# Plot the model loss of the prediction 2 training data
lines(history_functional$metrics$pred_2_loss, col="red")

# Plot the model loss of the prediction 2 validation data
lines(history_functional$metrics$val_pred_2_loss, col="black")

# Add legend
legend("topright", c("training loss prediction 1","validation loss
prediction 1","training loss prediction 2","validation loss
prediction 2"), col=c("blue", "green","red","black"), lty=c(1,1))
```

The following plot shows the training and validation loss for both prediction 1 and prediction 2:

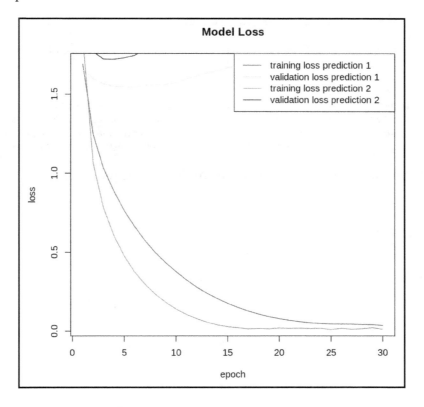

Now, let's plot the mean absolute error for the training and validation data of prediction 1 and prediction 2:

```
# Plot the model mean absolute error of the prediction 1 training
data
plot(history_functional$metrics$pred_1_mean_absolute_error,
main="Mean Absolute Error", xlab = "epoch", ylab="error",
col="blue", type="l")

# Plot the model mean squared error of the prediction 1 validation
data
lines(history_functional$metrics$val_pred_1_mean_absolute_error,
col="green")

# Plot the model mean squared error of the prediction 2 training
data
lines(history_functional$metrics$pred_2_mean_absolute_error,
col="red")

# Plot the model mean squared error of the prediction 2 validation
data
lines(history_functional$metrics$val_pred_2_mean_absolute_error,
col="black")

# Add legend
legend("topright", c("training mean absolute error prediction
1","validation mean absolute error prediction 1","training mean
absolute error prediction 2","validation mean absolute error
prediction 2"), col=c("blue", "green","red","black"), lty=c(1,1))
```

The following plot shows the mean absolute errors for prediction 1 and prediction 2:

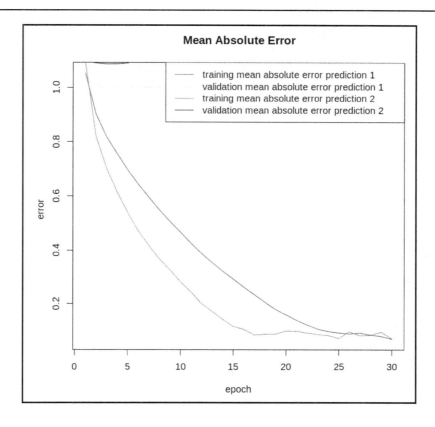

How it works...

To create a model using the functional API, we need to create the input and output layers independently, and then pass them to the `keras_model()` function in order to define the complete model. In the previous section, we created a model with two different output layers that share an input layer/tensor.

In *step 1*, we created an input tensor using the `layer_input()` function, which is an entry point into a computation graph that's been generated by the `keras` model. In *step 2*, we defined two different output layers. These output layers have different configurations; that is, activation functions and the number of perceptron units. The input tensor flows through these and produces two different outputs.

In *step 3*, we defined our model using the `keras_model()` function. It takes two arguments: `inputs` and `outputs`. These arguments specify which layers act as the input and output layers of the model. In the case of multi-input or multi-output models, you can use a vector of input layers and output layers, as shown here:

keras_model(inputs= c(input_layer_1, input_layer_2), outputs= c(output_layer_1, output_layer_2))

After we configured our model, we defined the learning process, trained our model, and visualized the loss and accuracy metrics. The `compile()` and `fit()` functions, which we used in *steps 4* and *5*, were described in detail in the *How it works* section of the *Sequential API* recipe.

There's more...

You will come across scenarios where you'll want the output of one model in order to feed it into another model alongside another input. The `layer_concatenate()` function can be used to do this. Let's define a new input that we will concatenate with the `predictions1` output layer we defined in the *How to do it* section of this recipe and build a model:

```
# Define new input of the model
new_input <- layer_input(shape = c(5), name = "new_input")

# Define output layer of new model
main_output <- layer_concatenate(c(predictions1, new_input)) %>%
  layer_dense(units = 64, activation = 'relu') %>%
  layer_dense(units = 1, activation = 'sigmoid', name = 'main_output')

# We define a multi input and multi output model
model <- keras_model(
  inputs = c(inputs, new_input),
  outputs = c(predictions1, main_output)
)
```

We can visualize the summary of the model using the `summary()` function.

It is good practice to give different layers unique names while working with complex models.

TensorFlow Estimator API

The Estimator is a high-level TensorFlow API that makes developing deep learning models much more manageable since you can use them to write models with high-level intuitive code. It builds a computation graph and provides an environment where we can initialize variables, load data, handle exceptions, and create checkpoints.

The `tfestimators` package is an R interface for the TensorFlow Estimator API. It implements various components of the TensorFlow Estimator API in R, as well as many pre-built canned models, such as linear models and deep neural networks (DNN classifiers and regressors). These are called **pre-made estimators**. The Estimator API does not have a direct implementation of recurrent neural networks or convolutional neural networks but supports a flexible framework for defining arbitrary new model types. This is known as the custom estimators framework.

Getting ready

In this recipe, we'll demonstrate how to build and fit a deep learning model using the Estimator API. To use the Estimator API in R, we need to install the `tfestimators` package.

First, let's install the library and then import it into our environment:

```
install.packages("tfestimators")
library(tfestimators)
```

Next, we need to simulate some dummy data for this exercise:

```
x_data_df <- as.data.frame( matrix(rnorm(1000*784), nrow = 1000, ncol =
784))
y_data_df <- as.data.frame(matrix(rnorm(1000), nrow = 1000, ncol = 1))
```

Let's rename the response variable to `target`:

```
colnames(y_data_df)<- c("target")
```

Now, let's bind the x and y data together to prepare the training data:

```
dummy_data_estimator <- cbind(x_data_df,y_data_df)
```

By doing this, we have created our input dataset.

How to do it...

In this recipe, we will use a pre-made `dnn_regressor` estimator. Let's get started and build and train a deep learning estimator model:

1. We need to execute some steps before building an estimator neural network. First, we need to create a vector of feature names:

```
features_set <- setdiff(names(dummy_data_estimator), "target")
```

Here, we construct the feature columns according to the Estimator API. The `feature_columns()` function is a constructor for feature columns, which defines the expected shape of the input to the model:

```
feature_cols <- feature_columns(
  column_numeric(features_set)
)
```

2. Next, we define an input function so that we can select feature and response variables:

```
estimator_input_fn <- function(data_,num_epochs = 1) {
  input_fn(data_, features = features_set, response =
"target",num_epochs = num_epochs )
}
```

3. Let's construct an estimator regressor model:

```
regressor <- dnn_regressor(
  feature_columns = feature_cols,
  hidden_units = c(5, 10, 8),
  label_dimension = 1L,
  activation_fn = "relu"
)
```

4. Next, we need to train the regressor we built in the previous step:

```
train(regressor, input_fn = estimator_input_fn(data_ =
dummy_data_estimator))
```

5. Similar to what we did for the training data, we need to simulate some test data and evaluate the model's performance:

```
x_data_test_df <- as.data.frame( matrix(rnorm(100*784), nrow = 100,
ncol = 784))
y_data_test_df <- as.data.frame(matrix(rnorm(100), nrow = 100, ncol
= 1))
```

We need to change the column name of the response variable, just like we did for the training data:

```
colnames(y_data_test_df)<- c("target")
```

We bind the x and y data together for the test data:

```
dummy_data_test_df <- cbind(x_data_test_df,y_data_test_df)
```

Now, we generate predictions for the test dataset using the regressor model we built previously:

```
predictions <- predict(regressor, input_fn =
estimator_input_fn(dummy_data_test_df), predict_keys =
c("predictions"))
```

Next, we evaluate the model's performance on the test dataset:

```
evaluation <- evaluate(regressor, input_fn =
estimator_input_fn(dummy_data_test_df))
evaluation
```

In the next section, you will gain a comprehensive understanding of the steps we implemented here.

How it works...

In this recipe, we implemented a DNN regressor using a pre-made estimator; the preceding program can be divided into a variety of subparts, as follows:

- **Define the feature columns**: In *step 1*, we created a vector of strings, which contains the names of our numeric feature columns. Next, we called the `feature_columns()` function, which defines the expected `shape` value of an input tensor and how features should be transformed (numeric or categorical) while they're being modeled. In our case, the shape of the input tensor was 784, and all the values of the input tensor were numerical. We transform the numeric features by providing the names of the numeric columns to the `column_numeric()` function within `feature_columns()`. If you have categorical columns in your data that have values such as `category_x`, `category_y` and you want to assign integer values (0, 1) to these, you can do this using the `column_categorical_with_identity()` function.

- **Write the dataset import functions**: In *step 2*, we defined how a pre-made estimator receives data. It is defined by the `input_fn()` function. It converts raw data sources into tensors and selects feature and response columns. It also configures how data is drawn during training; that is, shuffling, batch size, epochs, and so on.
- **Instantiate the relevant pre-made Estimator**: In *step 3*, we instantiated a pre-made **deep neural network (DNN)** estimator by calling `dnn_regressor()`. The `hidden_units` argument value of the function defines our network; that is, the hidden layers in the network and the number of perceptrons in each layer. It consists of dense, feedforward neural network layers. It takes vectors of integers as the argument value. In our model, we had three layers with 5, 10, and 8 perceptrons, respectively. We used `relu` as our activation function. The `label_dimension` argument of the `dnn_regrssor` function defines the shape of the regression target per example.
- **Call a training, evaluation method**: In *step 4*, we trained our model, and in the next step, we predicted the values for the test dataset and evaluated the performance of the model.

There's more...

Estimators provide a utility called run hooks so that we can track training, report progress, request early stopping, and more. One such utility is the `hook_history_saver()` function, which lets us save training history in every training step. While training an estimator, we pass our run hooks' definition to the hooks argument of the `train()` function, as shown in the following code block. It saves model progress after every two training iterations and returns saved training metrics.

The following code block shows how to implement run hooks:

```
training_history <- train(regressor,
  input_fn = estimator_input_fn(data_ = dummy_data_estimator),
  hooks = list(hook_history_saver(every_n_step = 2))
  )
```

Other pre-built run hooks are provided by the Estimator API. To find out more about them, please refer to the links in the *See also* section of this recipe.

See also

- **Custom estimators:** https://tensorflow.rstudio.com/tfestimators/articles/creating_estimators.html
- **Other pre-built run hooks:** https://tensorflow.rstudio.com/tfestimators/articles/run_hooks.html
- **Dataset API:** https://tensorflow.rstudio.com/tfestimators/articles/dataset_api.html

TensorFlow Core API

The TensorFlow Core API is a set of modules written in Python. It is a system where computations are represented as graphs. The R `tensorflow` package provides complete access to the TensorFlow API from R. TensorFlow represents computations as a data flow graph, where each node represents a mathematical operation, and directed arcs represent a multidimensional data array or tensor that operations are performed on. In this recipe, we'll build and train a model using the R interface for the TensorFlow Core API.

Getting ready

You will need the `tensorflow` library installed to continue with this recipe. You can install it using the following command:

```
install.packages("tensorflow")
```

After installing the package, load it into your environment:

```
library(tensorflow)
```

Executing the two preceding code blocks doesn't install `tensorflow` completely. Here, we need to use the `install_tensorflow()` function to install TensorFlow, as shown in the following code block:

```
install_tensorflow()
```

TensorFlow installation in R needs a Python environment with the `tensorflow` library installed in it. The `install_tensorflow()` function attempts to create an isolated python environment called `r-tensorflow` by default and installs `tensorflow` in it. It takes different values for the `method` argument, which provides various installation behaviors. These methods are explained at the following link: `https://tensorflow.rstudio.com/tensorflow/articles/installation.html#installation-methods`.

 The `virtualenv` and `conda` methods are available on Linux and OS X, while the `conda` and `system` methods are available on Windows.

How to do it...

After the initial installation and setup, we can start building deep learning models by simply loading the TensorFlow library into the R environment:

1. Let's start by simulating some dummy data:

```
x_data = matrix(runif(1000*2),nrow = 1000,ncol = 1)
y_data = matrix(runif(1000),nrow = 1000,ncol = 1)
```

2. Now, we need to initialize some TensorFlow variables; that is, the weights and biases:

```
W <- tf$Variable(tf$random_uniform(shape(1L), -1.0, 1.0))
b <- tf$Variable(tf$zeros(shape(1L)))
```

3. Now, let's define the model:

```
y_hat <- W * x_data + b
```

4. Then, we need to define the loss function and optimizer:

```
loss <- tf$reduce_mean((y_hat - y_data) ^ 2)
optimizer <- tf$train$GradientDescentOptimizer(0.5)
train <- optimizer$minimize(loss)
```

5. Next, we launch the computation graph and initialize the TensorFlow variables:

```
sess = tf$Session()
sess$run(tf$global_variables_initializer())
```

6. We train the model to fit the training data:

```
for (step in 1:201) {
  sess$run(train)
  if (step %% 20 == 0)
  cat(step, "-", sess$run(W), sess$run(b), "\n")
}
```

Finally, we close the session:

```
sess$close()
```

Here are the results of every 20th iteration:

```
20 - 0.02961582 0.477668
40 - 0.002623167 0.4924422
60 - -0.004212872 0.4961839
80 - -0.005944134 0.4971315
100 - -0.006382558 0.4973714
120 - -0.006493592 0.4974322
140 - -0.006521734 0.4974476
160 - -0.006528848 0.4974515
180 - -0.00653068 0.4974525
200 - -0.006531124 0.4974528
```

It is important that we close the session because resources are not released until we close it.

How it works...

TensorFlow programs generate a computation graph in which the nodes of the graph are called *ops*. These ops take tensors as input and perform computations and produce tensors (tensors are n-dimensional arrays or lists). TensorFlow programs are structured in two phases: the construction phase and the execution phase. In the construction phase, we assemble the graph, while in the execution phase, we execute the graphs in the context of the session. Calling the `tensorflow` package in R creates an entry point (the `tf` object) to the TensorFlow API, through which we can access the main TensorFlow module. The `tf$Variable()` function creates a variable that holds and updates trainable parameters. TensorFlow variables are in-memory buffers containing tensors.

In *step 1*, we created some dummy data. In the next step, we created two `tf` variables for the weights and bias with initial values. In *step 3*, we defined the model. In *step 4*, we defined the loss function, as per the following equation:

$$MSE = \frac{1}{n} \sum_{i=1}^{n} (Y_i - \hat{Y_i})^2$$

The `reduce_mean()` function computes the mean of the elements across the dimensions of a tensor. In our code, it calculates the average loss over the training set. In this step, we also defined the optimization algorithm we need to use to train our network. Here, we used the gradient descent optimizer with a learning rate of 0.5. Then, we defined the objective of each training step; that is, we minimize loss.

In *step 5*, we assembled the computation graph and provided TensorFlow with a description of the computations that we wanted to execute. In our implementation, we wanted TensorFlow to minimize loss; that is, minimize the mean squared error using the gradient descent algorithm. TensorFlow does not run any computations until the session is created and the `run()` function is called. We launched the session and added an ops (node) in order to run some `tf` variable initializers. `sessrun(tfrun(tfglobal_variables_initializer())` initializes all the variables simultaneously. We should only run this ops after we have fully constructed the graph and launched it in a session. Finally, in the last step, we executed the training steps in a loop and printed the `tf` variables (the weight and bias) at each iteration.

It is suggested that you use one of the higher-level APIs (Keras or Estimator) rather than the lower-level core TensorFlow API.

Implementing a single-layer neural network

An artificial neural network is a network of computing entities that can perform various tasks, such as regression, classification, clustering, and feature extraction. They are inspired by biological neural networks in the human brain. The most fundamental unit of a neural network is called a neuron/perceptron. A neuron is a simple computing unit that takes in a set of inputs and applies a function to these inputs in order to produce output.

The following diagram shows a simple neuron:

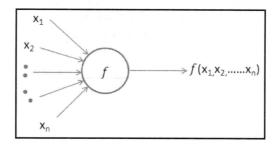

In 1957, Frank Rosenblatt proposed a classical perceptron model in which he associated weight with each input. He also proposed a method to realize these weights. A perceptron model is a simple computing unit with a threshold, θ, which can be defined by the following equation:

$$y = \begin{cases} 1 & \sum w_i * x_i \geq \theta \\ -1 & \sum w_i * x_i < \theta \end{cases}$$

The following diagram represents a perceptron:

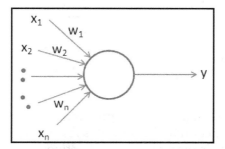

Perceptrons can only deal with linearly separable cases. The neural networks that we use today make use of activation functions rather than a harsh threshold, which are used in perceptrons. Unlike perceptrons, neural networks with non-linear activation functions can learn complex non-linear functional mappings between inputs and outputs, making them favorable for more complicated applications such as image recognition, language translation, speech recognition, and so on. The most popular activation functions are sigmoid, tanh, relu, and softmax.

We can implement various machine learning algorithms, such as simple linear regression, logistic regression, and so on, using neural networks. For example, we can think of logistic regression as a single-layer neural network. A logistic regression neural network uses a sigmoid ($\phi_{sigmoid}$) activation function. The following diagram shows a logistic regression neural network:

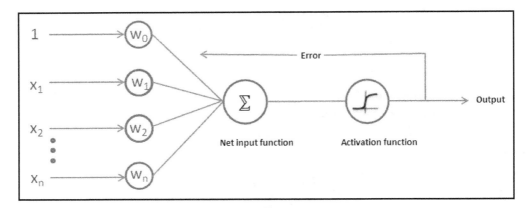

The output of the network is given as follows:

$$\phi_{\text{sigmoid}}(z) = \frac{1}{1 + e^{-z}}$$

$$\text{where } z \text{ is equal to } \sum_{1}^{n} w_i x_i$$

While implementing a multinomial logistic regression problem using neural networks, we place a softmax activation function in the output layer. The following equation shows the output of a multinomial logistic regression neural network:

$$P(y = j|z) = \phi_{softmax}(z) = \frac{e_j^z}{\sum_{n=1}^{N} e_n^z}$$

where z is the weighted sum of inputs for the jth class

In neural networks, the network error is calculated by comparing the model's output to the desired output. This error term is used to guide the training of neural networks. After each training iteration, the error is communicated backward in the network and the weights of the network are updated in order to minimize the error. This process is called **backpropagation**. In this recipe, we will build a multi-class classification neural network using the keras library in R.

Getting ready

We will use the iris dataset in this recipe. It is a multivariate dataset that consists of 50 samples that belong to three species of iris flower— setosa, virginica, and versicolor. Each sample contains four feature measurements; that is, the length and width of the sepals and petals in centimeters. We will use the keras package in order to utilize the deep learning functions for classification and the datasets library to import the iris dataset:

```
library(keras)
library(datasets)
```

In the next section, we will look at the data in more detail.

How to do it...

Before doing any transformations in the dataset, we will analyze the properties of the data, such as its dimensions, its variables, and its summary:

1. Let's start by loading the iris dataset from the datasets library:

    ```
    data <- datasets::iris
    ```

    Now, we can view the dimensions of the data:

    ```
    dim(data)
    ```

    Here, we can see that there are 150 rows and 5 columns in the data:

    Let's display the first five records of the data:

    ```
    head(data)
    ```

Let's have a glance at the data:

Sepal.Length	Sepal.Width	Petal.Length	Petal.Width	Species
5.1	3.5	1.4	0.2	setosa
4.9	3.0	1.4	0.2	setosa
4.7	3.2	1.3	0.2	setosa
4.6	3.1	1.5	0.2	setosa
5.0	3.6	1.4	0.2	setosa
5.4	3.9	1.7	0.4	setosa

Now, let's have a look at the datatypes of the variables in the dataset:

```
str(data)
```

Here, we can see that all the columns except **Species** are numeric. Species is the response variable for this classification exercise:

```
'data.frame':   150 obs. of  5 variables:
$ Sepal.Length: num  5.1 4.9 4.7 4.6 5 5.4 4.6 5 4.4 4.9 ...
$ Sepal.Width : num  3.5 3 3.2 3.1 3.6 3.9 3.4 3.4 2.9 3.1 ...
$ Petal.Length: num  1.4 1.4 1.3 1.5 1.4 1.7 1.4 1.5 1.4 1.5 ...
$ Petal.Width : num  0.2 0.2 0.2 0.2 0.2 0.4 0.3 0.2 0.2 0.1 ...
$ Species     : Factor w/ 3 levels "setosa","versicolor",..: 1 1 1 1 1 1 1 1 1 1 ...
```

Let's also look at a summary of the data to see the distribution of the variables:

```
summary(data)
```

We get the following output:

```
  Sepal.Length    Sepal.Width     Petal.Length    Petal.Width
 Min.   :4.300   Min.   :2.000   Min.   :1.000   Min.   :0.100
 1st Qu.:5.100   1st Qu.:2.800   1st Qu.:1.600   1st Qu.:0.300
 Median :5.800   Median :3.000   Median :4.350   Median :1.300
 Mean   :5.843   Mean   :3.057   Mean   :3.758   Mean   :1.199
 3rd Qu.:6.400   3rd Qu.:3.300   3rd Qu.:5.100   3rd Qu.:1.800
 Max.   :7.900   Max.   :4.400   Max.   :6.900   Max.   :2.500
        Species
 setosa    :50
 versicolor:50
 virginica :50
```

2. Now, we can work on the data transformation. To work with the `keras` package, we need to convert the data into an array or a matrix. The matrix data elements should be of the same basic type, but here, we have target values that are of the factor type, so we need to change this:

```
# Converting the data into a matrix for keras to consume
data[,5] <- as.numeric(data[,5]) -1
data <- as.matrix(data)

# Setting dimnames of data to NULL
dimnames(data) <- NULL
head(data)
```

3. Now, we need to split the data into training and testing datasets. The seed number is the starting point that's used when generating a sequence of random numbers. Using the same number inside the function ensures that we can reproduce the same data each time the code is run:

```
set.seed(76)

# Training and testing data sample size
indexes <- sample(2,nrow(data),replace = TRUE,prob = c(0.70,0.30))
```

We divide the data in the ratio of 70:30 for the training and testing datasets, respectively:

```
# Splitting the predictor variables into training and testing
data.train <- data[indexes==1, 1:4]
data.test <- data[indexes==2, 1:4]

# Splitting the label attribute(response variable)into training and
testing
data.trainingtarget <- data[indexes==1, 5]
data.testtarget <- data[indexes==2, 5]
```

4. Next, we one-hot encode the target column of the training and test data. The `to_categorical()` function converts a class vector into a binary class matrix:

```
data.trainLabels <- to_categorical(data.trainingtarget)
data.testLabels <- to_categorical(data.testtarget)
```

5. Now, let's build the model and compile it. First, we need to initialize a Keras sequential model object:

```
# Initialize a sequential model
model <- keras_model_sequential()
```

Next, we stack a dense layer. Since this is a single-layer network, we stack one layer:

```
model %>%
    layer_dense(units = 3, activation = 'softmax',input_shape =
ncol(data.train))
```

This layer is a three-node softmax layer that returns an array of three probability scores that sum to 1. Now, let's have a look at the summary of the model:

```
summary(model)
```

The output of the preceding code is as follows:

```
Layer (type)                       Output Shape                Param #
====================================================================
dense_10 (Dense)                   (None, 3)                   15
====================================================================
Total params: 15
Trainable params: 15
Non-trainable params: 0
```

Compiling the model prepares it for training. When compiling the model, we specify a loss function and an optimizer name and metric in order to evaluate the model during training and testing:

```
# Compile the model
model %>% compile(
loss = 'categorical_crossentropy',
optimizer = 'adam',
metrics = 'accuracy'
)
```

6. Now, we train the model:

```
# Fit the model
model %>% fit(data.train,
data.trainLabels,
epochs = 200,
batch_size = 5,
validation_split = 0.2
)
```

7. Let's visualize the metrics of the trained model:

```
history <- model %>% fit(data.train,
data.trainLabels,
epochs = 200,
batch_size = 5,
validation_split = 0.2
)

# Plotting the model metrics - loss and accuracy
plot(history)
```

In the following plot, **loss** and **acc** indicate the loss and accuracy of the model for the training and validation data:

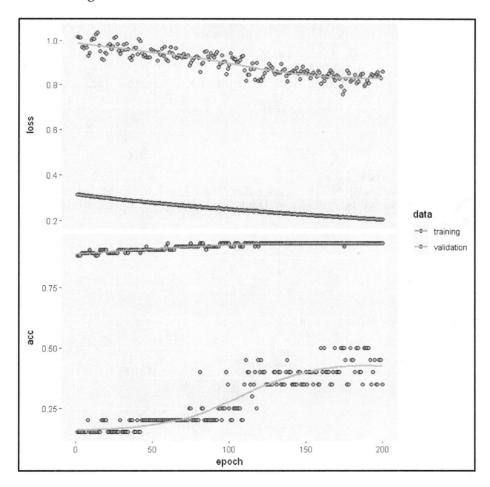

8. Now, we generate predictions for the test data. Here, we use the `predict_classes()` function to predict the classes for the test data. We're using a batch size of `128`:

```
classes <- model %>% predict_classes(data.test, batch_size = 128)
```

The following code provides us with the confusion matrix, which lets us see the correct and incorrect predictions:

```
table(data.testtarget, classes)
```

The following table shows the confusion matrix for the test data:

```
                       classes
data.testtarget  0   1   2
              0  17   0   0
              1   0  18   0
              2   0  13   5
```

Finally, let's evaluate the model's performance on the test data:

```
score <- model %>% evaluate(data.test, data.testLabels, batch_size = 128)
```

Now, we print the model scores:

```
print(score)
```

The following screenshot shows the loss and accuracy of the model on the test data:

```
$loss
[1]  0.3954425

$acc
[1]  0.754717
```

We can see that our model's accuracy is about 75%.

How it works...

In *step* 1, we loaded the `iris` data from the `datasets` library in R. It is always advised to be aware of the data and its characteristics before we start building models. Hence, we studied the structure and type of the variables in the data. We saw that apart from Species (our response (target) variable), all the other variables were numeric. Then, we checked the dimensions of our dataset.

The `summary()` function shows us the distribution of variables and the central tendency metric for each of these variables in the data. The `head()` function, by default, displays only the first five rows of the dataset.

 You can use `head()` to display any number of records. To do this, you need to pass the number of records as an argument in the head function. If you want to see the records from the end of the data, use the `tail()` function.

In *step* 2, we did the required data transformations. To work with the `keras` package, we need to convert the data into an array or a matrix. In our example, we changed our target column from the `factor` datatype to `numeric` and converted the data into a matrix format. From the summary of the dataset, it was clear that we did not need to normalize this data.

 If we need to deal with some data that hasn't been normalized, we can use the `normalize()` function from `keras`.

Next, in *step* 3, we divided the data into training and testing sets in the ratio of 70:30. Note that before dividing the data into training and testing, we set the seed, with a random integer being passed as an argument to it. The `seed()` function helps generate the same sequence of random numbers when we supply the same number (seed) inside the function.

While building a multi-class classification model with neural networks, it is recommended to transform the target attribute from a vector that contains values for each class value into a matrix with a boolean value for each class, indicating the presence or absence of that class value in an instance. To achieve this, in *step* 4, we used the `to_categorical()` function from the `keras` library.

In *step* 5, we built the model. First, we initialized a sequential model using the `keras_model_sequential()` function. Then, we added layers to the model. The model needs to know what input shape it should expect, so we specified the input shape in the first layer in our sequential model. The number of units is three because the number of output classes in our multi-class classification problem is three. Note that the activation function in this layer is `softmax`. This activation function is used when we need to predict probability values ranging between 0 and 1 as output. Then, we used the `summary()` function to get a summary of our model. There are a few more functions that can help us investigate the model, such as `get_config()` and `get_layer()`.

Once we set up the architecture of our model, we compiled it. To compile the model, we need to provide a few settings:

- **Loss function**: This measures the accuracy of the model during training. We need to minimize this function to reach convergence.
- **Optimizer**: This metric helps update the model based on the data it sees and its loss function.
- **Metrics**: These are used to evaluate the training and testing steps.

Other popular optimization algorithms include SGD, ADAM, and RMSprop. Choosing a loss function depends on the problem statement you are dealing with. For a classification problem, we generally use cross-entropy, while for a binary classification problem, we use the `binary_crossentropy()` loss function.

In *step 6*, we trained the model using the `fit()` method. An epoch refers to a single pass through the entire training set. The batch size defines the number of samples passed through the network.

In *step 7*, we plotted the model's metrics using the `plot()` function and analyzed the accuracy and loss of the training and validation data.

In the last step, we generated predictions for the test dataset and evaluated our model's performance. Note that since this is a classification model, we used the `predict_classes()` function to predict the outcomes. In the case of a regression exercise, we use the `predict()` function. We used the `evaluate()` function to check the accuracy of our model on the test data. By doing this, we saw that our model's accuracy was around 75.4%.

There's more...

Activation functions are used to learn non-linear and complex functional mappings between the inputs and the response variable in an artificial neural network. One thing to keep in mind is that an activation function should be differentiable so that backpropagation optimization can be performed in the network while computing gradients of error (loss) with respect to weights, in order to optimize weights and reduce errors. Let's have a look at some of the popular activation functions and their properties:

- **Sigmoid:**
  - A sigmoid function ranges between 0 and 1.
  - It is usually used in an output layer of a binary classification problem.
  - It is better than linear activation because the output of the activation function is in the range of (0,1) compared to (-inf, inf), so the output of the activation is bound. It scales down large negative numbers toward 0 and large positive numbers toward 1.
  - Its output is not zero centered, which makes gradient updates go too far in different directions and makes optimization harder.
  - It has a vanishing gradient problem.
  - It also has slow convergence.

    The sigmoid function is defined as follows:

    $$f(x) = \frac{1}{1 + e^{-x}}$$

    Here is the graph of the sigmoid function:

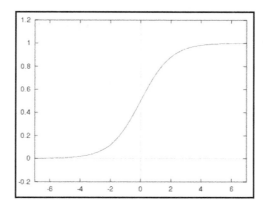

- **Tangent Hyperbolic (tanh):**
    - The tanh function scales the values between -1 and 1.
    - The gradient for tanh is steeper than it is for sigmoid.
    - Unlike sigmoid, it is centered around zero, which makes optimization easier.
    - It is usually used in hidden layers.
    - It has a vanishing gradient problem.

    The tanh function is defined as follows:

    $$f(x) = \frac{e^x - e^{-x}}{e^x + e^{-x}}$$

    The following diagram is the graph of the tanh function:

    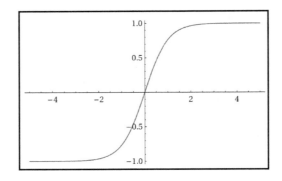

- **Rectified linear units (ReLU):**
    - It is a non-linear function
    - It ranges from 0 to infinity
    - It does not have a vanishing gradient problem
    - Its convergence is faster than sigmoid and tanh
    - It has a dying ReLU problem
    - It is used in hidden layers

    The ReLU function is defined as follows:

    $$f(x) = \begin{cases} x & x \geq 0 \\ 0 & x < 0 \end{cases}$$

Here is the graph for the ReLU function:

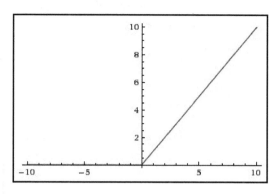

Now, let's look at the **variants of ReLU**:

- **Leaky ReLU:**
    - It doesn't have a dying ReLU problem as it doesn't have zero-slope parts
    - Leaky ReLU learns faster then ReLU

    Mathematically, the Leaky ReLU function can be defined as follows:

    $$f(x) = \begin{cases} x & x \geq 0 \\ \alpha x & x < 0 \end{cases}$$

    Here is a graphical representation of the Leaky ReLU function:

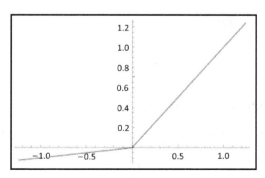

- **Exponential Linear Unit (ELU):**
    - It doesn't have the dying ReLU problem
    - It saturates for large negative values

    Mathematically, the ELU function can be defined as follows:

    $$f(x) = \begin{cases} \alpha(e^x - 1) & x < 0 \\ x & x \geq 0 \end{cases}$$

    Here is a graphical representation of the ELU function:

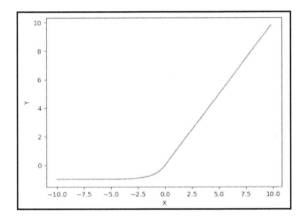

- **Parametric Rectified Linear Unit (PReLu):**
    - PReLU is a type of leaky ReLU, where the value of alpha is determined by the network itself.

    The mathematical definition of the PReLu function is as follows:

    $$f(x) = \begin{cases} \alpha x & x < 0 \\ x & x \geq 0 \end{cases}$$

- **Thresholded Rectified linear unit:**

    The mathematical definition of the PReLu function is as follows:

    $$f(x) = \begin{cases} 0 & x \leq \theta \\ x & x > \theta \end{cases}$$

- **Softmax:**
    - It is non-linear.
    - It's usually used in the output layer of a multiclass classification problem.
    - It calculates the probability distribution of the event over "n" different events (classes). It outputs values between 0 to 1 for all the classes and the sum of all the probabilities is 1.

    The mathematical definition of the softmax function is as follows:

    $$\sigma(z)_i = \frac{e^{z_i}}{\sum_{j=1}^{K} e^{z_j}} \text{ for i} = 1, ..., \text{K and } \mathbf{z} = (z_1, \dots, z_K) \in \mathbb{R}^K$$

    Here, K is the number of possible outcomes.

See also

- You can read more about gradient descent optimization algorithms and some variants here: `https://arxiv.org/pdf/1609.04747.pdf`.
- You can find a good article about vanishing gradients and choosing the right activation function here: `https://blog.paperspace.com/vanishing-gradients-activation-function/`.

Training your first deep neural network

In the previous recipe, *Implementing a single-layer neural network,* we implemented a simple baseline neural network for a classification task. Continuing with that model architecture, we will create a deep neural network. A deep neural network consists of several hidden layers that can be interpreted geometrically as additional hyperplanes. These networks learn to model data in complex ways and learn complex mappings between inputs and outputs.

The following diagram is an example of a deep neural network with two hidden layers:

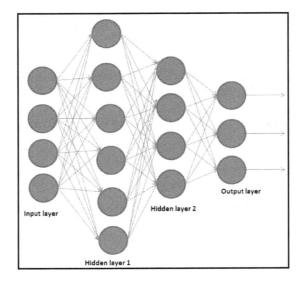

In this recipe, we will learn how to implement a deep neural network for a multi-class classification problem.

Getting ready

In this recipe, we will use the MNIST digit dataset. This is a database of handwritten digits that consists of 60,000 28x28 grayscale images of the 10 digits, along with a test set of 10,000 images. We will build a model that will recognize handwritten digits from this dataset.

To start, let's load the keras library:

```
library(keras)
```

Now, we can do some data preprocessing and model building.

How to do it...

The MNIST dataset is included in `keras` and can be accessed using the `dataset_mnist()` function:

1. Let's load the data into the R environment:

```
mnist <- dataset_mnist()
x_train <- mnist$train$x
y_train <- mnist$train$y
x_test <- mnist$test$x
y_test <- mnist$test$y
```

2. Our training data is of the form (images, width, height). Due to this, we'll convert the data into a one-dimensional array and rescale it:

```
# Reshaping the data
x_train <- array_reshape(x_train , c(nrow(x_train),784))
x_test <- array_reshape(x_test , c(nrow(x_test),784))

# Rescaling the data
x_train <- x_train/255
x_test <- x_test/255
```

3. Our target data is an integer vector and contains values from 0 to 9. We need to one-hot encode our target variable in order to convert it into a binary matrix format. We use the `to_categorical()` function from `keras` to do this:

```
y_train <- to_categorical(y_train,10)
y_test <- to_categorical(y_test,10)
```

4. Now, we can build the model. We use the Sequential API from `keras` to configure this model. Note that in the first layer's configuration, the `input_shape` argument is the shape of the input data; that is, it's a numeric vector of length 784 and represents a grayscale image. The final layer outputs a length 10 numeric vector (probabilities for each digit from 0 to 9) using a softmax activation function:

```
model <- keras_model_sequential()
model %>%
  layer_dense(units = 256, activation = 'relu', input_shape =
c(784)) %>%
  layer_dropout(rate = 0.4) %>%
  layer_dense(units = 128, activation = 'relu') %>%
  layer_dropout(rate = 0.3) %>%
  layer_dense(units = 10, activation = 'softmax')
```

Let's look at the details of the model:

```
summary(model)
```

Here's the model's summary:

```
Layer (type)                    Output Shape              Param #
================================================================
dense_1 (Dense)                 (None, 256)               200960
_____
dropout_1 (Dropout)             (None, 256)               0
_____
dense_2 (Dense)                 (None, 128)               32896
_____
dropout_2 (Dropout)             (None, 128)               0
_____
dense_3 (Dense)                 (None, 10)                1290
================================================================
Total params: 235,146
Trainable params: 235,146
Non-trainable params: 0
_____
```

5. Next, we go ahead and compile our model by providing some appropriate
   arguments, such as the loss function, optimizer, and metrics. Here, we have used
   the `rmsprop` optimizer. This optimizer is similar to the gradient descent
   optimizer, except that it can increase our learning rate so that our algorithm can
   take larger steps in the horizontal direction, thus converging faster:

```
model %>% compile(
loss = 'categorical_crossentropy',
optimizer = optimizer_rmsprop(),
metrics = c('accuracy')
)
```

6. Now, let's fit the training data to the configured model. Here, we've set the
   number of epochs to `30`, the batch size to `128`, and the validation percentage to
   `20`:

```
history <- model %>% fit(
    x_train, y_train,
    epochs = 30, batch_size = 128,
    validation_split = 0.2
)
```

7. Next, we visualize the model metrics. We can plot the model's accuracy and loss metrics from the history variable. Let's plot the model's accuracy:

```
# Plot the accuracy of the training data
plot(history$metrics$acc, main="Model Accuracy", xlab = "epoch",
ylab="accuracy", col="blue",
type="l")

# Plot the accuracy of the validation data
lines(history$metrics$val_acc, col="green")

# Add Legend
legend("bottomright", c("train","validation"), col=c("blue",
"green"), lty=c(1,1))
```

The following plot shows the model's accuracy on the training and test dataset:

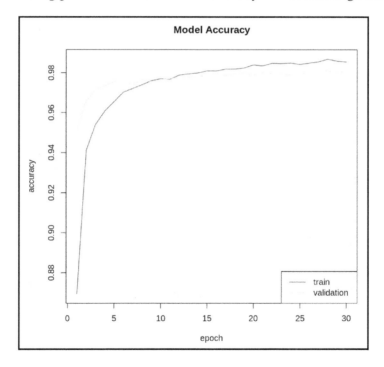

Now, let's plot the model's loss:

```
# Plot the model loss of the training data
plot(history$metrics$loss, main="Model Loss", xlab = "epoch",
ylab="loss", col="blue", type="l")
```

```
# Plot the model loss of the validation data
lines(history$metrics$val_loss, col="green")

# Add legend
legend("topright", c("train","validation"), col=c("blue", "green"),
lty=c(1,1))
```

The following plot shows the model's loss on the training and test dataset:

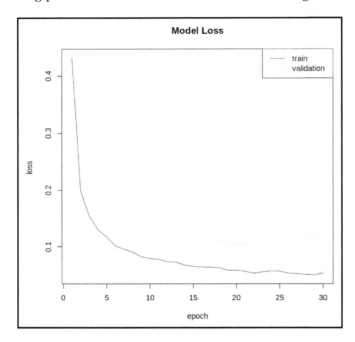

8. Now, we predict the classes for the test data instances using the trained model:

```
model %>% predict_classes(x_test)
```

9. Let's check the accuracy of the model on the test data:

```
model %>% evaluate(x_test, y_test)
```

The following diagram shows the model metrics on the test data:

```
$loss
[1] 0.1062629

$acc
[1] 0.9793
```

Here, we got an accuracy of around 97.9 %.

How it works...

In *step* 1, we loaded the MNIST dataset. The x data was a 3D array of grayscale values of the form (images, width, height). In *step* 2, we flattened these 28x28 images into a vector of length 784. Then, we normalized the grayscale values between 0 and 1. In *step* 3, we one-hot encoded the target variable using the `to_categorical()` function from `keras` to convert this into a binary format matrix.

In *step* 4, we built a sequential model by stacking dense and dropout layers. In a dense layer, every neuron receives input from all the neurons of the previous layer, which is why it's known as being densely connected. In our model, each layer took input from the previous layer and applied an activation to the output of our previous layer. We used the `relu` activation function in the hidden layers and the softmax activation function in the last layer since we had 10 possible outcomes. **Dropout** layers are used for regularizing deep learning models. Dropout refers to the process of not considering certain neurons in the training phase during a particular forward or backward pass in order to prevent overfitting. The `summary()` function provides us with a summary of the model; it gives us information about each layer, such as the shape of the output and the parameters in each layer.

In *step* 5, we compiled the model using the `compile()` function from `keras`. We applied the `rmsprop()` optimizer to find the weights and biases that minimize our objective loss function, `categorical_crossentropy`. The `metrics` argument calculates the metric to be evaluated by the model during training.

In *step* 6, we trained our model for a fixed number of iterations, which is defined by the `epochs` argument. The `validation_split` argument can take float values between 0 and 1 and specifies the fraction of the data to be used as validation data. Finally, `batch_size` defines the number of samples that will be propagated through the network. The history object records the training metrics for each epoch and contains two lists, `params` and `metrics`. The params contains the model's parameters, such as batch size, steps, and so on, while `metrics` contains model metrics such as loss and accuracy.

In *step* 7, we visualized the model's accuracy and loss metrics. In *step* 8, we used our model to generate predictions for the test data using the `predict_classes()` function. Lastly, we evaluated the model's accuracy on the test data using the `evaluate()` function.

There's more...

Tuning is the process of maximizing a model's performance without overfitting or underfitting. This can be achieved by setting appropriate values for the model parameters. A deep neural network has multiple parameters that can be tuned; layers, hidden units optimization parameters such as an optimizer, the learning rate, and the number of epochs.

To tune Keras model parameters, we need to define `flags` for the parameters that we want to optimize. These are defined by the `flags()` function of the `keras` package, which returns an object of the `tfruns_flags` type. This contains information about the parameters to be tuned. In the following code block, we have declared four flags that will tune the dropout rate and the number of neurons in the first and second layers of the model. `flag_integer("dense_units1",8)` tunes the number of units in layer 1, `dense_units1` is the name of the flag, and 8 is the default number of neurons:

```
# Defining flags
FLAGS <- flags(
  flag_integer("dense_units1",8),
  flag_numeric("dropout1",0.4),
  flag_integer("dense_units2",8),
  flag_numeric("dropout2", 0.3)
)
```

Once we have defined the flags, we use them in the definition of our model. In the following code block, we have defined our model using the parameters that we want to tune:

```
# Defining model
model <- keras_model_sequential()
model %>%
  layer_dense(units = FLAGS$dense_units1, activation = 'relu', input_shape =
```

```
c(784)) %>%
  layer_dropout(rate = FLAGS$dropout1) %>%
  layer_dense(units = FLAGS$dense_units2, activation = 'relu') %>%
  layer_dropout(rate = FLAGS$dropout2) %>%
  layer_dense(units = 10, activation = 'softmax')
```

The preceding two code blocks are code snippets from
the `hyperparamexcter_tuning_model.R` script, which is available in this book's GitHub
repository. In the script, we have implemented a model for classifying MNIST digits.
Executing this script does not tune your hyperparameters; it just defines the parameterized
training runs to create the best model.

The following code block shows how we can fine-tune the model defined
in `hyperparameter_tuning_model.R`. Here, we used the `tuning_run()` function from
the `tfruns` package. The `tfruns` package provides a suite of tools for tracking, visualizing,
and managing TensorFlow training runs and experiments from R. The `file` argument of
the function should be the path to the training script and should contain flags and the
model definition. The `flags` argument takes a list of key-value pairs where the key names
must match the names of the different flags that we defined in our model. The
`tuning_run()` function executes training runs for every combination of the specified flags.
By default, all the runs go into the `runs` subdirectory of the current working directory. It
returns a dataframe that contains summary information about all the runs, such as
evaluation, validation and performance loss (`categorical_crossentropy`), and metrics
(`accuracy`):

```
library(tfruns)

# training runs
runs <- tuning_run(file = "hypereparameter_tuning_model.R", flags = list(
  dense_units1 = c(8,16),
  dropout1 = c(0.2, 0.3, 0.4),
  dense_units2 = c(8,16),
  dropout2 = c(0.2, 0.3, 0.4)
))
runs
```

Here are the results from each run during hyperparameter tuning:

```
Data frame: 36 x 29
              run_dir eval_loss eval_acc metric_loss metric_acc metric_val_loss metric_val_acc
1  runs/2019-04-15T15-51-53Z   0.3611   0.9130    0.8188     0.7376       0.3464        0.9170
2  runs/2019-04-15T15-49-55Z   0.6040   0.8665    1.1354     0.6021       0.5855        0.8748
3  runs/2019-04-15T15-47-54Z   0.3282   0.9166    0.7001     0.7755       0.3056        0.9184
4  runs/2019-04-15T15-45-55Z   0.4942   0.8898    0.9931     0.6697       0.4844        0.8936
5  runs/2019-04-15T15-43-53Z   0.3065   0.9245    0.5879     0.8200       0.3005        0.9232
6  runs/2019-04-15T15-41-57Z   0.4713   0.8882    0.8418     0.7317       0.4499        0.8922
7  runs/2019-04-15T15-40-00Z   0.4764   0.9107    1.1170     0.6125       0.4624        0.9092
8  runs/2019-04-15T15-38-04Z   0.8189   0.8235    1.3665     0.5032       0.8022        0.8332
9  runs/2019-04-15T15-36-06Z   0.4649   0.9034    1.0160     0.6569       0.4585        0.9051
10 runs/2019-04-15T15-34-10Z   0.7296   0.8442    1.3047     0.5189       0.6953        0.8537
# ... with 26 more rows
# ... with 22 more columns:
#   flag_dense_units1, flag_dropout1, flag_dense_units2, flag_dropout2, samples, validation_samples, batch_size, epochs,
#   epochs_completed, metrics, model, loss_function, optimizer, learning_rate, script, start, end, completed, output,
#   source_code, context, type
```

For each training run, we get the model metrics for the training and validation data.

See also

- Vectorization of operations in deep neural networks: `http://ufldl.stanford.edu/wiki/index.php/Neural_Network_Vectorization` and `https://peterroelants.github.io/posts/neural-network-implementation-part04/`

2
Working with Convolutional Neural Networks

Convolutional Neural Networks (CNNs) are the most popular and widely used deep neural networks for computer vision problems. They are used in a variety of applications including image classification, face recognition, document analysis, medical image analysis, action recognition, and natural language processing. In this chapter, we will focus on learning convolutional operations, and concepts such as padding and strides, to optimize CNNs. The idea behind this chapter is to make you well versed with the functioning of the CNN and learn techniques such as data augmentation and batch normalization to fine-tune your network and prevent overfitting. We will also provide a brief discussion about how we can leverage transfer learning to boost model performance.

In this chapter, we will cover the following recipes:

- Introduction to the convolution operation
- Understanding strides and padding
- Getting familiar with pooling layers
- Implementing transfer learning

Introduction to convolutional operations

The generic architecture of CNN is comprised of convolutional layers followed by fully connected layers. Like other neural networks, a CNN also contains input, hidden and output layers, but it works by restructuring the data into tensors that consist of the image, and the width and height of the image. In CNN, each volume in one layer is connected only to a spatially relevant region in the next layer to ensure that when the number of layers increases, each neuron has a local influence on its specific location. A CNN may also contain pooling layers along with few fully connected layers.

The following is an example of a simple CNN with convolution and pooling layers. In this recipe, we will work with convolution layers. We will introduce the concept of pooling layers in the *Getting familiar with pooling layers* recipe of this chapter:

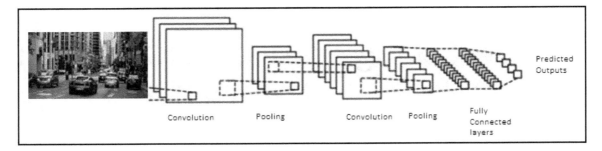

The convolution operation is an element-wise multiplication and summation between the input matrix and the filter used. Here is an example of a convolution operation:

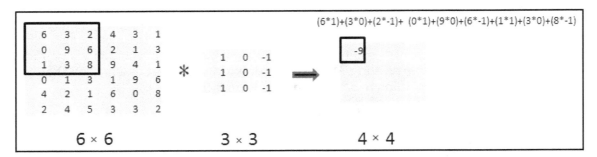

Now we understand how a convolution layer works. Let's move on to building a convolutional neural network to classify clothing and accessories.

Getting ready

Let's start with importing the `keras` library:

```
library(keras)
```

In this recipe, we will work with the Fashion-MNIST dataset, which we can import directly from keras.

How to do it...

The Fashion-MNIST dataset contains images of 10 different types of items of clothing and accessories. It consists of 60,000 examples in the training set and 10,000 examples in the testing dataset. Each example is a 28 × 28 grayscale image, associated with a label from the 10 classes.

1. We import the Fashion-MNIST dataset in our environment:

```
fashion <- dataset_fashion_mnist()
x_train <- fashion$train$x
y_train <- fashion$train$y
x_test <- fashion$test$x
y_test <- fashion$test$y
```

We can check the dimensions of the train and test datasets using the commands:

```
dim(x_train)
dim(x_test)
```

Now let's take a look at the data for a sample image:

```
x_test[1,,]
```

In the following screenshot, we can see that the sample image data is in the form of a matrix:

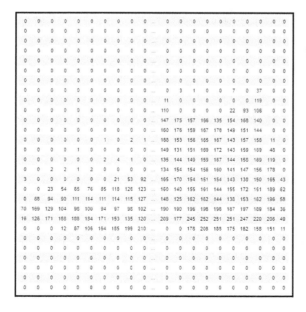

We check the label of the preceding screenshot using the following code:

```
paste("label of first image is:  " ,y_train[1])
```

In the following screenshot, we can see that the sample image belongs to class 9:

'label of first image is: 9'

Now we define the label names for the different classes in the data:

```
label_names = c('T-shirt/top', 'Trouser', 'Pullover', 'Dress',
'Coat',  'Sandal',
 'Shirt', 'Sneaker', 'Bag', 'Ankle boot')
```

If you are using the Jupyter notebook, you can use the repr library to set the plot window size using the following code: `options(repr.plot.width=5, repr.plot.height=3)`

Let's visualize a few sample images from the different classes:

```
# Visualize images

par(mfcol=c(3,3))
par(mar=c(2,2,2,2),xaxs = "i",yaxs = "i")
for (idx in 1:9) {
 img <- x_train[idx,,]
 img <- t(apply(img, 2, rev))
 image(1:28,1:28,img, main=paste(label_names[y_train[idx]+1]),xaxt
= 'n',yaxt = 'n',col= gray((0:255)/255))
 }
```

In the following screenshot, we can see sample images along with their label names:

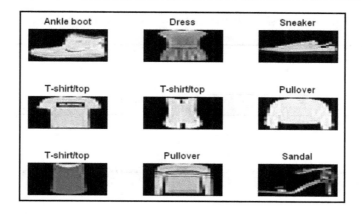

2. Next, we reshape the data, normalize it, and convert the target label to a binary class matrix:

```
# Resize the shape of inputs
x_train <- array_reshape(x_train, c(nrow(x_train), 28, 28, 1))
x_test <- array_reshape(x_test, c(nrow(x_test), 28, 28, 1))

# Transform RGB values into [0,1] range
x_train <- x_train / 255
x_test <- x_test / 255

# Convert class vectors to binary class matrices
y_train <- to_categorical(y_train, 10)
y_test <- to_categorical(y_test, 10)
```

3. Once we are done with data preparation, we build, compile, and train our CNN model:

```
# Define model
cnn_model <- keras_model_sequential() %>%
 layer_conv_2d(filters = 8, kernel_size = c(4,4), activation =
'relu',
 input_shape = c(28,28,1)) %>%
 layer_conv_2d(filters = 16, kernel_size = c(3,3), activation =
'relu') %>%
 layer_flatten() %>%
 layer_dense(units = 16, activation = 'relu') %>%
 layer_dense(units = 10, activation = 'softmax')
```

Let's look at the summary of the model:

```
cnn_model %>% summary()
```

The following screenshot shows the details about the model:

```
Layer (type)                    Output Shape               Param #
==================================================================
conv2d (Conv2D)                 (None, 25, 25, 8)          136

conv2d_1 (Conv2D)               (None, 23, 23, 16)         1168

flatten (Flatten)               (None, 8464)               0

dense (Dense)                   (None, 16)                 135440

dense_1 (Dense)                 (None, 10)                 170
==================================================================
Total params: 136,914
Trainable params: 136,914
Non-trainable params: 0
```

Before compiling the model, let's define its loss function:

```
loss_entropy <- function(y_pred, y_true) {
  loss_categorical_crossentropy(y_pred, y_true)
  }
```

Now we compile the model:

```
# Compile model
cnn_model %>% compile(
  loss = loss_entropy,
  optimizer = optimizer_sgd(),
  metrics = c('accuracy')
)
```

After compiling the model, we train it with a batch size of 128, number of epochs set to 5, and a validation split of 20%:

```
# train the model
cnn_model %>% fit(
  x_train, y_train,
  batch_size = 128,
  epochs = 5,
  validation_split = 0.2
)
```

4. Finally, we evaluate the performance of the trained model and print the evaluation metrics:

```
scores <- cnn_model %>% evaluate(x_test,
  y_test,
  verbose = 0
```

```
    )
    # Output metrics
    paste('Test loss:', scores[[1]])
    paste('Test accuracy:', scores[[2]])
```

In the following screenshot, we can see the evaluation metrics of the model on test data:

'Test loss: 0.537091252660751 \n'

'Test accuracy: 0.816399991512299 \n'

Once we are satisfied with the model's accuracy, we can use it for predicting classes for the testing dataset:

```
    #prediction
    predicted_label <- cnn_model %>% predict_classes(x_test)
```

In the preceding screenshot, we can see our model achieves a good accuracy of 81.63% on test data.

How it works...

The `keras` library in R provides various datasets, using which we can develop deep learning models. In *step 1*, we imported the Fashion-MNIST dataset, using the `dataset_fashion_mnist()` function and checked the dimensions of its training and testing partitions. We also looked at the data and label of a sample image. Next, we defined the label names for the data and visualized one sample image for each label.

 Base R graphics provide functions to plot interesting plots. The `par()` function is used to set various graphical parameters, and the `image()` function creates a grid of colored or grayscale rectangles with colors corresponding to the values in the image matrix.

In *step 2*, we reshaped our data and normalized it within the range of 0 to 1. We also one-hot encoded the target label matrix using the `to_categorical()` function. After we completed the data preparation, in *step 3*, we configured our CNN model and looked at its summary. In the model configuration, we added two convolutional layers with 8 and 16 filters of sizes 4 × 4 and 3 × 3 respectively, and each layer used the **ReLU** activation function.

Next, we used `layer_flatten()` to convert the output matrix of the convolutional layer into a linear array, which gets fed as an input into the nodes of our dense neural network. Our dense network contained a hidden layer with 16 units and an output layer with 10 units because we had 10 target labels. Next, we looked at the summary of the model; it gave us the information about output shape and number of parameters in each layer. The following are the formulas to calculate these for the convolutional layer:

- The output shape of each layer: If the input to our convolutional layer is $n \times n \times n_c$ and we apply m filters of $f_{row} \times f_{column}$, then the output shape is given by the following formula:
  $(n - f_{row} + 1, n - f_{column} + 1, m)$
- The number of parameters in each layer can be calculated by the following formula:
  $(f_{row} \times f_{column} \times n_c \times m) + m$

After the model configuration, we compiled the model using a stochastic gradient descent optimizer and a categorical cross-entropy loss function. Next, we trained the model. Lastly, in *step 4*, we evaluated the performance of the model on the testing dataset and printed the evaluation metrics and generated predictions for the testing dataset.

There's more...

Until now, we have predominantly used two-dimensional convolutional layers. Apart from two-dimensional convolutions, there are one-dimensional and three-dimensional implementations of CNNs, depending upon the type of input data used.

One-dimensional CNNs are widely used for textual data analysis, for example, classifying customer reviews. Unlike images, which are mostly two-dimensional in nature, text data has one-dimensional input data. You can refer to the following example for one-dimensional convolutions, available at `https://keras.rstudio.com/articles/examples/imdb_cnn.html` here.

See also

- You can refer to the Keras documentation for more details about three-dimensional convolutional layers, at `https://keras.rstudio.com/reference/layer_conv_3d.html`

Understanding strides and padding

In this recipe, we will learn about two key configuration hyperparameters of CNN, which are strides and padding. Strides are used mainly to reduce the size of the output volume. Padding is another technique that lets us preserve the dimensions of the input volume in the output volume, thus enabling us to extract the low-level features efficiently.

Strides: Stride, in very simple terms, means the step of the convolution operation. Stride specifies the amount by which filters convolve around the input. For example, if we specify the value of stride argument as 1, that means the filter will shift one unit at a time over the input matrix.

Strides can be used for multiple purposes, primarily the following:

- To avoid feature overlapping
- To achieve smaller spatial dimensionality of the output volume

In the following diagram, you can see an example of a convolution operation on a 7 × 7 input data with a filter size of a 3 × 3 and a stride of 1:

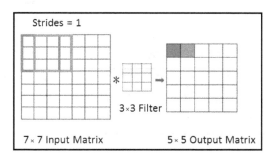

Padding: For better modeling performance, we need to preserve the information about the low-level features of the input volume in the early layers of the network. As we keep applying convolutional layers, the size of the output volume decreases faster. Also, the pixels at corners of the input matrix are traversed a lesser number of times, compared to the pixels in the middle of the input matrix, which leads to throwing away a lot of the information near the edge of the image. To avoid this, we use zero padding. Zero padding symmetrically pads the input volume with zeros around the border.

There are two types of padding:

- **Valid**: If we specify valid padding, our convolutional layer is not going to pad anything around the input matrix and the size of the output volume will keep decreasing on adding layers.

- **Same**: This pads the original input with zeros around the edges of the input matrix before we convolve it so that the output size is the same size as the input size.

In the following screenshot, we can see a pictorial representation of zero padding:

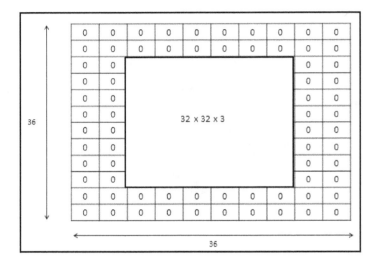

Now that we are aware of the concepts of strides and padding, let's move further to the implementation part.

How to do it...

In this section, we will use the same Fashion-MNIST dataset that was used in the previous *Introduction to the convolution operation* recipe of this chapter. The data exploration and transformation will remain the same, hence we directly jump to the model configuration:

1. Let's define our model with strides and padding:

```
cnn_model_sp <- keras_model_sequential() %>%
    layer_conv_2d(filters = 8, kernel_size = c(4,4), activation =
```

```
'relu',
input_shape = c(28,28,1),
strides = c(2L, 2L),,padding = "same") %>%
layer_conv_2d(filters = 16, kernel_size = c(3,3), activation =
'relu') %>%
layer_flatten() %>%
layer_dense(units = 16, activation = 'relu') %>%
layer_dense(units = 10, activation = 'softmax')
```

Let's look at the summary of the model:

```
cnn_model_sp %>% summary()
```

The following screenshot shows the details about the model created:

```
Layer (type)                    Output Shape                   Param #
================================================================================
conv2d (Conv2D)                 (None, 14, 14, 8)              136

conv2d_1 (Conv2D)               (None, 12, 12, 16)             1168

flatten (Flatten)               (None, 2304)                   0

dense (Dense)                   (None, 16)                     36880

dense_1 (Dense)                 (None, 10)                     170
================================================================================
Total params: 38,354
Trainable params: 38,354
Non-trainable params: 0
```

2. After configuring our model, we define its objective loss function, then compile and train it:

```
# loss function
loss_entropy <- function(y_pred, y_true) {
  loss_categorical_crossentropy(y_pred, y_true)
}

# Compile model
cnn_model_sp %>% compile(
  loss = loss_entropy,
  optimizer = optimizer_sgd(),
  metrics = c('accuracy')
)
```

```
# Train model
cnn_model_sp %>% fit(
  x_train, y_train,
  batch_size = 128,
  epochs = 5,
  validation_split = 0.2
)
```

Let's evaluate the performance of the model on the test data and print the evaluation metrics:

```
scores <- cnn_model_sp %>% evaluate(x_test,
  y_test,
  verbose = 0
)
```

Now we print the model loss and accuracy on the test data:

```
# Output metrics
paste('Test loss:', scores[[1]], '\n')
paste('Test accuracy:', scores[[2]], '\n')
```

We can see that the model's accuracy on test data is around 78%:

```
'Test loss: 0.564140768718719 \n'
'Test accuracy: 0.788699984550476 \n'
```

We can see that the model did a good job in the classification task.

How it works...

In the previous recipe, *Introduction to convolution operation*, we built a simple CNN model. Apart from **filter size** and the **number of filters**, there are two more parameters of a convolution layer that can be configured for better feature extraction, and these are **strides** and **padding**. In *step 1*, we passed a vector of two integers (width and height), specifying the strides of the convolution along the width and height. The padding argument takes two values, **valid**, and **same**, with **valid** meaning no padding, and **same** means that the input and output sizes remain the same. Next, we printed a summary of the model.

The output shape and number of trainable parameters of a convolutional layer can be given by the following formula:

- Output shape: If the input to our convolutional layer is $n \times n \times n_c$ and we apply m filters of $f_{row} \times f_{column}$ and s strides and p padding, then the output shape is given by the following formula:

$$(\frac{n - f_{row} + 2p}{s} + 1, \frac{n - f_{column} + 2p}{s} + 1, m)$$

- The number of parameters in each layer is calculated as follows:

$$(f_{row} \times f_{column} \times n_c \times m) + m$$

In *step 2*, we defined the loss function of our model, then compiled and trained it. We then tested the model's performance on the testing dataset and printed the model's loss and accuracy.

Getting familiar with pooling layers

CNNs use pooling layers to reduce the size of the representation, to speed up the computation of the network, and to ensure robust feature extraction. The pooling layer is mostly stacked on top of the convolutional layer and this layer heavily downsizes the input dimension to reduce the computation in the network and also reduce overfitting.

There are two most commonly used types of pooling techniques :

- **Max pooling**: This type of pooling does downsampling by dividing the input matrix into pooling regions followed by computing the max values of each region.

Here's an example:

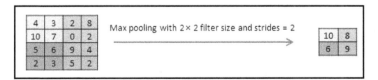

- **Average pooling**: This type of pooling does downsampling by dividing the input matrix into pooling regions followed by computing the average values of each region.

Here's an example:

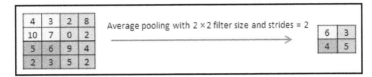

In this recipe, we will learn how to fit pooling layers in a CNN model architecture.

Getting ready

In this example, we will work on a sample of the Fruits 360 dataset. The dataset is credited to Horea Muresan and Mihai Oltean. The dataset was introduced in their paper, *Fruit recognition from images using deep learning,* which presents the results of a numerical experiment for training a neural network to detect fruits. The dataset can be downloaded from Kaggle at https://www.kaggle.com/moltean/fruits. The Fruits 360 dataset contains colored images of 103 fruits of size 100 × 100, but in our example, we will work on images of only 23 fruits. It has two subsets: a training set and a test set with samples of each fruit in directories corresponding to the fruit name.

We will start by loading the keras library:

```
library(keras)
```

We have our dataset in the folder named as fruits in our current working directory. This folder contains train and test subfolders that contain fruit images in folders named after that particular fruit. Let's store the paths of the train and test data into variables:

```
# path to train and test directories
train_path <- "fruits/train/"
test_path <- "fruits/test/"
```

Let's create a vector of names of the fruits that are present in our data:

```
class_label <- list.dirs(path = train_path, full.names = FALSE, recursive =
TRUE)[-1]
```

Now we print the names of fruits (class labels) of our data:

```
class_label
```

The following screenshot shows the names of fruits in our data:

```
'Apricot'  'Avocado'  'Banana'  'Cactus fruit'  'Cherry Wax Red'  'Chestnut'  'Dates'  'Guava'  'Kiwi'  'Lemon'  'Lychee'  'Mango'  'Orange'  'Papaya'
'Peach'  'Pear'  'Physalis with Husk'  'Pineapple'  'Pomegranate'  'Raspberry'  'Strawberry'  'Tomato Cherry Red'  'Walnut'
```

For looking at the number of classes of fruits, you can use the following code:

```
length(class_label)
```

Now let's set the image width and height, we will scale down the size of the image from 100×100 to 20×20:

```
img_width = 20
img_height = 20
img_size = c(img_width,img_height)
```

We are now familiar with the dataset and the transformations we want to do. Let's move on to implement these transformations.

How to do it...

We will use the `flow_images_from_directory()` function from keras to read and manipulate data on the fly.

1. Let's read the images from the train and test directory and do the required transformations:

```
# Reading train data
train_data <- flow_images_from_directory(directory = train_path,
 target_size = img_size,
 color_mode = "rgb",
 class_mode = "categorical",
 classes = class_label,
 batch_size = 20)

# Reading  test data
test_data <- flow_images_from_directory(directory = test_path,
```

```
target_size = img_size,
color_mode = "rgb",
class_mode = "categorical",
classes = class_label,
batch_size = 20)
```

Let's see how many images we have in train and test sets:

```
print(paste("Number of images in train and test
is",train_data$n,"and ",test_data$n,"repectively"))
```

We can see that the training dataset contains 11,397 images and the test data contains 3,829 images:

```
"Number of images in train and test is 11397 and  3829 repectively"
```

Now let's also have a look at the number of images per class in the train and test data:

```
table(factor(train_data$classes))
```

This is the distribution of images per class in the training data:

```
  0   1   2   3   4   5   6   7   8   9  10  11  12  13  14
492 427 490 450 490 492 479 492 492 490 492 490 492 492 735
```

```
table(factor(test_data$classes))
```

This is the distribution of images per class in the test data:

```
  0   1   2   3   4   5   6   7   8   9  10  11  12  13  14
164 143 166 153 166 164 160 164 164 166 164 166 164 164 249
```

Note that the class labels are numeric. Let's look at the mapping of the class label and class label names. These would be the same for the train and test data:

```
train_data$class_indices
```

The screenshot shows the class labels in the data:

```
$Apricot
0
$Avocado
1
$Banana
2
$`Cactus fruit`
3
$`Cherry Wax Red`
4
$Chestnut
5
$Dates
6
$Guava
7
$Kiwi
8
$Lemon
9
$Lychee
10
$Mango
11
$Orange
12
$Papaya
13
$Peach
14
$Pear
15
$`Physalis with Husk`
16
$Pineapple
17
$Pomegranate
18
$Raspberry
19
$Strawberry
20
$`Tomato Cherry Red`
21
$Walnut
22
```

Similarly, we can look at the test label and label names. Now let's print the shape of the image we loaded into our environment:

```
train_data$image_shape
```

The screenshot shows the dimensions of the image loaded:

```
1. 20
2. 20
3. 3
```

2. Next, we define the Keras model with pooling layers:

```
cnn_model_pool <- keras_model_sequential() %>%
  layer_conv_2d(filters = 32, kernel_size = c(3,3), activation =
'relu',
  input_shape = c(img_width,img_height,3),padding = "same") %>%
  layer_conv_2d(filters = 16, kernel_size = c(3,3), activation =
'relu',padding = "same") %>%
  layer_max_pooling_2d(pool_size = c(2,2)) %>%
  layer_flatten() %>%
  layer_dense(units = 50, activation = 'relu') %>%
  layer_dense(units = 23, activation = 'softmax')
```

Let's look at the model summary:

```
cnn_model_pool %>% summary()
```

The following screenshot shows the summary of the model:

Layer (type)	Output Shape	Param #
conv2d (Conv2D)	(None, 20, 20, 32)	896
conv2d_1 (Conv2D)	(None, 20, 20, 16)	4624
max_pooling2d (MaxPooling2D)	(None, 10, 10, 16)	0
flatten (Flatten)	(None, 1600)	0
dense (Dense)	(None, 50)	80050
dense_1 (Dense)	(None, 23)	1173

```
Total params: 86,743
Trainable params: 86,743
Non-trainable params: 0
```

3. After defining our model, we compile and train it.

While compiling the model, we set the loss function, model metric, learning rate, and decay rate of our optimizer:

```
cnn_model_pool %>% compile(
  loss = "categorical_crossentropy",
  optimizer = optimizer_rmsprop(lr = 0.0001,decay = 1e-6),
  metrics = c('accuracy')
)
```

Now we train the model:

```
cnn_model_pool %>% fit_generator(generator = train_data,
  steps_per_epoch = 20,
  epochs = 5)
```

After training the model, we evaluate its performance on test data and print the performance metrics:

```
scores <- cnn_model_pool %>% evaluate_generator(generator =
test_data,steps = 20)

# Output metrics
paste('Test loss:', scores[[1]], '\n')
paste('Test accuracy:', scores[[2]], '\n')
```

The following screenshot shows the model performance on the test data:

'Test loss: 2.9508512192228 \n'

'Test accuracy: 0.789501190185547 \n'

We can see that the accuracy of the model on test data is around 79%.

How it works...

In *step 1*, we used the `flow_images_from_directory()` function to load the images from a directory. To use this functionality, we must structure our data as we did for the Fruits 360 dataset. This function gives us the flexibility to transform our images while loading them in R. In our implementation, we reshaped each image to a size of 20 × 20 and changed the color mode to RGB channel. Next, we explored the data and looked at the distribution of images in the training and test datasets.

In the next step, we defined our model. In this model, we fit a max-pooling layer followed by two dense layers. The last layer of the network had **softmax** activation with 23 units since we had 23 output labels. Next, we looked at the summary of the model, and we observed that the number of trainable parameters in the pooling layer is zero because it has no weights and biases to train. The output shape of the pooling layer can be determined by: *floor(input size/pool size)*.

In the last step, we compiled and trained the model. To train the model, we used the `fit_generator()` function because we had to train our model on the generator object returned by `flow_images_from_directory()`. Next, we evaluated our model's performance on the test dataset and printed the evaluation metrics.

There's more...

Overfitting is a common challenge in scenarios where we have only a few data samples to learn from. This prevents our model from performing robustly on unseen data. There are a few techniques that help us deal with this issue:

Data augmentation: It is a technique that reduces overfitting by generating more training data from existing samples in the data and augmenting the samples via several random transformations that produce believable-looking images. It creates modified versions by applying operations like shifting, flipping, zooming, and so on. It also enriches our data, which helps to generalize our model and make it more robust. Data augmentation is done only on the training set.

The `keras` library in R provides the `image_data_generator()` function to implement real-time data augmentation in batches. The following example shows how we can augment data from the Fruits 360 dataset. The augmented images will be rotated randomly by between 0 and 50 degrees, and their width/height will vary between 0% and 10% of the total width/height. We have specified a zoom range of 0.2:

```
train_data_generator <- image_data_generator(rotation_range = 50,
width_shift_range = 0.1,
height_shift_range = 0.1,
zoom_range = 0.2,
horizontal_flip = TRUE,
fill_mode = "nearest")
```

The following code block demonstrates how to load images from a directory with data augmentation on the fly:

```
train_data <- flow_images_from_directory(directory = train_path,
generator = train_data_generator,
target_size = img_size,
color_mode = "rgb",
class_mode = "categorical",
classes = class_label,
batch_size = 20)
```

Note that we have used the `rgb` color mode; other color modes include `grayscale`.

Batch normalization: While training deep neural networks, the distribution of each layer's inputs changes and slows down the training since we need to keep lower learning rates and do careful parameter initialization to train the model correctly. This phenomenon is referred to as **internal covariate shift** and is addressed by performing the normalization for each training mini-batch. Batch normalization normalizes each batch by both mean and variance reference, allowing us to use higher learning rates. It also acts as a regularizer, in some cases eliminating the need for dropout. Batch normalization makes weight initializations easy. For more details about the `layer_batch_normalization()` function and its arguments, please refer to `https://keras.rstudio.com/reference/layer_batch_normalization.html`.

If we were to use batch normalization in our CNN model, here is how we could have done it:

```
cnn_model_batch_norm <- keras_model_sequential() %>%
 layer_conv_2d(filters = 32, kernel_size = c(4,4),input_shape =
c(img_width,img_height,3),padding = "same") %>%
 layer_batch_normalization()%>%
 layer_activation("relu") %>%
 layer_conv_2d(filters = 16, kernel_size = c(3,3))%>%
 layer_batch_normalization()%>%
 layer_activation("relu")%>%
 layer_max_pooling_2d(pool_size = c(2,2)) %>%
 layer_flatten() %>%
 layer_dense(units = 50, activation = 'relu') %>%
 layer_dense(units = 23, activation = 'softmax')
```

Let's see the summary of the model with batch normalization:

```
summary(cnn_model_batch_norm)
```

The screenshot shows the description of the model with batch normalization:

Layer (type)	Output Shape	Param #
conv2d (Conv2D)	(None, 20, 20, 32)	1568
batch_normalization_v1 (BatchNormal	(None, 20, 20, 32)	128
activation (Activation)	(None, 20, 20, 32)	0
conv2d_1 (Conv2D)	(None, 18, 18, 16)	4624
batch_normalization_v1_1 (BatchNorm	(None, 18, 18, 16)	64
activation_1 (Activation)	(None, 18, 18, 16)	0
max_pooling2d (MaxPooling2D)	(None, 9, 9, 16)	0
flatten (Flatten)	(None, 1296)	0
dense (Dense)	(None, 50)	64850
dense_1 (Dense)	(None, 23)	1173

```
Total params: 72,407
Trainable params: 72,311
Non-trainable params: 96
```

Thus, in this recipe, we focused on max pooling and average pooling. Another famous technique of pooling is known as **global average pooling**, which performs extreme dimensionality reduction. In the *See also* section of this recipe, a link to more information about global average pooling is provided.

See also

- Sometimes, we also use global average pooling layers to prevent overfitting. The keras library provides an implementation of these layers. To read more, click on `https://keras.rstudio.com/reference/layer_global_max_pooling_2d.html`.
- To know more about how to set a custom learning rate decay for our optimizer, refer to the example implemented at `https://tensorflow.rstudio.com/tfestimators/articles/examples/iris_custom_decay_dnn.html`.

Implementing transfer learning

Transfer learning helps us solve a new problem using fewer examples by using information gained from solving other related tasks. It is a technique where we reuse a learned model trained on a different dataset to solve a similar but different problem. In transfer learning, we extend the learning of a pre-trained model in our network and build a new model to solve a new learning problem. The keras library in R provides many pre-trained models; we will be using one such model called as **VGG16** to train our network.

Getting ready

We will start by importing the `keras` library into our environment:

```
library(keras)
```

In this example, we will work with a subset of the Dogs versus Cats dataset from Kaggle (`https://www.kaggle.com/c/dogs-vs-cats`), which contains images of dogs and cats in different sizes. This dataset was developed as a partnership between Petfinder and Microsoft. We have divided our data into train, test, and validation sets, each containing images of cats and dogs in their respective folders. Our train and test data has 1,000 pictures of cats and dogs each, and the test and validation set has 500 images each of dogs and cats.

Let's define the train, test, and validation paths of our data:

```
train_path <- "dogs_cats_small/train/"
test_path <- "dogs_cats_small/test/"
validation_path <- "dogs_cats_small/validation/"
```

We have set the paths of our dataset.

How to do it...

Now let's proceed to data processing:

1. We start by defining a generator for the training and testing data. We will use these generators while loading data into our environment and perform real-time data augmentation:

```
# train generator
train_augmentor = image_data_generator(
  rescale = 1/255,
  rotation_range = 300,
  width_shift_range = 0.15,
  height_shift_range = 0.15,
  shear_range = 0.2,
  zoom_range = 0.2,
  horizontal_flip = TRUE,
  fill_mode = "nearest"
)

# test generator
test_augmentor <- image_data_generator(rescale = 1/255)
```

Now let's load the training, testing, and validation data into our environment:

```
# load train data
train_data <- flow_images_from_directory(
  train_path,
  train_augmentor,
  target_size = c(150, 150),
  batch_size = 20,
  class_mode = "binary")

# load test data
test_data <- test_generator <- flow_images_from_directory(
  test_path,
  test_augmentor,
  target_size = c(150, 150),
```

```
batch_size = 20,
class_mode = "binary")

# load validation data
validation_data <- flow_images_from_directory(
 validation_path,
 test_augmentor,
 target_size = c(150, 150),
 batch_size = 20,
 class_mode = "binary"
 )
```

We can print the shape of the rescaled image using the following code:

```
train_data$image_shape
```

2. After loading our data, let's instantiate a pre-trained VGG16 model. Going further, we will refer to this model as the base model:

```
pre_trained_base <- application_vgg16(
 weights = "imagenet",
 include_top = FALSE,
 input_shape = c(150, 150, 3)
 )
```

Let's now take a look at the summary of the base model:

```
summary(pre_trained_base)
```

Here is the description of the base model:

```
Layer (type)                    Output Shape              Param #
=================================================================
input_1 (InputLayer)            (None, 150, 150, 3)       0
block1_conv1 (Conv2D)           (None, 150, 150, 64)      1792
block1_conv2 (Conv2D)           (None, 150, 150, 64)      36928
block1_pool (MaxPooling2D)      (None, 75, 75, 64)        0
block2_conv1 (Conv2D)           (None, 75, 75, 128)       73856
block2_conv2 (Conv2D)           (None, 75, 75, 128)       147584
block2_pool (MaxPooling2D)      (None, 37, 37, 128)       0
block3_conv1 (Conv2D)           (None, 37, 37, 256)       295168
block3_conv2 (Conv2D)           (None, 37, 37, 256)       590080
block3_conv3 (Conv2D)           (None, 37, 37, 256)       590080
block3_pool (MaxPooling2D)      (None, 18, 18, 256)       0
block4_conv1 (Conv2D)           (None, 18, 18, 512)       1180160
block4_conv2 (Conv2D)           (None, 18, 18, 512)       2359808
block4_conv3 (Conv2D)           (None, 18, 18, 512)       2359808
block4_pool (MaxPooling2D)      (None, 9, 9, 512)         0
block5_conv1 (Conv2D)           (None, 9, 9, 512)         2359808
block5_conv2 (Conv2D)           (None, 9, 9, 512)         2359808
block5_conv3 (Conv2D)           (None, 9, 9, 512)         2359808
block5_pool (MaxPooling2D)      (None, 4, 4, 512)         0
=================================================================
Total params: 14,714,688
Trainable params: 14,714,688
Non-trainable params: 0
```

After instantiating the base model, we add dense layers to it and build a holistic model:

```
model_with_pretrained <- keras_model_sequential() %>%
  pre_trained_base %>%
  layer_flatten() %>%
  layer_dense(units = 8, activation = "relu") %>%
  layer_dense(units = 16, activation = "relu") %>%
  layer_dense(units = 1, activation = "sigmoid")
```

Now we visualize the summary of the model:

```
summary(model_with_pretrained)
```

The screenshot shows a summary of the holistic model:

```
Layer (type)                        Output Shape              Param #
=====================================================================
vgg16 (Model)                       (None, 4, 4, 512)         14714688
_____
flatten (Flatten)                   (None, 8192)              0
_____
dense (Dense)                       (None, 8)                 65544
_____
dense_1 (Dense)                     (None, 16)                144
_____
dense_2 (Dense)                     (None, 1)                 17
=====================================================================
Total params: 14,780,393
Trainable params: 14,780,393
Non-trainable params: 0
```

We can print the number of trainable kernels and biases we have in our model using the following code:

```
length(model_with_pretrained$trainable_weights)
```

Let's freeze the pre-realized weights of the base model:

```
freeze_weights(pre_trained_base)
```

We can check how many trainable weights we have after freezing the base model by executing the following code:

```
length(model_with_pretrained$trainable_weights)
```

3. After configuring the model, we then compile and train it.

Let's compile the model using binary cross-entropy as the loss function and `RMSprop()` as the optimizer:

```
model_with_pretrained %>% compile(
  loss = "binary_crossentropy",
  optimizer = optimizer_rmsprop(lr = 0.0001),
  metrics = c('accuracy')
)
```

After compiling, we now train the model:

```
model_with_pretrained %>% fit_generator(generator = train_data,
  steps_per_epoch = 20,
  epochs = 10,
  validation_data = validation_data)
```

Next, we evaluate the performance of the trained model on the test data and print the evaluation metrics:

```
scores <- model_with_pretrained %>% evaluate_generator(generator =
test_data, steps = 20)

# Output metrics
paste('Test loss:', scores[[1]], '\n')
paste('Test accuracy:', scores[[2]], '\n')
```

The screenshot shows the model performance on the test data:

'Test loss: 0.385350868999958'

'Test accuracy: 0.830999970436096'

The test accuracy is around 83%.

How it works...

In *step 1*, we defined our train and test generators to set the parameters for data augmentation. Then, we loaded the datasets into our environment and simultaneously performed real-time data augmentation while resizing the images to 150 × 150.

In the next step, we instantiated a pre-trained base model, **VGG16**, with weights trained on ImageNet data. ImageNet is a large visual database that contains images of 1,000 different classes. Note that we had set the value of include_top as FALSE. Setting it to false does not include the default densely connected layers of the VGG16 network, which correspond to 1,000 classes of the ImageNet data. Further, we defined a sequential Keras model that contains the base model along with a few custom dense layers to build a binary classifier. Next, we printed out a summary of our model and the number of kernels and biases in it. Then we froze the layers of the base model because we did not want to modify its weights while training on our dataset.

In the last step, we compiled our model with binary_crossentropy as the loss function and trained it using the RMSprop optimizer. Once we had trained our model, we printed its performance metrics on the test data.

There's more...

There are mainly three ways to implement transfer learning:

- Use a pre-trained model with pre-realized weights and biases; that is, completely freeze the pre-trained model of your network and train on a new dataset.
- Partially freeze a few layers of the pre-trained model of our network and train it on a new dataset.
- Retain only the architecture of the pre-trained model and train your complete network for new weights and biases.

The following code snippet demonstrates how to partially freeze the pre-trained part of the network. Before we unfreeze selected layers of the pre-trained network, we must define the holistic model and freeze the pre-trained part:

```
unfreeze_weights(pre_trained_base, from = "block5_conv1", to =
"block5_conv3")
```

The `from` and `to` arguments of the `unfreeze_weights()` function let us define the layers between which we want to unfreeze the weights. Please note that both the `from` and `to` layers are inclusive.

 We should use a very low learning rate while we are tuning layers of a pre-trained model on a new dataset. A low learning rate is advised because, on the layers that we are fine-tuning, we should restrict the magnitude of the modifications we make to the representations.

See also

We can leverage other pre-trained models to solve various deep learning problems, and Keras provides many such models. For more information, check out the page at `https://tensorflow.rstudio.com/keras/reference/#section-applications`.

3
Recurrent Neural Networks in Action

Sequence data is data where the order matters, such as in audio, video, and speech. Learning sequential data is one of the most challenging problems in the field of pattern recognition because of the nature of the data. The dependencies between the parts of sequences and their varying length add further complexity when processing sequential data. With the advent of sequence models and algorithms such as **recurrent neural networks (RNN)**, **long short-term memory models (LSTM)**, and **gated recurrent units (GRU)**, sequence data modeling is being utilized in multiple applications, such as sequence classification, sequence generation, speech to text conversion, and many more.

In sequence classification, the goal is to predict the category of the sequence, whereas in sequence generation, we generate a new output sequence based on the input sequence. In this chapter, you will learn how to implement sequence classification and generation, as well as time series forecasting, using different flavors of RNN.

In this chapter, we will cover the following recipes:

- Sentiment classification using RNNs
- Text generation using LSTMs
- Time series forecasting using GRUs
- Implementing bidirectional recurrent neural networks

Sentiment classification using RNNs

RNN is a unique network because of its ability to remember inputs. This ability makes it perfectly suited for problems that deal with sequential data, such as time series forecasting, speech recognition, machine translation, and audio and video sequence prediction. In RNNs, data traverses in such a way that, at each node, the network learns from both the current and previous inputs, sharing the weights over time. It's like performing the same task at each step, just with different inputs that reduce the total number of parameters we need to learn.

For example, if the activation function is *tanh*, then the weight at the recurrent neuron is W_{aa} and the weight at the input neuron is W_{ax}. Here, we can write the equation for the state, h, at time t as follows:

$$h_t = tanh(W_{aa}h_{t-1} + W_{ax}X_t)$$

The gradient at each output depends on the computations of the current and previous time steps. For example, to calculate the gradient at $t=6$, we would need to backpropagate five steps and add the gradients. This is known as **Backpropagation Through Time** (**BPTT**). During BPTT, while iterating over the training examples, we modify the weights in order to reduce errors.

RNNs can handle data with various input and output types through the different architectures it supports. The main ones are as follows:

- **One-to-Many:** One input is mapped to a sequence with multiple steps as output. An example of this is music generation:

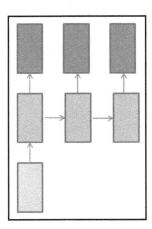

- **Many-to-One**: A sequence of inputs is mapped to a class or quantity prediction. An example of this is sentiment classification:

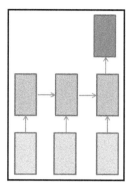

- **Many-to-Many**: A sequence of inputs is mapped to a sequence of outputs. An example of this is language translation:

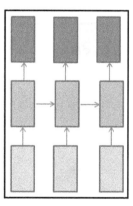

In this recipe, we will build an RNN model that will classify the sentiments of movie reviews.

Getting ready

In this section, we will use the IMDb dataset, which contains movie reviews and sentiment associated with it. We can import dataset from the `keras` library. These reviews are preprocessed and encoded as a sequence of word indexes. These words are indexed by their overall frequency in the dataset; for example, the word index *8*, refers to the 8th most frequent word in the data.

Now, let's import the `keras` library and the `imdb` dataset:

```
library(keras)
imdb <- dataset_imdb(num_words = 1000)
```

Let's divide the data into training and testing sets:

```
train_x <- imdb$train$x
train_y <- imdb$train$y
test_x <- imdb$test$x
test_y <- imdb$test$y
```

Now, we can have a look at the number of reviews in the train and test data:

```
# number of samples in train and test set
cat(length(train_x), 'train sequences\n')
cat(length(test_x), 'test sequences')
```

Here, we can see that there are 25000 reviews each in the train and test sets:

```
25000 train sequences
25000 test sequences
```

Let's also look at the structure of the train data:

```
str(train_x)
```

The following screenshot shows a description of the predictor variables in the training data:

```
List of 25000
 $ : int [1:218] 1 14 22 16 43 530 973 2 2 65 ...
 $ : int [1:189] 1 194 2 194 2 78 228 5 6 2 ...
 $ : int [1:141] 1 14 47 8 30 31 7 4 249 108 ...
 $ : int [1:550] 1 4 2 2 33 2 4 2 432 111 ...
 $ : int [1:147] 1 249 2 7 61 113 10 10 13 2 ...
 $ : int [1:43] 1 778 128 74 12 630 163 15 4 2 ...
 $ : int [1:123] 1 2 365 2 5 2 354 11 14 2 ...
 $ : int [1:562] 1 4 2 716 4 65 7 4 689 2 ...
 $ : int [1:233] 1 43 188 46 5 566 264 51 6 530 ...
 $ : int [1:130] 1 14 20 47 111 439 2 19 12 15 ...
 $ : int [1:450] 1 785 189 438 47 110 142 7 6 2 ...
 $ : int [1:99] 1 54 13 2 14 20 13 69 55 364 ...
 $ : int [1:117] 1 13 119 954 189 2 13 92 459 48 ...
 $ : int [1:238] 1 259 37 100 169 2 2 11 14 418 ...
 $ : int [1:109] 1 503 20 33 118 481 302 26 184 52 ...
 $ : int [1:129] 1 6 964 437 7 58 43 2 11 6 ...
 $ : int [1:163] 1 2 2 11 4 2 9 4 2 4 ...
 $ : int [1:752] 1 33 4 2 7 4 2 194 2 2 ...
 $ : int [1:212] 1 13 28 64 69 4 2 7 319 14 ...
 $ : int [1:177] 1 2 26 9 6 2 731 939 44 6 ...
 $ : int [1:129] 1 617 11 2 17 2 14 966 78 20 ...
 $ : int [1:140] 1 466 49 2 204 2 40 4 2 732 ...
 $ : int [1:256] 1 13 784 886 857 15 135 142 40 2 ...
```

Similarly, we will take a look at the structure of the training label:

```
str(train_y)
```

The following screenshot shows the description of the target variable in the training data:

```
int [1:25000] 1 0 0 1 0 0 1 0 1 0 ...
```

Here, we can see that our training set is a list of reviews and sentiment labels. Let's look at the first review and the number of words in it:

```
train_x[[1]]
cat("Number of words in the first review is",length(train_x[[1]]))
```

The following screenshot shows the first review in encoded form:

```
  1  14  22  16  43  530 973  2  2  65  458  2  66  2  4  173  36  256  5  25  100  43  838  112  50  670  2  9  35  480  284  5
150  4  172 112 167  2  336 385 39  4  172  2  2  17 546 38  13  447  4  192  50  16  6  147  2  19  14  22  4  2  2  469  4
 22  71  87  12  16  43  530 38  76  15  13  2  4  22  17 515 17  12  16  626 18  2  5  62  386  12  8  316  8  106  5  4  2  2
 16 480  66  2  33  4  130 12  16  38 619  5  25 124 51  36 135 48  25  2  33  6  22  12 215  28  77  52  5  14 407  16
 82  2  8  4  107 117  2  15 256  4  2  7  2  5 723 36  71  43 530 476  26 400 317  46  7  4  2  2  13 104  88  4 381 15
297  98  32  2  56  26 141  6 194  2  18  4 226  22  21 134 476 26 480  5 144  30  2  18  51  36  28 224  92  25 104  4
226  65  16  38  2  88  12  16 283  5  16  2 113 103  32 15  16  2  19 178  32

Number of words in the first review is 218
```

Please note that when we imported our dataset, we set the value of the `num_words` argument to `1000`. This means that only the top thousand frequent words are kept in the encoded reviews. Just to check this, let's look at the maximum encoded value in our list of reviews:

```
cat("Maximum encoded value in train ",max(sapply(train_x, max)),"\n")
cat("Maximum encoded value in test ",max(sapply(test_x, max)))
```

Executing the preceding code gives us the maximum encoded values in the train and test data.

How to do it...

Now that we're familiar with the data, let's look at it in more detail:

1. Let's import the word index for the `imdb` data:

   ```
   word_index = dataset_imdb_word_index()
   ```

We can look at the head of the word index using the following code:

```
head(word_index)
```

Here, we can see that there's is a list of key-value pairs, where the key is the word and the value is the integer that it's mapped to:

```
$fawn
34701
$tsukino
52006
$nunnery
52007
$sonja
16816
$vani
63951
$woods
1408
```

Let's also look at the number of unique words in our word index:

```
length((word_index))
```

Here, we can see that there are 88,584 unique words in the word index:

```
88584
```

2. Now, we create a reversed list of key-value pairs of the word index. We will use this list to decode the reviews in the IMDb dataset:

```
reverse_word_index <- names(word_index)
names(reverse_word_index) <- word_index
head(reverse_word_index)
```

Here, we can see that the reversed word index list is a list of key-value pairs, where the key is the integer index and the value is the associated word:

34701	'fawn'
52006	'tsukino'
52007	'nunnery'
16816	'sonja'
63951	'vani'
1408	'woods'

3. Now, we decode the first review. Note that the word encodings are offset by three because 0,1,2 are reserved for padding, the start of the sequence, and out of vocabulary words, respectively:

```
decoded_review <- sapply(train_x[[1]], function(index) {

  word <- if (index >= 3) reverse_word_index[[as.character(index
-3)]]
  if (!is.null(word)) word else "?"

})

cat(decoded_review)
```

The following screenshot shows the decoded version of the first review:

```
? this film was just brilliant casting ? ? story direction ? really ? the part they played and you could just imagi
ne being there robert ? is an amazing actor and now the same being director ? father came from the same ? ? as myse
lf so i loved the fact there was a real ? with this film the ? ? throughout the film were great it was just brillia
nt so much that i ? the film as soon as it was released for ? and would recommend it to everyone to watch and the ?
? was amazing really ? at the end it was so sad and you know what they say if you ? at a film it must have been goo
d and this definitely was also ? to the two little ? that played the ? of ? and paul they were just brilliant child
ren are often left out of the ? ? i think because the stars that play them all ? up are such a big ? for the whole
film but these children are amazing and should be ? for what they have done don't you think the whole story was so
? because it was true and was ? life after all that was ? with us all
```

4. Let's pad all the sequences to make them uniform in length:

```
train_x <- pad_sequences(train_x, maxlen = 80)
test_x <- pad_sequences(test_x, maxlen = 80)
cat('x_train shape:', dim(train_x), '\n')
cat('x_test shape:', dim(test_x), '\n')
```

All the sequences are padded to a length of 80:

```
x_train shape: 25000 80
x_test shape: 25000 80
```

Now, let's look at the first review after padding it:

```
train_x[1,]
```

Here, you can see that the review only has 80 indexes after padding:

```
15  256   4   2   7   2   5  723  36  71  43  530  476  26  400  317  46   7   4   2   2  13  104  88   4  381  15  297  98  32   2  56  26
141   6  194   2  18   4  226  22  21  134  476  26  480   5  144  30   2  18  51  36  28  224  92  25  104   4  226  65  16  38   2  88
12  16  283   5  16   2  113  103  32  15  16   2  19  178  32
```

5. Now, we build the model for sentiment classification and view its summary:

```
model <- keras_model_sequential()
model %>%
  layer_embedding(input_dim = 1000, output_dim = 128) %>%
  layer_simple_rnn(units = 32) %>%
  layer_dense(units = 1, activation = 'sigmoid')

summary(model)
```

Here is the description of the model:

```
Layer (type)                    Output Shape               Param #
================================================================
embedding (Embedding)           (None, None, 128)          256000
_____
simple_rnn (SimpleRNN)          (None, 32)                 5152
_____
dense (Dense)                   (None, 1)                  33
================================================================
Total params: 261,185
Trainable params: 261,185
Non-trainable params: 0
```

6. Now, we compile the model and train it:

```
# compile model
model %>% compile(
  loss = 'binary_crossentropy',
  optimizer = 'adam',
  metrics = c('accuracy')
)

# train model
model %>% fit(
  train_x,train_y,
  batch_size = 32,
```

```
    epochs = 10,
    validation_split = .2
)
```

7. Finally, we evaluate the model's performance on the test data and print the metrics:

```
scores <- model %>% evaluate(
  test_x, test_y,
  batch_size = 32
)

cat('Test score:', scores[[1]],'\n')

cat('Test accuracy', scores[[2]])
```

The following screenshot shows the performance metrics on the test data:

```
Test score: 0.8564493
Test accuracy 0.71648
```

By doing this, we achieved an accuracy of around 71% on the test data.

How it works...

In this example, we used the built-in dataset of IMDb reviews from the `keras` library. We loaded the training and testing partitions of the data and had a look at the structure of these data partitions. We saw that the data had been mapped to a specific sequence of integer values, each integer representing a particular word in a dictionary. This dictionary has a rich collection of words arranged based on the frequency of each word getting used in the corpus. From this, we could see that the dictionary is a list of key-value pairs, with the keys representing the words and the values representing the index of the word in the dictionary. To discard the words that are not frequently used, we provided a threshold of 1,000; that is, we kept only the top 1,000 most frequent words in our training dataset and ignored the rest. Then, we moved to the data processing part.

In *step 1*, we imported the word index for the IMDb dataset. In this word index, the words in the data were encoded and indexed by the overall frequency in the dataset. In *step 2*, we created a reversed list of key-value pairs of the word index that was used to decode the sentences back into their original version from a series of encoded integers. In *step 3*, we showcased how to regenerate a sample review.

In *step 4*, we prepared the data so that it could be fed into the model. Since we cannot directly pass a list of integers into the model, we converted them into uniformly shaped tensors. To make the length of all the reviews uniform, we can follow either of these two approaches:

- **One-hot encoding**: This will convert the sequences into tensors of the same length. The size of the matrix will be *number of words * number of reviews*. This approach is computationally heavy.
- **Pad the reviews**: Alternatively, we can pad all the sequences so that they all have the same length. This will create an integer tensor of the shape *num_examples * max_length*. The *max_length* argument is used to cap the maximum number of words that we want to keep in all the reviews.

Since the second approach is less memory- and computationally-intensive, we went for the second approach; that is, we padded the sequences to a maximum length of 80.

In *step 5*, we defined a sequential Keras model and configured its layers. The first layer is the embedding layer and is used to generate the context of the word sequences from our data and provide information about the relevant features. In an embedding, the words are represented by dense vector representations. Each vector represents the projection of the word into a continuous vector space, which is then learned from the text and is based on the words that surround a particular word. The position of the word in the vector space is referred to as its **embedding**. When we do embedding, we represent each review in terms of some latent factors. For example, the word *brilliant* can be represented by a vector; let's say, [.32, .02, .48, .21, .56, .15]. This is computationally efficient when we're using massive datasets since it reduces dimensionality. The embedded vectors also get updated during the training process of the deep neural network, which helps in identifying similar words in a multi-dimensional space. Word embeddings also reflect how words are related to each other semantically. For example, words such as **talking** and **talked** can be thought of as related in the same way as **swimming** is related to **swam**.

The following diagram shows a pictorial representation of word embedding:

The embedding layer is defined by specifying three arguments:

- `input_dim`: This is the size of the vocabulary in the text data. In our example, the text data is an integer that's been encoded to values between 0-999. Due to this, the size of the vocabulary is 1,000 words.
- `output_dim`: This is the size of the vector space in which words will be embedded. We specified it as 128.
- `input_length`: This is the length of input sequences, as we define it for any input layer of a Keras model.
  In the next layer, we defined a simple RNN model with 32 hidden units. If n is the number of input dimensions and d is the number of hidden units in the RNN layer, then the number of trainable parameters can be given by the following equation:

$$((n + d) * d) + d$$

The last layer is densely connected with a single output node. Here, we used the sigmoid activation function since this is a binary classification task. In *step 6,* we compiled the model. We specified `binary_crossentropy` as the loss function since we were dealing with binary classification and **adam** as the optimizer. Then, we trained our model with a validation split of 20%. Finally, in the last step, we evaluated the test accuracy of our model to see how our model performed on the test data.

There's more...

By now, you are aware of how BPTT works in an RNN. We traverse the network backward, calculating gradients of errors with respect to the weights in each iteration. During backpropagation, as we move closer to the early layers of the network, these gradients become too small, thus making the neurons in these layers learn very slowly. For an accurate model, it is crucial for the early layers to get trained accurately since these layers are responsible for learning simple patterns from the input and passing the relevant information to the following layers accordingly. RNNs often face this challenge when we train huge networks with more dependencies within the layers. This challenge is referred to as the **vanishing gradient problem**, which makes the network learn too slowly. This also means that the results aren't as accurate as they could be. It is often advised to use the RELU activation function to avoid the vanishing gradient problem in large networks. Another very common way to deal with this issue is to use a **long short-term memory (LSTM)** model. We will talk about this in the next recipe.

Another challenge that RNNs encounter is the **exploding gradient problem**. In this case, we can see large gradient values, which in turn make the model learn too fast and inaccurately. In some cases, gradients can also become NaN due to numerical overflows in computations. When this happens, the weights in the network increase by huge margins within less time while training. The most commonly used remedy to prevent this problem is **gradient clipping**, which prevents the gradients from increasing beyond a specified threshold.

See also

To find out more about regularization in recurrent neural networks, go to https://arxiv. org/pdf/1409.2329.pdf.

Text generation using LSTMs

Recurrent neural networks face difficulties in carrying information properly, especially when there are long order dependencies between layers in large networks. **Long-short term memory** networks, generally referred to as **LSTM** networks, are an extension of RNNs that are capable of learning long-term dependencies and are widely used in deep learning to avoid the vanishing gradient problem that's faced by RNNs. LSTMs combat vanishing gradients through a gating mechanism and are able to remove or add information to the cell state. This cell state is carefully regulated by the gates, which control the information that's passed through them. LSTMs have three kinds of gates: input, output, and forget. The forget gate controls how much information from the previous state we want to pass to the next cell. The input state defines how much information of the newly computed state we want to pass to the succeeding states for the current input, x_t, while the output gate defines how much of the internal state information we want to pass to the next state.

The following diagram shows a pictorial representation of the LSTM network's architecture:

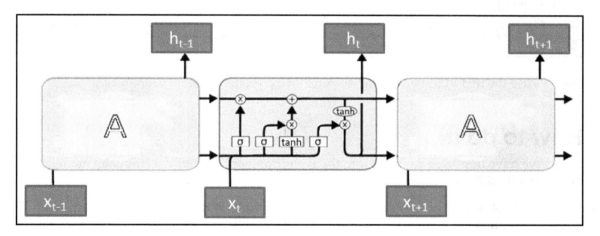

In this recipe, we will implement an LSTM model for sequence prediction (many-to-one, in this example). The model will predict the occurrence of a word based on the previous sequence of words. This is known as text generation.

Getting ready

In this example, we will use the *Jack and Jill* nursery rhyme as our source text so that we can build a language model. We'll create a text file with the rhyme in it and save it in the directory. Our language model will take two words as input to predict the next word.

We'll start by importing the required libraries and reading our text file:

```
library(keras)
library(readr)
library(stringr)

data <- read_file("data/rhyme.txt") %>% str_to_lower()
```

In NLP, we refer to our data as a corpus. A corpus is a large collection of text. Let's have a look at our corpus:

```
data
```

The following screenshot shows the text in our corpus:

'jack and jill went up the hill\nto fetch a pail of water.\njack fell down and broke his crown,\nand jill came tumbling after.\n\nup jack got and home did trot\nas fast as he could caper;\nand went to bed to mend his head\nwith vinegar and brown paper.\n'

We will use the text in the preceding screenshot for sequence generation.

How to do it...

So far, we have imported a corpus into the R environment. To build a language model, we need to convert it into a sequence of integers. Let's start doing some data preprocessing:

1. First, we define our tokenizer. We will use it later to convert text into integer sequences:

   ```
   tokenizer = text_tokenizer(num_words = 35,char_level = F)
   tokenizer %>% fit_text_tokenizer(data)
   ```

   Let's look at the number of unique words in our corpus:

   ```
   cat("Number of unique words", length(tokenizer$word_index))
   ```

   We have 37 unique words in our corpus. To look at the first few records of the vocabulary, we can use the following command:

   ```
   head(tokenizer$word_index)
   ```

Let's convert our corpus into an integer sequence using the tokenizer we defined previously:

```
text_seqs <- texts_to_sequences(tokenizer, data)
str(text_seqs)
```

The following image displays the structure of the returned sequences:

```
List of 1
 $ : int [1:48] 2 1 4 5 6 9 10 3 11 12 ...
```

Here, we can see that `texts_to_sequences()` returns a list. Let's convert it into a vector and print its length:

```
text_seqs <- text_seqs[[1]]
length(text_seqs)
```

The length of our corpus is 48:

```
48
```

2. Now, let's convert our text sequence into input (feature) and output (labels) sequences, where the input will be a sequence of two consecutive words and the output will be the next word that appears in the sequence:

```
input_sequence_length <- 2
feature <- matrix(ncol = input_sequence_length)
label <- matrix(ncol = 1)

for(i in seq(input_sequence_length, length(text_seqs))){
    if(i >= length(text_seqs)){
        break()
    }
    start_idx <- (i - input_sequence_length) +1
    end_idx <- i +1
    new_seq <-  text_seqs[start_idx:end_idx]
    feature <- rbind(feature,new_seq[1:input_sequence_length])
    label <- rbind(label,new_seq[input_sequence_length+1])
}
feature <- feature[-1,]
label <- label[-1,]

paste("Feature")
head(feature)
```

The following screenshot shows the feature sequence that we formulated:

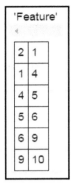

Let's have a look at the label sequences that we created:

```
paste("label")
head(label)
```

The following screenshot shows the first few label sequences:

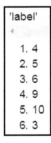

Let's one-hot encode our label and look at the dimensions of our features and labels:

```
label <- to_categorical(label,num_classes = tokenizer$num_words )
```

Here, we can see the dimensions of our feature and label data:

```
cat("Shape of features",dim(feature),"\n")
cat("Shape of label",length(label))
```

The following screenshot shows the dimensions of our features and label sequences:

```
Shape of features 46 2
Shape of label 1610
```

3. Now, we create a model for text generation and print its summary:

```
model <- keras_model_sequential()
model %>%
    layer_embedding(input_dim = tokenizer$num_words,output_dim =
10,input_length = input_sequence_length) %>%
    layer_lstm(units = 50) %>%
    layer_dense(tokenizer$num_words) %>%
    layer_activation("softmax")

summary(model)
```

The following screenshot shows the summary of the model:

Layer (type)	Output Shape	Param #
embedding (Embedding)	(None, 2, 10)	350
lstm (LSTM)	(None, 50)	12200
dense (Dense)	(None, 35)	1785
activation (Activation)	(None, 35)	0

```
Total params: 14,335
Trainable params: 14,335
Non-trainable params: 0
```

Next, we compile the model and train it:

```
# compile
model %>% compile(
    loss = "categorical_crossentropy",
    optimizer = optimizer_rmsprop(lr = 0.001),
    metrics = c('accuracy')
)

# train
model %>% fit(
  feature, label,
#   batch_size = 128,
```

```
    epochs = 500
)
```

4. In the following code block, we implement a function that will generate a sequence from a language model:

```
generate_sequence <-function(model, tokenizer, input_length,
seed_text, predict_next_n_words){
    input_text <- seed_text
    for(i in seq(predict_next_n_words)){
        encoded <- texts_to_sequences(tokenizer,input_text)[[1]]
        encoded <- pad_sequences(sequences = list(encoded),maxlen =
input_length,padding = 'pre')
        yhat <- predict_classes(model,encoded, verbose=0)
        next_word <- tokenizer$index_word[[as.character(yhat)]]
        input_text <- paste(input_text, next_word)
    }
    return(input_text)
}
```

Now, we can use our custom function, generate_sequence(), to generate text from the integer sequences:

```
seed_1 = "Jack and"
cat("Text generated from seed 1: "
,generate_sequence(model,tokenizer,input_sequence_length,seed_1,11)
,"\n ")
seed_2 = "Jack fell"
cat("Text generated from seed 2:
",generate_sequence(model,tokenizer,input_sequence_length,seed_2,11
))
```

The following screenshot shows the text that was generated by the model from the input text:

```
Text generated from seed 1:  Jack and jill went up the hill to fetch a pail of water
 Text generated from seed 2:  Jack fell down and broke his crown and jill went up the hill
```

From this, we can see that our model did a good job of predicting sequences.

How it works...

To build any language model, we need to clean the input text and break it into tokens. Tokens are individual words, and breaking text into its different words is called tokenization. By default, the `keras` tokenizer splits the corpus into a list of tokens (" " is used for splitting sentences into words), removes all punctuation, converts the words into lowercase, and builds an internal vocabulary based on the input text. The vocabulary that's generated by the tokenizer is an indexed list where the words are indexed by their overall frequency in the dataset. In this recipe, we saw that in the nursery rhyme, "and" is the most frequent word, while "up" is the 5th most frequent word. There are 37 unique words in total.

In *step 1*, we converted our corpus into an integer sequence. Please note that the `num_words` argument of `text_tokenizer()` defines the maximum number of words to keep, based on word frequency. This means that only the top "n" frequent words are kept in the encoded sequence. In *step 2*, we prepared the features and labels for our corpus.

In *step 3*, we defined our LSTM neural network. First, we initialized a sequential model and then added an embedding layer to it. The embedding layer transforms the input feature space into a latent feature with an "d" dimension; in our example, it transformed it into 128 latent features. Next, we added the LSTM layer with 50 units. Word prediction is a classification problem where we predict the next word from the vocabulary. Due to this, we added a dense layer with units equal to the number of words in the vocabulary with a softmax activation function.

In *step 4*, we defined a function that would generate text from a given initial set of two words. Our model predicts the next word from the original preceding two words. In our example, the initial seed is "Jack and" and the predicted word is "jill", thus creating a three-word sequence. In the next iteration, we took the last two words of the sentence, "and jill", and predicted the next word, "went". The function continues to generate text until we have generated words equal to the value of the `predict_next_n_words` argument.

There's more...

While working on NLP applications, we construct meaningful features from the text data. There are many techniques we can use to construct these features, such as count vectorization, binary vectorization, **term frequency-inverse document frequency (tf-idf)**, word embeddings, and more. The following code block demonstrates how to build a tf-idf feature matrix for various NLP applications using the `keras` library in R:

```
texts_to_matrix(tokenizer, input, mode = c("tfidf"))
```

Other modes that are available include *binary, count,* and *freq*.

See also

- To find out more about stacked RNNs/LSTMs for encoder-decoder networks, go to `https://cs224d.stanford.edu/reports/Lambert.pdf`.
- To find out more about the word2vec class of neural networks, go to `http://mccormickml.com/assets/word2vec/Alex_Minnaar_Word2Vec_Tutorial_Part_I_The_Skip-Gram_Model.pdf`.

Time series forecasting using GRUs

Unlike LSTMs, GRUs do not use a memory unit to control the flow of information and can directly make use of all the hidden states. Instead of using a cell state, GRUs use the hidden state to transfer information. GRUs usually train faster than other memory-based neural networks because of the fact that they have fewer parameters to train, fewer tensor operations, and can work well with fewer data. GRUs have two gates. These are known as the *reset gate* and the *update gate*. The reset gate is used to determine how to combine new inputs with the previous memory, while the update gate determines how much information to keep from the previous state. If you compare this with LSTMs, the update gate in a GRU is comparable to what the input and forget gates do in an LSTM. It decides what information to add or remove. GRUs also merge the cell state and hidden state in such a way that the resulting models are simple.

The following diagram is a pictorial representation of a GRU:

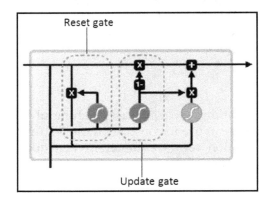

In this recipe, we will build a model using GRUs to forecast shampoo sales.

Getting ready

For this recipe, we need to analyze the trend of the data prior to building the model.

First, let's import the `keras` library:

```
library(keras)
```

In this recipe, we will use the shampoo sales data, which can be downloaded from this book's GitHub repository. This dataset contains the monthly sales of shampoo over a 3-year period and consists of 36 rows. The original dataset is credited to Makridakis, Wheelwright, and Hyndman (1998):

```
data = read.table("data/shampoo_sales.txt",sep = ',')
data <- data[-1,]
rownames(data) <- 1:nrow(data)
colnames(data) <- c("Year_Month","Sales")
head(data)
```

The following screenshot shows a few records from the data:

Year_Month	Sales
1-01	266.0
1-02	145.9
1-03	183.1
1-04	119.3
1-05	180.3
1-06	168.5

Let's analyze the trend in the `Sales` column of the data:

```
# Draw a line plot to show the trend of data
library(ggplot2)
q = ggplot(data = data, aes(x = Year_Month, y = Sales,group =1))+
geom_line()
q = q+theme(axis.text.x = element_text(angle = 90, hjust = 1))
q
```

The following plot gives us an understanding of the trend in the data:

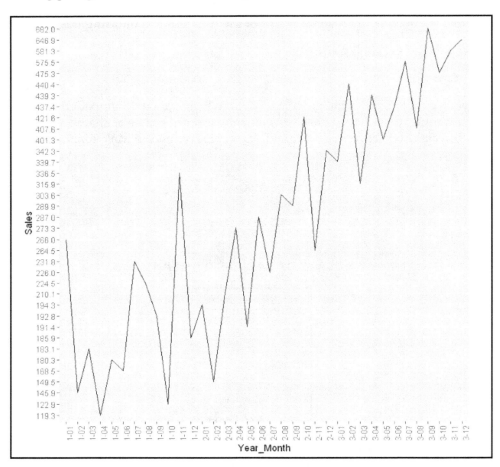

Here, we can see that there is an increasing trend in the data.

How to do it...

Let's move on to the data processing part:

1. First, we check the datatype of the `Sales` column in our data:

```
class(data$Sales)
```

Note that, in the data, the `Sales` column is of the factor datatype. We need to make this a numeric datatype in order to use it in our analysis:

```
data$Sales <- as.numeric(as.character(data$Sales))
class(data$Sales)
```

Now, the class of the `Sales` column has been changed into a numeric datatype.

2. To implement a time series forecast, we need to convert the data into stationary data. We can do this using the `diff()` function, which will calculate the iterated difference. We pass the value of the argument differences as 1 since we want the differencing to have a lag of 1:

```
data_differenced = diff(data$Sales, differences = 1)
head(data_differenced)
```

The following screenshot shows a piece of the data after differencing:

```
-120.1  37.2  -63.8  61  -11.8  63.3
```

3. Next, we create a supervised dataset so that we can apply GRU. We transform the `data_differenced` series by creating a lag in the series with an order of 1; that is, the value at time (t-1) as the input will have the value at time *t* as the output:

```
data_lagged = c(rep(NA, 1),
data_differenced[1:(length(data_differenced)-1)])
data_preprocessed =
as.data.frame(cbind(data_lagged,data_differenced))
colnames(data_preprocessed) <- c( paste0('x-', 1), 'x')
data_preprocessed[is.na(data_preprocessed)] <- 0
head(data_preprocessed)
```

Here is how our supervised dataset looks:

x-1	x
0.0	-120.1
-120.1	37.2
37.2	-63.8
-63.8	61.0
61.0	-11.8
-11.8	63.3

4. Now, we need to split the data into training and testing sets. In time series problems, we can't do random sampling on the data since the order of the data matters. Thus, we need to split the data by taking the first 70% of the series as training data and the remaining 30% of the data as test data:

```
N = nrow(data_preprocessed)
n = round(N *0.7, digits = 0)
train = data_preprocessed[1:n, ]
test = data_preprocessed[(n+1):N,]
print("Training data snapshot :")
head(train)
print("Testing data snapshot :")
head(test)
```

The following screenshot shows a few records from the training dataset:

[1] "Training data snapshot :"

x-1	x
0.0	-120.1
-120.1	37.2
37.2	-63.8
-63.8	61.0
61.0	-11.8
-11.8	63.3

The following screenshot shows a few records from the test dataset:

[1] "Testing data snapshot :"

x-1	x
-2.6	100.7
100.7	-124.5
-124.5	123.4
123.4	-38.0
-38.0	36.1
36.1	138.1

5. Next, we normalize the data within the scale of the activation function that we are going to use. Since we are going with *tanh* as our choice of activation function, which ranges from -1 to +1, we scale the data using **min-max normalization**. Here, we normalize with respect to the training data:

```
scaling_data = function(train, test, feature_range = c(0, 1)) {
 x = train
 fr_min = feature_range[1]
 fr_max = feature_range[2]
 std_train = ((x - min(x) ) / (max(x) - min(x) ))
 std_test = ((test - min(x) ) / (max(x) - min(x) ))

 scaled_train = std_train *(fr_max -fr_min) + fr_min
 scaled_test = std_test *(fr_max -fr_min) + fr_min

 return( list(scaled_train = as.vector(scaled_train), scaled_test =
as.vector(scaled_test) ,scaler= c(min =min(x), max = max(x))) )

}

Scaled = scaling_data(train, test, c(-1, 1))
y_train = Scaled$scaled_train[, 2]
x_train = Scaled$scaled_train[, 1]

y_test = Scaled$scaled_test[, 2]
x_test = Scaled$scaled_test[, 1]
```

Then, we write a function to revert the predicted values to the original scale. We will use this function while predicting the values:

```
## inverse-transform
invert_scaling = function(scaled, scaler, feature_range = c(0, 1)){
 min = scaler[1]
 max = scaler[2]
 t = length(scaled)
 mins = feature_range[1]
 maxs = feature_range[2]
 inverted_dfs = numeric(t)

 for( i in 1:t){
 X = (scaled[i]- mins)/(maxs - mins)
 rawValues = X *(max - min) + min
 inverted_dfs[i] <- rawValues
 }
 return(inverted_dfs)
}
```

6. Now, we define the model and configure the layers. We reshape our data into a 3D format so that it can be fed into the model:

```
# Reshaping the input to 3-dimensional
dim(x_train) <- c(length(x_train), 1, 1)

# specify required arguments
batch_size = 1
units = 1

model <- keras_model_sequential()
model%>%
  layer_gru(units, batch_input_shape = c(batch_size,
dim(x_train)[2], dim(x_train)[3]),         stateful=TRUE)%>%
  layer_dense(units = 1)
```

Let's have a look at the summary of the model:

```
summary(model)
```

The following screenshot shows a description of the model:

```
Layer (type)                     Output Shape                     Param #
=========================================================================
gru_1 (GRU)                      (1, 1)                           9
_____
dense_1 (Dense)                  (1, 1)                           2
=========================================================================
Total params: 11
Trainable params: 11
Non-trainable params: 0
_____
```

Next, we compile the model:

```
model %>% compile(
  loss = 'mean_squared_error',
  optimizer = optimizer_adam( lr= 0.01, decay = 1e-6 ),
  metrics = c('accuracy')
  )
```

7. Now, in each epoch, we fit our training data into the model and reset the states. We train the model for 50 epochs:

```
for(i in 1:50 ){
  model %>% fit(x_train, y_train, epochs=1, batch_size=batch_size,
verbose=1, shuffle=FALSE)
```

```
model %>% reset_states()
}
```

8. Finally, we predict the values for the test dataset and use
   the `inverse_scaling` function to scale back the predictions to the original scale:

```
scaler = Scaled$scaler
predictions = vector()

for(i in 1:length(x_test)){
  X = x_test[i]
  dim(X) = c(1,1,1)
  yhat = model %>% predict(X, batch_size=batch_size)
  # invert scaling
  yhat = invert_scaling(yhat, scaler, c(-1, 1))
  # invert differencing
  yhat = yhat + data$Sales[(n+i)]
  # store
  predictions[i] <- yhat
}
```

Let's look at the `predictions` for the test data:

```
predictions
```

The following screenshot shows the values that were predicted for the test dataset:

348.112441666424	359.491248017549	379.598579031229	354.127689468861	413.616816712916	423.328302359581	455.889744898677
461.995177252591	513.082208752632	505.667284664512	502.387261849642			

From the predicted values for the test data, we can infer that the model did a decent job.

How it works...

In *step 1*, we checked the datatype of the column whose values are to be forecasted; here, we used the `Sales` column. We changed its datatype to numeric. In *step 2*, we converted the input data into stationary data. This is done to get rid of time-dependent components in the data. We saw that our input data has an increasing trend. In time series forecasting, it is advised to get rid of the trend component before building the model. These trends can be added back to the forecasted values later so that we can get our predictions in the original scale. In this example, we removed the trend by differencing the data with an order of 1; that is, we subtracted the previous observation from the current one.

While using algorithms such as LSTM and GRU, we need to feed data in a supervised form; that is, in the form of predictors and target variables. In time series problems, we deal with data where the value at time (t-k) acts as the input for the value at time *t* for any *k* stepped lagged dataset. In our example, *k* was equal to 1, so in *step 3*, we created a lagged dataset by transforming the current data into a lagged data of order 1. By doing this, we saw the X=t-1 and Y=t pattern in the data. The lagged dataset series that we created acted as the predictor variable.

In *step 4*, we split the data into training and testing datasets. Random sampling does not allow us to maintain the order of the observations in a time series data. Hence, we split the data while keeping the order of observations intact. To do this, we took the first 70% of the data as training and the other 30% as testing data. *n* represents the split point, which is the last index of training, while *n+1* represents the starting index of the testing data. In *step 5*, we normalized our data. GRUs expect data to be within the scale of the activation function being used by the network. Since we were using *tanh* as the activation function, which gives outputs in the range of (-1,1), hence, we scaled the training and testing dataset within the range of (-1,1) too. We used min-max scaling in this case:

$$z_i = \frac{x_i - x_{min}}{x_{max} - x_{min}}$$

The scaling coefficient values should be calculated on the training dataset and applied to scale the test dataset. This is done to avoid bias in the experiment due to any kind of knowledge from the test dataset. That is why, here, min and max values of training data are used as the reference to scale both training and testing data and also the predicted values. We also created a function called `invert_scaling` to inversely scale the scaled values and map them back to the original scale.

GRUs expect data in a specific format of the form [`batch_size`, `timesteps`, `features`]. The `batch_size` defines the number of observations to be fed to the model in each batch. `timesteps` represents the number of time steps the model needs to look back in the historical data for prediction. In this example, we set it to 1. The `features` argument represents the number of predictors we will use, which is 1 in our case. In *step 6*, we reshaped the input data in the required format and fed this into the GRU layer. Note that we specified the argument `stateful` = TRUE so that the last state for each sample at index *i* in a batch will be used as the initial state for the sample of index *i* in the following batch.

This assumes a one-to-one mapping between the samples in different successive batches. The `units` argument represents the dimension of the output space. Since we were dealing with predicting continuous values, we took units *=1* in this case. Once we defined the model, we compiled it. We specified `mean_squared_error` as the loss function and adam as the optimization algorithm with a learning rate of 0.01. We used accuracy as the metric to assess the model's performance. Next, we had a look at the summary of the model.

Let's say that we have the following:

- *f* is the number of **feedforward neural networks** (**FFNN**) in a unit (in GRU, it is 3)
- *h* is the size of hidden units
- *i* is the dimension or size of the input

Since every FFNN has $h(h+i) + h$ parameters, we can calculate the number of training parameters in the GRU as follows:

$$num\_params = f \times [h(h+i) + h] \ ; \ f = 3 \ for \ GRU$$

In *step 7*, for each epoch, we fit the training data into the model. We specified the value of the `shuffle` argument as false to avoid any kind of shuffling in the training data while building the model. This is done to prevent time dependencies between the observations. We also reset the network state after each epoch via the `reset_states()` function. Since we specified the value of the `stateful = True` argument, we needed to manually reset the states of the LSTM after each epoch to have a clean setup for the next one.

In the last step, we predicted the values for the test dataset. To scale the predicted values back to the original scale, we used the `inverse_scaling` function, which was defined in *step 5*.

There's more...

While working with large datasets, we often run out of memory while training a deep learning model. The `keras` library in R provides various generator utility functions, which generate batches of training data on the fly during the training process. It also provides a utility function for creating batches of temporal data. The following code creates a supervised form of data similar to what we created in the *How to do it..* section of this recipe, using a generator utility:

```
# importing required libraries
library(reticulate)
library(keras)

# generating dummy data
data =  seq(from = 1,to = 10)

# timseries generator
gen = timeseries_generator(data = data,targets = data,length = 1,batch_size
= 5)

# Print first batch
iter_next(as_iterator(gen))
```

The following screenshot displays the first batch of the generator. Here, we can see that a generator object yields a list of two sequences; the first sequence is a feature vector, while the second sequence is the corresponding label vector:

```
1. 1
   2
   3
   4
   5
2. 2  3  4  5  6
```

The following code implements a custom generator for time series data. It gives us the flexibility to define `lookback`; that is, how many past values we should use to predict the future value or sequence. `future_steps` defines the number of future time steps to predict:

```
generator <- function (data,lookback =3 ,future_steps = 3,batch_size = 3 ){
    new_data = data
    for(i in seq(1,3)){
        data_lagged = c(rep(NA, i), data[1:(length(data)-i)])
        new_data = cbind(data_lagged,new_data)
    }
    targets = new_data[future_steps:length(data),(ncol(new_data)-
(future_steps-1)):ncol(new_data)]
    gen = timeseries_generator(data = data[1:(length(data)-
(future_steps-1))],targets = targets,length = lookback,batch_size =
batch_size)
}

cat("First batch of generator:")
iter_next(as_iterator(generator(data = data,lookback = 3,future_steps =
2)))
```

The following screenshot shows the first batch that was produced by the custom generator:

```
First batch of generator:
    1. 1  2  3
       2  3  4
       3  4  5
    2. 4  5
       5  6
       6  7
```

Here, we can see that at the first index of the list, we have `lookback` data points, while the second index contains the corresponding future time steps.

See also

To find out how to leverage LSTMs for time series data with multiple seasonal patterns, go to https://arxiv.org/pdf/1909.04293.pdf.

Implementing bidirectional recurrent neural networks

Bidirectional recurrent neural networks are an extension of RNNs, where the input data is fed in both normal and reverse time order into two networks. The output that's received from both networks is combined in each time step using various kinds of merge modes, such as summation, concatenation, multiplication, and averaging. Bidirectional RNNs are mostly used in challenges where the context of the whole statement or text is dependent on the entire sequence and not just a linear interpretation. Bidirectional RNNs are costly to train due to their long gradient chains.

The following diagram is a pictorial representation of a bidirectional RNN:

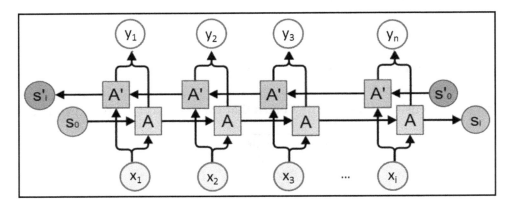

In this recipe, we will implement a bidirectional RNN for the sentiment classification of IMDb reviews.

How to do it...

In this section, we will work with the IMDb reviews dataset. The data preparation steps for this are the same as they were for the *Sentiment classification using RNNs* section. This means we can move straight onto the model-building part:

1. Let's start by instantiating our sequential model:

```
model <- keras_model_sequential()
```

2. Now, we add some layers to our model and print its summary:

```
model %>%
    layer_embedding(input_dim = 2000, output_dim = 128) %>%
    bidirectional(layer_simple_rnn(units = 32),merge_mode = "concat")
%>%
    layer_dense(units = 1, activation = 'sigmoid')

summary(model)
```

The following screenshot shows the summary of the model:

Layer (type)	Output Shape	Param #
embedding (Embedding)	(None, None, 128)	256000
bidirectional (Bidirectional)	(None, 64)	10304
dense (Dense)	(None, 1)	65

Total params: 266,369
Trainable params: 266,369
Non-trainable params: 0

3. Let's compile and train our model:

```
# compile model
model %>% compile(
  loss = "binary_crossentropy",
  optimizer = "adam",
  metrics = c("accuracy")
)

# train model
model %>% fit(
  train_x,train_y,
  batch_size = 32,
  epochs = 10,
  validation_split = .2
)
```

4. Let's evaluate the model and print the metrics:

```
scores <- model %>% evaluate(
  test_x, test_y,
  batch_size = 32
)
```

```
cat('Test score:', scores[[1]],'\n')
cat('Test accuracy', scores[[2]])
```

The following screenshot shows the performance metric on the test data:

```
Test score: 1.067133
Test accuracy 0.75688
```

We get an accuracy of 75% on the test data.

How it works...

Before building the model, we need to prepare the data. You can refer to the *Sentiment classification using RNNs* section of this chapter if you want to learn more about the data preprocessing part.

In *step 1*, we instantiated a Keras sequential model. In *step 2*, we added layers to the sequential model. First, we added an embedding layer, which reduced the dimensionality of the input feature space. Then, we added a simple RNN in a bidirectional wrapper with `merge_mode` equal to `concat`. Merge mode defines how to combine outputs of the forward and backward RNNs. Other modes include `sum`, `mul`, `ave`, and `NULL`. Finally, we added a dense layer with one hidden unit and used sigmoid as the activation function.

In *step 3*, we compiled the model with `binary_crossentropy` as the loss function since we were solving a binary classification problem. We used the `adam` optimizer for this. Then, we trained our model on the training dataset. In *step 4*, we evaluated the test accuracy of our model to see how our model performed on the test data.

There's more...

Although bidirectional RNNs are kind of a state of the art technologies, there are several limitations of using them. Since bidirectional RNNs operate in both positive and negative directions, they are extremely slow since the gradients have a long dependency chain.

Also, bidirectional RNNs are used in very specific applications, such as filling in the missing word, machine translation, and so on. Another major issue with this algorithm is that it is challenging to train because of memory-bandwidth-bound computations.

4
Implementing Autoencoders with Keras

An **autoencoder** is a special kind of feedforward neural network capable of learning efficient encoding of input data. These encodings can be of a lower or higher dimension than the input. Autoencoder is an unsupervised deep learning technique that learns to represent input data into a latent feature space. Autoencoders can be leveraged for multiple applications such as dimensionality reduction, image compression, image denoising, image generation, and feature extraction.

In this chapter, we will cover the following recipes:

- Implementing vanilla autoencoders
- Dimensionality reduction using autoencoders
- Denoising autoencoders
- Changing black and white to color

Implementing vanilla autoencoders

An autoencoder comprises of the following two networks:

- **Encoder**: An encoder encodes its input, x_i, into a hidden representation, h. The output of an encoder unit is as follows:

$$h = g(Wx_i + b)$$

  where, $x_i \in R^n$, $W \in R^{d \times n}$, $b \in R^d$.

- **Decoder**: A decoder reconstructs the input from the hidden representation, h. The output of a decoder unit is as follows:

$$\hat{x}_i = f(W * h + c)$$

  where, $W^* \in R^{n \times d}$, $h \in R^d$, $c \in R^n$.

An autoencoder neural network tries to reconstruct the original input, x_i, from the encoded representation, h, of d dimension to produce an output, $\hat{x}_i$, such that $\hat{x}_i$ approximates to x_i. The network is trained to minimize the reconstruction error (loss function). It is a measure of the difference between the original input and the predicted output, and can be denoted as, $\mathcal{L}(x_i, \hat{x}_i)$. An autoencoder with a dimension of encoded representation less than the input dimension is known as an under-complete autoencoder, whereas an autoencoder with a dimension of encoded representation more than the input dimension is known as an overcomplete autoencoder.

The following diagram shows examples of an under-complete and an over-complete autoencoder:

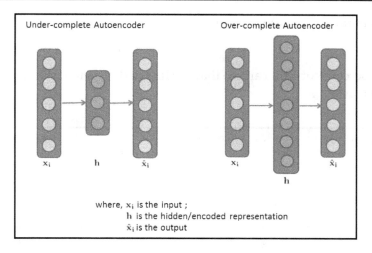

where, x_i is the input ;
 h is the hidden/encoded representation
 $\hat{x}_i$ is the output

In the following section, we will implement an under-complete autoencoder.

Getting ready

In this recipe, we will use the MNIST handwritten digit dataset. It has a training set of 60,000 examples and a test set of 10,000 examples.

We start by importing the required libraries:

```
library(keras)
library(abind)
library(grid)
```

Let's import the training and testing partitions of the data:

```
data = dataset_mnist()
x_train = data$train$x
x_test = data$test$x
cat("Train data dimnsions",dim(x_train),"\n")
cat("Test data dimnsions",dim(x_test))
```

In the following screenshot, we can see that the MNIST data has 60,000 train and 10,000 test images of a size of 28x28:

```
Train data dimnsions 60000 28 28
Test data dimnsions 10000 28 28
```

Let's take a look at the data of the first image:

```
x_train[1,,]
```

In the following screenshot, you can see that the image data is in the form of a multidimensional array:

0	0	0	0	0	0	0	0	0	0	...	0	0	0	0	0	0	0	0	0	0
0	0	0	0	0	0	0	0	0	0	...	0	0	0	0	0	0	0	0	0	0
0	0	0	0	0	0	0	0	0	0	...	0	0	0	0	0	0	0	0	0	0
0	0	0	0	0	0	0	0	0	0	...	0	0	0	0	0	0	0	0	0	0
0	0	0	0	0	0	0	0	0	0	...	0	0	0	0	0	0	0	0	0	0
0	0	0	0	0	0	0	0	0	0	...	175	26	166	255	247	127	0	0	0	0
0	0	0	0	0	0	0	0	30	36	...	225	172	253	242	195	64	0	0	0	0
0	0	0	0	0	0	0	49	238	253	...	93	82	82	56	39	0	0	0	0	0
0	0	0	0	0	0	0	18	219	253	...	0	0	0	0	0	0	0	0	0	0
0	0	0	0	0	0	0	0	80	156	...	0	0	0	0	0	0	0	0	0	0
0	0	0	0	0	0	0	0	0	14	...	0	0	0	0	0	0	0	0	0	0
0	0	0	0	0	0	0	0	0	0	...	0	0	0	0	0	0	0	0	0	0
0	0	0	0	0	0	0	0	0	0	...	0	0	0	0	0	0	0	0	0	0
0	0	0	0	0	0	0	0	0	0	...	0	0	0	0	0	0	0	0	0	0
0	0	0	0	0	0	0	0	0	0	...	25	0	0	0	0	0	0	0	0	0
0	0	0	0	0	0	0	0	0	0	...	150	27	0	0	0	0	0	0	0	0
0	0	0	0	0	0	0	0	0	0	...	253	187	0	0	0	0	0	0	0	0
0	0	0	0	0	0	0	0	0	0	...	253	249	64	0	0	0	0	0	0	0
0	0	0	0	0	0	0	0	0	0	...	253	207	2	0	0	0	0	0	0	0
0	0	0	0	0	0	0	0	0	0	...	250	182	0	0	0	0	0	0	0	0
0	0	0	0	0	0	0	0	0	0	...	78	0	0	0	0	0	0	0	0	0
0	0	0	0	0	0	0	0	23	66	...	0	0	0	0	0	0	0	0	0	0
0	0	0	0	0	0	18	171	219	253	...	0	0	0	0	0	0	0	0	0	0
0	0	0	0	55	172	226	253	253	253	...	0	0	0	0	0	0	0	0	0	0
0	0	0	0	136	253	253	253	212	135	...	0	0	0	0	0	0	0	0	0	0
0	0	0	0	0	0	0	0	0	0	...	0	0	0	0	0	0	0	0	0	0
0	0	0	0	0	0	0	0	0	0	...	0	0	0	0	0	0	0	0	0	0
0	0	0	0	0	0	0	0	0	0	...	0	0	0	0	0	0	0	0	0	0

We normalize the values of our train and test datasets within 0 and 1 and flatten each image of a size of 28X28 into a 1-dimensional array of 784 elements:

```
x_train = x_train/ 255
x_test = x_test / 255

x_train <- array_reshape(x_train, c(nrow(x_train), 784))
x_test <- array_reshape(x_test, c(nrow(x_test), 784))
```

Now that we have seen how the data looks, let's move to model building.

How to do it...

Now, we move on to building our model:

1. We first define a variable, the value of which will be equal to the dimension of the compressed encoded representation of the input. Then, we set the input layer of our model:

```
encoding_dim = 32
input_img = layer_input(shape=c(784),name = "input")
```

2. Let's build an encoder and decoder and combine them to build an autoencoder:

```
encoded = input_img %>% layer_dense(units = encoding_dim,
activation='relu',name = "encoder")
decoded = encoded %>% layer_dense(units = c(784),
activation='sigmoid',name = "decoder")

# this model maps an input to its reconstruction
autoencoder = keras_model(input_img, decoded)
```

Now, we visualize the summary of the autoencoder model:

```
summary(autoencoder)
```

The summary of the model is as follows:

Layer (type)	Output Shape	Param #
input (InputLayer)	(None, 784)	0
encoder (Dense)	(None, 32)	25120
decoder (Dense)	(None, 784)	25872

Total params: 50,992
Trainable params: 50,992
Non-trainable params: 0

3. We then compile and train our model:

```
# compiling the model
autoencoder %>% compile(optimizer='adadelta',
loss='binary_crossentropy')
# training the model
```

```
autoencoder %>% fit(x_train, x_train,
 epochs=50,
 batch_size=256,
 shuffle=TRUE,
 validation_data=list(x_test, x_test))
```

4. Now, we predict the output of our model on the test set and print out a sample of test and predicted images:

```
# predict
predicted <- autoencoder %>% predict(x_test)

# Original images from test data
grid = array_reshape(x_test[20,],dim = c(28,28))
for(i in seq(1,5)){
 grid = abind(grid,array_reshape(x_test[i,],dim = c(28,28)),along =
2)
}
grid.raster(grid,interpolate=FALSE)

# Reconstructed images
grid1 = array_reshape(predicted[20,],dim = c(28,28))
for(i in seq(1,5)){
    grid1 = abind(grid1,array_reshape(predicted[i,],dim =
c(28,28)),along = 2)
}
grid.raster(grid1, interpolate=FALSE)
```

Here are some sample images from the test data:

The following screenshot shows the predicted images for the sample test images displayed previously:

We can see that all of the images have been reconstructed accurately by our model.

How it works...

In *step 1*, we initialized a variable, `encoded_dim`, to set the dimensionality of the encoded representation of the input. Since we implemented an under-complete autoencoder, which compresses input feature space to a lower dimension, `encoded_dim` is less than the input dimension. Next, we defined the input layer of the autoencoder, which took an array of a size of 784 as input.

In the next step, we built an autoencoder model. We first defined an encoder and a decoder network and then combined them to create an autoencoder. Note that the number of units in the encoder layer is equal to `encoded_dim` because we wanted to compress the input feature space of 784 dimensions to 32 dimensions. The number of units in the decoder layer is the same as the input dimension because the decoder tries to reconstruct the input. After building the autoencoder, we visualized the summary of the model. In *step 3*, we configured our model to minimize **binary cross-entropy** loss with the **Adadelta** optimizer and then trained the model. We set the input and target value as `x_train`.

In the last step, we visualized the predicted images for a few sample images from the test dataset.

There's more...

In a simple autoencoder, the decoder and encoder networks have fully connected dense layers. A convolutional autoencoder extends this underlying autoencoder architecture by replacing its dense layers with convolutional layers. Like simple autoencoders, the size of the input layer is the same as the output layers in a convolutional autoencoder. The encoder network of this autoencoder has convolutional layers, while the decoder network has transposed convolutional layers or an upsampling layer coupled with a convolutional layer.

In the following code block, we have implemented a convolutional autoencoder, where the decoder network consists of an upsampling layer combined with a convolutional layer. This approach scales up the input and then applies a convolution operation. In the *Denoising autoencoders* recipe, we have implemented an autoencoder with a transposed convolutional layer.

The following code shows an implementation of a convolutional autoencoder:

```
x_train = x_train/ 255
x_test = x_test / 255

x_train = array_reshape(x_train, c(nrow(x_train), 28,28,1))
x_test = array_reshape(x_test, c(nrow(x_test), 28,28,1))

input_img = layer_input(shape=c(28, 28, 1))

x = input_img %>% layer_conv_2d(32, c(3, 3), activation='relu',
padding='same')
x = x %>% layer_max_pooling_2d(c(2, 2), padding='same')
x = x %>% layer_conv_2d(18, c(3, 3), activation='relu', padding='same')
x = x %>%layer_max_pooling_2d(c(2, 2), padding='same')
x = x %>% layer_conv_2d(8, c(3, 3), activation='relu', padding='same')
encoded = x %>% layer_max_pooling_2d(c(2, 2), padding='same')


x = encoded %>% layer_conv_2d(8, c(3, 3), activation='relu',
padding='same')
x = x %>% layer_upsampling_2d(c(2, 2))
x = x %>% layer_conv_2d(8, c(3, 3), activation='relu', padding='same')
x = x %>% layer_upsampling_2d(c(2, 2))
x = x %>% layer_conv_2d(16, c(3, 3), activation='relu')
x = x %>% layer_upsampling_2d(c(2, 2))
decoded = x %>% layer_conv_2d(1, c(3, 3), activation='sigmoid',
padding='same')

autoencoder = keras_model(input_img, decoded)
summary(autoencoder)

autoencoder %>% compile(optimizer='adadelta', loss='binary_crossentropy')

autoencoder %>% fit(x_train, x_train,
    epochs=20,
    batch_size=128,
    validation_data=list(x_test, x_test))
predicted <- autoencoder %>% predict(x_test)
```

Here are some sample test images reconstructed using a convolutional autoencoder:

From the preceding screenshot, we can say that our model did a great job of reconstructing the original images.

Dimensionality reduction using autoencoders

Autoencoders can practically learn very interesting data projections that can help to reduce the dimensionality of the data without much data loss in the lower dimensional space. The encoder compresses the input and selects the most important features, also known as latent features, during compression. The decoder is the opposite of encoder, and it tries to recreate the original input as closely as possible. While encoding the original input data, autoencoders try to capture the maximum variance of the data using lesser features.

In this recipe, we will build a deep autoencoder to extract low dimensional latent features and demonstrate how we can use this lower-dimensional feature set to solve various learning problems such as regression, classification, and more. Dimensionality reduction decreases training time significantly. While reducing the dimensionality, autoencoders also learn non-linear features present in the data, hence enhancing the model's performance.

Getting ready

In the previous recipe, *Implementing vanilla autoencoders*, we implemented the simplest autoencoder. In this recipe, we will build a deep autoencoder using MNIST digits data to demonstrate dimensionality reduction. The data preprocessing will be the same as that of the previous recipe, *Implementing vanilla autoencoders*. We will extract encoded features (low dimensional) from the encoder network and then use these encoded features in the decoder to reconstruct the original input and evaluate the reconstruction error. We use these encoded features to build a digit classification model.

How to do it...

We will now move on to build our deep autoencoder. A deep autoencoder has multiple layers in its encoder and decoder network:

1. Let's build an autoencoder:

```
encoded_dim = 32

# input layer
input_img <- layer_input(shape = c(784),name = "input")

# encoder
encoded = input_img %>%
```

```
      layer_dense(128, activation='relu',name = "encoder_1") %>%
      layer_dense(64, activation='relu',name = "encoder_2") %>%
      layer_dense(encoded_dim, activation='relu',name = "encoder_3")

# decoder
decoded = encoded %>%
    layer_dense(64, activation='relu',name = "decoder_1")%>%
    layer_dense(128, activation='relu',name = "decoder_2")%>%
    layer_dense(784,activation = 'sigmoid',name = "decoder_3")

# autoencoder
autoencoder = keras_model(input_img, decoded)
summary(autoencoder)
```

The summary of the autoencoder model is shown in the following screenshot:

Layer (type)	Output Shape	Param #
input (InputLayer)	(None, 784)	0
encoder_1 (Dense)	(None, 128)	100480
encoder_2 (Dense)	(None, 64)	8256
encoder_3 (Dense)	(None, 32)	2080
decoder_1 (Dense)	(None, 64)	2112
decoder_2 (Dense)	(None, 128)	8320
decoder_3 (Dense)	(None, 784)	101136

```
Total params: 222,384
Trainable params: 222,384
Non-trainable params: 0
```

2. Let's create a separate encoder model; this model maps an input to its encoded representation:

```
encoder = keras_model(input_img, encoded)
summary(encoder)
```

The following screenshot shows the summary of the encoder network:

Layer (type)	Output Shape	Param #
input (InputLayer)	(None, 784)	0
encoder_1 (Dense)	(None, 128)	100480
encoder_2 (Dense)	(None, 64)	8256
encoder_3 (Dense)	(None, 32)	2080

```
Total params: 110,816
Trainable params: 110,816
Non-trainable params: 0
```

3. Let's also create the decoder model:

```
# input layer for decoder
encoded_input = layer_input(shape=c(32),name = "encoded_input")

# retrieve the layer of the autoencoder model for decoder
decoder_layer1 <- get_layer(autoencoder,name= "decoder_1")
decoder_layer2 <- get_layer(autoencoder,name= "decoder_2")
decoder_layer3 <- get_layer(autoencoder,name= "decoder_3")

# create the decoder model from retreived layers
decoder = keras_model(encoded_input,
  decoder_layer3(decoder_layer2(decoder_layer1(encoded_input)))))

summary(decoder)
```

The following screenshot shows the summary of the decoder network:

```
Layer (type)                    Output Shape              Param #
=================================================================
encoded_input (InputLayer)      (None, 32)                0
_____
decoder_1 (Dense)               (None, 64)                2112
_____
decoder_2 (Dense)               (None, 128)               8320
_____
decoder_3 (Dense)               (None, 784)               101136
=================================================================
Total params: 111,568
Trainable params: 111,568
Non-trainable params: 0
```

4. We then compile and train our autoencoder model:

```
# compiling the model
autoencoder %>% compile(optimizer =
'adadelta',loss='binary_crossentropy')

# training the model
autoencoder %>% fit(x_train, x_train,
    epochs=50,
    batch_size=256,
    shuffle=TRUE,
    validation_data=list(x_test, x_test))
```

5. Let's now encode the test images:

```
encoded_imgs = encoder %>% predict(x_test)
```

6. After encoding our test images, we reconstruct the original input test images from the encoded representation using the decoder network and calculate the reconstruction error:

```
# reconstructing images
decoded_imgs = decoder %>% predict(encoded_imgs)

# calculating reconstruction error
reconstruction_error =
metric_mean_squared_error(x_test,decoded_imgs)
paste("reconstruction error: "
,k_get_value(k_mean(reconstruction_error)))
```

We can see that we have achieved a satisfactory reconstruction error of 0.228:

```
'reconstruction error:  0.228853663540732'
```

7. Let's now encode training images. We will use the encoded data to train a digit classifier:

```
encoded_train_imgs = encoder %>% predict(x_train)
```

8. We now build a digit classifier network and compile it:

```
# Building the model
model <- keras_model_sequential()
model %>%
  layer_dense(units = 256, activation = 'relu', input_shape =
c(encoded_dim)) %>%
  layer_dropout(rate = 0.4) %>%
  layer_dense(units = 128, activation = 'relu') %>%
  layer_dropout(rate = 0.3) %>%
  layer_dense(units = 10, activation = 'softmax')

# compiling the model
model %>% compile(
  loss = 'categorical_crossentropy',
  optimizer = optimizer_rmsprop(),
  metrics = c('accuracy')
)
```

9. We proceed to process train labels and then we will train the network:

```
# extracting class labels
y_train <- mnist$train$y
y_test <- mnist$test$y
```

```
# Converting class vector (integers) to binary class matrix.
y_train <- to_categorical(y_train, 10)
y_test <- to_categorical(y_test, 10)

# training the model
history <- model %>% fit(
  encoded_train_imgs, y_train,
  epochs = 30, batch_size = 128,
  validation_split = 0.2
)
```

10. Let's evaluate the model performance:

```
model %>% evaluate(encoded_imgs, y_test, batch_size = 128)
```

The following screenshot shows the model's accuracy and loss:

\$loss
0.654463641643524
\$acc
0.79040002822876

From the previous screenshot, it is clear that our autoencoder model did a great job at learning encoded representation of data. Using these encoded features we trained a classifier with 79% accuracy.

How it works...

In *step 1*, we built a Keras functional autoencoder model. We first defined an input layer and an encoder and decoder network and then combined them to create a deep autoencoder. The encoder network reduces the input of 784 dimensions to 32 dimensions. The decoder network reconstructs 32 dimensions (the input to the decoder) to 784 dimensions. In step 2, we built a separate encoder model. The encoder model shared the encoder layers of the autoencoder, which means the weights are shared.

In the next step, we defined a separate decoder model. This model shared the decoder layers of the autoencoder. We first defined an encoded input layer and then extracted dense layers from the autoencoder to create the decoder. In *step 4*, we configured our model to minimize binary cross-entropy loss with the Adadelta optimizer and then trained the model for 50 epochs. In *step 5*, we encoded the test images into reduced dimensions.

In *step 6*, we used the decoder model to reconstruct the test data and calculated the reconstruction error. In the next step, we encoded training images. In *step 8*, we configured and compiled a classification network for digit recognition. In *step 9*, we processed train labels and trained the network. In the last step, we evaluated the performance of our digit classification model.

There's more...

We often come across problems where the dimensions of the data are huge. We might need to reduce the dimensions of the data in such a way that the reduced dimensional data best represents the original data. **Principal Component Analysis (PCA)** and autoencoders are some of the popular techniques to achieve this.

Although the intention of both these algorithms is the same for dimensionality reduction, there are some key differences in these two techniques:

- Unlike PCAs, autoencoders can learn non-linear feature representations from the data, which leads to enhanced model performance.
- PCAs are easier to train and more interpretable than autoencoders. The underlying math in autoencoders is also complex.
- PCA takes less time to run as compared to the autoencoders, which require more computation.

Denoising autoencoders

Autoencoders are widely used for feature selection and extraction. They try to apply transformations on the input data to reconstruct the input accurately. When the nodes of the hidden layers are equal to or more than the nodes in the input layer, autoencoders carry the risk of learning the identity function where the output simply equals the input, hence making the autoencoder of no use. **Denoising** refers to adding random noise to the raw input intentionally before feeding it to the network. By doing this, the identity-function risk is addressed, and the encoder learns significant features from the data and learns a robust representation of the input data. While working with denoising autoencoders, it is essential to note that the loss function is calculated by comparing the output values with the original input and not with the corrupted input.

Here is a sample representation of a denoising autoencoder:

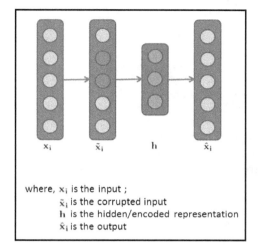

where, x_i is the input ;
$\tilde{x}_i$ is the corrupted input
h is the hidden/encoded representation
$\hat{x}_i$ is the output

In this recipe, we will implement a denoising autoencoder.

Getting ready

In this recipe, we will use the MNIST data set that was used in the previous recipes, *Implementing vanilla autoencoder* and *Dimensionality reduction using autoencoders*. We will add random Gaussian noise to the normalized MNIST images and denoise them with a denoising autoencoder. We will refer to the normalized train and test datasets as x_train_norm and x_test_norm.

How to do it...

Let's begin by adding noise to the input data:

1. We add a normal random noise to the input data before feeding it into the network. We generate corrupted images by adding noise with a normal distribution centered at 0.5 and a standard deviation of 0.5:

```
# noise for train dataset
noise_train <- array(data = rnorm(seq(0, 1, by = 0.02),mean =
0.5,sd = 0.5) ,dim = c(n_train,28,28,1))
dim(noise_train)
```

```
# noise for test dataset
noise_test <- array(data = rnorm(seq(0, 1, by = 0.02),mean = 0.5,sd
= 0.5) ,dim = c(n_test,28,28,1))
dim(noise_test)

# adding noise to train
x_train_norm_noise <- x_train_norm + noise_train

# adding noise to test
x_test_norm_noise <- x_test_norm + noise_test
```

2. We clip the corrupted input data (input data + noise) for maintaining the pixel values in the range of 0 and 1. Values less than 0 are clipped to 0 and values greater than 1 are clipped to 1:

```
# clipping train set
x_train_norm_noise[x_train_norm_noise < 0] <- 0
x_train_norm_noise[x_train_norm_noise > 1] <- 1

# clipping test set
x_test_norm_noise[x_test_norm_noise < 0] <- 0
x_test_norm_noise[x_test_norm_noise > 1] <- 1
```

Let's now visualize the sample corrupted image:

```
grid.raster(x_train_norm_noise[2,,,])
```

The following screenshot shows an image after it has been corrupted. Similarly, all of the other images will also be corrupted after adding noise:

3. We first create the encoder part. We start by creating an input layer using the `layer_input` function:

```
# input layer
inputs <- layer_input(shape = c(28, 28, 1))
x = inputs
```

Next, we configure the layers for the encoder model:

```
# outputs compose input + dense layers
x <- x %>%
  layer_conv_2d(filter = 32, kernel_size = 3,padding = "same",
input_shape = c(28, 28, 1)) %>%
  layer_activation("relu") %>%
  layer_conv_2d(filter = 64, kernel_size = 3) %>%
  layer_activation("relu")
```

We extract the shape of the output tensor from the network created in the preceding codeblock. This information will be needed to build the decoder model:

```
shape = k_int_shape(x)
shape
```

The following screenshot shows the shape of the output tensor from the encoder model:

```
1. NULL
2. 26
3. 26
4. 64
```

The final layer of the encoder is a dense layer with 16 units. Let's add a flattened layer and a dense layer at the end of the encoder model:

```
x = x %>% layer_flatten()
latent = x %>% layer_dense(16,name = "latent")
```

We instantiate the encoder model now. This model maps an input to its encoded representation:

```
encoder = keras_model(inputs, latent)
```

Let's now have a look at the summary of the encoder model:

```
summary(encoder)
```

The following screenshot shows the summary of the encoder model:

Layer (type)	Output Shape	Param #
input_1 (InputLayer)	(None, 28, 28, 1)	0
conv2d (Conv2D)	(None, 28, 28, 32)	320
activation (Activation)	(None, 28, 28, 32)	0
conv2d_1 (Conv2D)	(None, 26, 26, 64)	18496
activation_1 (Activation)	(None, 26, 26, 64)	0
flatten (Flatten)	(None, 43264)	0
latent (Dense)	(None, 16)	692240

```
Total params: 711,056
Trainable params: 711,056
Non-trainable params: 0
```

4. The output of the encoder is fed as input for the decoder part. The decoder is the opposite of an encoder in terms of layer configuration:

```
latent_inputs = layer_input(shape=16, name='decoder_input')

x = latent_inputs %>% layer_dense(shape[[2]] * shape[[3]] *
shape[[4]]) %>%
    layer_reshape(c(shape[[2]],shape[[3]], shape[[4]]))
```

Next, we configure the layers for the decoder part:

```
x <- x %>%
 layer_conv_2d_transpose(
 filter = 64, kernel_size = 3, padding = "same",
 input_shape = c(28, 28, 1)
 ) %>%
 layer_activation("relu") %>%
 # Second hidden layer
 layer_conv_2d_transpose(filter = 32, kernel_size =3) %>%
 layer_activation("relu")

x = x %>% layer_conv_2d_transpose(filters=1,
 kernel_size= 3,
 padding='same')

outputs = x %>% layer_activation('sigmoid', name='decoder_output')
```

We now instantiate the decoder model and see its summary:

```
decoder = keras_model(latent_inputs, outputs)
summary(decoder)
```

The following screenshot shows the summary of the decoder model:

Layer (type)	Output Shape	Param #
decoder_input (InputLayer)	(None, 16)	0
dense (Dense)	(None, 43264)	735488
reshape (Reshape)	(None, 26, 26, 64)	0
conv2d_transpose (Conv2DTranspose)	(None, 26, 26, 64)	36928
activation_2 (Activation)	(None, 26, 26, 64)	0
conv2d_transpose_1 (Conv2DTranspose	(None, 28, 28, 32)	18464
activation_3 (Activation)	(None, 28, 28, 32)	0
conv2d_transpose_2 (Conv2DTranspose	(None, 28, 28, 1)	289
decoder_output (Activation)	(None, 28, 28, 1)	0

```
Total params: 791,169
Trainable params: 791,169
Non-trainable params: 0
```

5. Now, we build the autoencoder model. We can see that the shape of the input and the output in the autoencoder model are of the same dimension:

```
# Autoencoder = Encoder + Decoder ; instantiating autoencoder model
autoencoder = keras_model(inputs, decoder(encoder(inputs)))
summary(autoencoder)
```

The following screenshot shows the summary of the autoencoder model:

Layer (type)	Output Shape	Param #
input_1 (InputLayer)	(None, 28, 28, 1)	0
model (Model)	(None, 16)	711056
model_1 (Model)	(None, 28, 28, 1)	791169

```
Total params: 1,502,225
Trainable params: 1,502,225
Non-trainable params: 0
```

6. Now, we compile the autoencoder model and fit the training data into the model to train the autoencoder:

```
autoencoder %>% compile(loss = 'mse',optimizer = 'adam')

autoencoder %>% fit(x_train_norm_noise,
 x_train_norm,
 validation_data=list(x_test_norm_noise, x_test_norm),
 epochs=30,batch_size= 128
 )
```

7. Next, we generate predictions for the test data:

```
prediction <- autoencoder %>% predict(x_test_norm_noise)
```

The following screenshot shows MNIST digits with noise and predicted images from denoising the autoencoder:

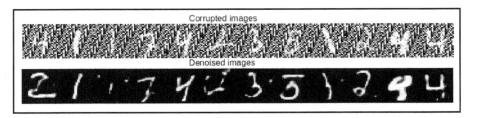

From the previous screenshot, we can say that our model did a decent job of denoising the digits.

How it works...

In *step 1*, we generated a random Gaussian noise with a mean of 0.5 and a standard deviation of 0.5. The shape of the noise data has to be similar to the shape of the data to which we add it.

We want our pixel values to be in the range of 0 and 1, but after introducing noise in the input data, the pixel values might change and no longer be in the required range. To avoid this, in *step 2*, we clipped the values in the corrupted input data within a range of 0 and 1. Clipping converted all of the negative values into 0 and values greater than one into 1, while the rest of the values remain as is. In *step 3*, we created the encoder part of the autoencoder model. In our example, the encoder model was a stack of two convolutional layers.

The first convolutional layer had 32 filters of a size of 3x3, followed by another second convolutional layer with 64 filters of a size of 3x3. The activation function used was `relu`. In the next step, we built the decoder part of the autoencoder model. Note that, in the decoder model, the layer configuration is just the opposite of the encoder model. The input to the decoder model is the compressed representation of the data that was provided by the encoder. The output of the decoder model will have the same dimensions as the input dimension. In *step 5*, we combined the encoder and decoder and built an autoencoder model. In the next step, we compiled and trained the autoencoder. We used **mean squared error** as the loss function and `adam` as the optimizer. The overall objective is to make the model robust:

Noise + Data → Denoising Autoencoder → Data

In the last step, we generated predictions for the test data and visualized reconstructed images after predictions.

There's more...

Autoencoders can learn internal representations from raw input data. One of the challenges with these autoencoders is that they can be too specialized for the training data, that is, they overfit and do not generalize for new data. Regularization makes an autoencoder less sensitive to the input but, at the same time, minimizing reconstruction errors forces it to remain sensitive to capture more variations. Applying penalties to the loss function appropriately makes the model more robust and learn generalized features.

In this section, we will learn about two types of regularized autoencoders:

- Contractive autoencoders
- Sparse autoencoders

Contractive autoencoders: These are regularized autoencoders where a penalty is applied to the reconstruction cost function, $L(x, \bar{x})$, for a robust learned representation that is less sensitive to small variations in the data. This penalty term is the Frobenius norm of the Jacobian matrix of the encoder activations with respect to the training data inputs:

$$L = |x - g(f(x))| + \lambda ||J_f(x)||_F^2$$
$$where, \quad ||J_f(x)||_F^2 = \sum_{ij} (\frac{\partial h_j(x)}{\partial x_i})^2 \ and$$
$$h = f(Wx + b) \ and$$
$$\bar{x} = g(h)$$

Adding this penalty results in a localized space contraction, which leads to robust feature extraction in the activation layer. Contractive autoencoders extract the local directions of variation dictated by the data, which belong to a lower-dimensional non-linear manifold and are more steady in the directions orthogonal to the manifold. One significant difference between denoising autoencoders and contractive autoencoder is that the denoising autoencoder makes both encoder and decoder networks robust, while contractive autoencoder only makes the encoder portion robust.

Sparse autoencoders: In an autoencoder while training, the hidden units in the middle layer fire very frequently for most of the training samples. We don't want this characteristic. In sparse autoencoders, we add a sparsity constraint to lower the activation rate of the hidden neurons to make them activated only for a small fraction of the training examples. This is called sparse because each hidden unit activates only to a particular type of inputs and not all of them. By forcing a neuron to fire for only a specific type of inputs in the training samples, the unit would work robustly and learn useful representations in the data. This is a different approach of regularization as, here, we regularize the activations, unlike the other approaches where we regularize the weights of a network. In a trained sparse autoencoder model, different inputs will result in activations of different nodes in the network.

There are mainly two ways for imposing the sparsity constraint in sparse autoencoders, and both penalize the excessive activations by adding some term to the loss function:

- **L1 Regularization:** In this regularization technique, we add a penalizing term to the loss function that penalizes the absolute value of the activation vectors in layer h for observation i, scaled by a tuning parameter, λ:

$$L(x, \bar{x}) + \lambda \sum_i |a_i^{(h)}|$$

- **KL-Divergence:** We add a sparsity parameter, ρ, which is the average activation of a neuron over a collection of training samples:

$$L(x, \bar{x}) + \lambda \sum_j KL(\rho || \hat{\rho}_j)$$

$$where, \ \hat{\rho}_j = \frac{1}{m} \lambda \sum_i |a_{(i)}^{(h)}(x)|$$

- Here, the subscript *j* denotes a specific neuron in layer *h*, and *m* denotes the number of training observations that can be individually denoted as *x*. The KL divergence between two Bernoulli distributions can be written as follows:

$$\sum_{j=1}^{l^{(h)}} = \rho log \frac{\rho}{\hat{\rho}_j} + (1 - \rho) log \frac{1 - \rho}{1 - \hat{\rho}_j}$$

See also

If you are interested to know more about stacked denoising autoencoders, please refer to the following link: http://www.jmlr.org/papers/volume11/vincent10a/vincent10a.pdf.

Changing black and white into color

Image colorization using deep learning techniques is a common real-world application nowadays. In image coloring, a black and white, that is, a grayscale, image is converted into a colored image that best represents the semantic colors of the input image. For example, the color of the sky on a clear sunny day must be colored as blue and not red by the model. There are many colorization algorithms and techniques available; these techniques mostly differ in the way they treat the data and map the grayscale to colors. Some of the parametric methods learn representations by doing training on huge datasets of colored images, posing the problem as regression or classification, and providing proper loss function. Other methods rely on defining one or more color reference images.

In this recipe, we will use autoencoders to achieve this task. We will train the autoencoder with a sufficient number of grayscale photos as input and the corresponding colored pictures as output so that it could discover the hidden structure on correctly applying colors.

Getting ready

In this example, we will use the CIFAR-10 dataset, which consists of color images of a size of 32x32. There are 50,000 training images and 10,000 test images. We will preprocess its images to grayscale and then build an autoencoder to color them.

Let's first load the required libraries into the environment:

```
library(keras)
library(wvtool)
library(grid)
library(abind)
```

We load the training and testing datasets and store them into variables:

```
data <- dataset_cifar10()
x_train = data$train$x
x_test = data$test$x
```

Let's store relevant dimension data into respective variables:

```
num_images = dim(x_train)[1]
num_images_test = dim(x_test)[1]
img_width = dim(x_train)[2]
img_height = dim(x_train)[3]
```

Let's convert all of the images in the train and test data into grayscale images using the `rgb2gray()` function from `wvtools`:

```
# grayscale train set
x_train_gray <- apply(x_train[1:num_images,,,], c(1), FUN = function(x){
  rgb2gray(x, coefs=c(0.299, 0.587, 0.114))
})
x_train_gray <- t(x_train_gray)
x_train_gray = array(x_train_gray,dim = c(num_images,img_width,img_height))

# grayscale test set
x_test_gray <- apply(x_test[1:num_images_test,,,], c(1), FUN = function(x){
  rgb2gray(x, coefs=c(0.299, 0.587, 0.114))
})
x_test_gray <- t(x_test_gray)
x_test_gray = array(x_test_gray,dim =
c(num_images_test,img_width,img_height))
```

Next, we normalize the train and test colored images and the grayscale images within the range of 0 and 1:

```
# normalize train and test coloured images
x_train = x_train / 255
x_test = x_test / 255

# normalize train and test grayscale images
x_train_gray = x_train_gray / 255
x_test_gray = x_test_gray / 255
```

Then, we reshape each grayscale image into the shape of the image height, image width, and number of channels:

```
x_train_gray <- array_reshape(x_train_gray,dim =
c(num_images,img_height,img_width,1))
x_test_gray <- array_reshape(x_test_gray,dim =
c(num_images_test,img_height,img_width,1))
```

Note that, in the case of grayscale images, the number of channels is 1.

How to do it...

We have converted images in the CIFAR-10 dataset into grayscale. Now, let's build an autoencoder to colorize them:

1. Let's define variables to set the parameters of the autoencoder:

```
# network parameters
input_shape = c(img_height, img_width, 1)
batch_size = 32
kernel_size = 3
latent_dim = 256
```

Next, we create an input layer of the autoencoder:

```
inputs = layer_input(shape = input_shape,name = "encoder_input")
```

2. We have created our input layer, so now let's define and configure layers of the encoder part of the network:

```
x = inputs
x <- x %>% layer_conv_2d(filters = 64,kernel_size =
kernel_size,strides = 2,
 activation = "relu",padding = "same") %>%
 layer_conv_2d(filters = 128,kernel_size = kernel_size,strides = 2,
 activation = "relu",padding = "same") %>%
 layer_conv_2d(filters = 256,kernel_size = kernel_size,strides = 2,
 activation = "relu",padding = "same")
```

We also extract the shape of the output tensor from the network created in the preceding codeblock. This information will be needed to build the decoder model:

```
shape = k_int_shape(x)
```

Let's add a flattened layer and a dense layer at the end of the encoder and build the encoder model:

```
x <- x %>% layer_flatten()
latent <- x %>% layer_dense(units = latent_dim,name = "latent")
encoder = keras_model(inputs, latent)
```

We now see the summary of the encoder model:

```
summary(encoder)
```

The following screenshot shows the summary of the encoder network:

Layer (type)	Output Shape	Param #
encoder_input (InputLayer)	(None, 32, 32, 1)	0
conv2d (Conv2D)	(None, 16, 16, 64)	640
conv2d_1 (Conv2D)	(None, 8, 8, 128)	73856
conv2d_2 (Conv2D)	(None, 4, 4, 256)	295168
flatten (Flatten)	(None, 4096)	0
latent (Dense)	(None, 256)	1048832

```
Total params: 1,418,496
Trainable params: 1,418,496
Non-trainable params: 0
```

3. Next, we build the decoder model. The output of the encoder is input for the decoder part; hence, the output shape of the encoder should be set equal to the input of the decoder. Note that the decoder network is the opposite of the encoder in terms of layer configuration:

```
# decoder input layer
latent_inputs = layer_input(shape = c(latent_dim),
name='decoder_input')

# adding layers to input layer
x = latent_inputs %>% layer_dense(shape[[2]] * shape[[3]] *
shape[[4]])
x = x %>% layer_reshape(c(shape[[2]], shape[[3]], shape[[4]]))
x <- x %>% layer_conv_2d_transpose(filters = 256,kernel_size =
kernel_size,strides = 2,
  activation = "relu",padding = "same") %>%
  layer_conv_2d_transpose(filters = 128,kernel_size =
kernel_size,strides = 2,
  activation = "relu",padding = "same") %>%
```

```
layer_conv_2d_transpose(filters = 64,kernel_size =
kernel_size,strides = 2,
 activation = "relu",padding = "same")

# output layer
outputs = x %>% layer_conv_2d_transpose(filters=3,
 kernel_size=kernel_size,
 activation='sigmoid',
 padding='same',
 name='decoder_output')

# decoder
decoder = keras_model(latent_inputs, outputs)
```

Let's see the summary of the decoder model:

```
summary(decoder)
```

The following screenshot shows the summary of the decoder network:

```
Layer (type)                    Output Shape            Param #
=================================================================
decoder_input (InputLayer)      (None, 256)             0
_____
dense (Dense)                   (None, 4096)            1052672
_____
reshape (Reshape)               (None, 4, 4, 256)       0
_____
conv2d_transpose (Conv2DTranspose) (None, 8, 8, 256)    590080
_____
conv2d_transpose_1 (Conv2DTranspose (None, 16, 16, 128)  295040
_____
conv2d_transpose_2 (Conv2DTranspose (None, 32, 32, 64)   73792
_____
decoder_output (Conv2DTranspose) (None, 32, 32, 3)      1731
=================================================================
Total params: 2,013,315
Trainable params: 2,013,315
Non-trainable params: 0
```

4. The next step is to combine the encoder and decoder into one autoencoder model:

```
# autoencoder = encoder + decoder
autoencoder = keras_model(inputs, decoder(encoder(inputs)))
```

Let's see the summary of the complete autoencoder model:

```
summary(autoencoder)
```

The following screenshot shows the summary of the autoencoder network:

```
Layer (type)                      Output Shape              Param #
================================================================
encoder_input (InputLayer)        (None, 32, 32, 1)         0

model (Model)                     (None, 256)               1418496

model_1 (Model)                   (None, 32, 32, 3)         2013315
================================================================
Total params: 3,431,811
Trainable params: 3,431,811
Non-trainable params: 0
```

5. We now compile and train the autoencoder:

    ```
    # compile
    autoencoder %>% compile(loss='mse', optimizer='adam')

    # train the autoencoder
    autoencoder %>% fit(x_train_gray,
      x_train,
      validation_data= list(x_test_gray, x_test),
      epochs=20,
      batch_size=batch_size)
    ```

6. We use the trained model to generate predictions for test data:

    ```
    predicted <- autoencoder %>% predict(x_test_gray)
    ```

The following screenshot depicts how our autoencoder colorized the grayscale images:

In the next section, we will get down to the nitty-gritty of all of the steps we implemented.

How it works...

In *step 1*, we initialized variables to set model parameters. The `latent_dim` variable sets the dimensionality of the encoded features. Then, we created an input layer of the autoencoder. In *step* 2, we built an encoder model. We first created convolutional layers of the encoder and then extracted the output shape of the last convolutional layer. Next, we added a flattened layer and then connected a dense layer with units equal to the `latent_dim` variable. In the next step, we built the decoder model. We defined an input layer for the decoder, which receives an input of a shape equal to `latent_dim`.

Next, we added layers in the decoder such that we reverse the operations of an encoder. In *step* 4, we combined encoder and decoder and built an autoencoder. In the next step, we compiled and trained the autoencoder for 20 epochs. We used mean squared error as the loss function and adam as the optimizer. In the last step, we input black and white images and colorized them.

See also

To read about lossy image compression using autoencoders, please refer to this paper: `https://arxiv.org/pdf/1703.00395.pdf`.

5
Deep Generative Models

Deep generative neural networks are a popular form of unsupervised deep learning models. These models aim to learn the process that generates the data. Generative models not only learn to extract patterns from the data but also estimate the underlying probability distribution. These models are used to create synthetic data, which follows the same probability distribution as that of the given training dataset. This chapter will give you an idea of deep generative models and how they work.

In this chapter, we will cover the following recipes:

- Generating images with GANs
- Implementing DCGANs
- Implementing variational autoencoders

Generating images with GANs

Generative adversarial networks (GANs) are widely used for learning any data distribution and imitating it. GANs consist of two networks; one is the generator, which generates new synthetic instances of data from a normal or uniform distribution, while the other is the discriminator, which evaluates the generated instances and checks if they are authentic – that is, they belong to the original training data distribution or not. The generator and discriminator are pitted against each other in a counterfeiter and cop scenario where the goal of the counterfeiter is to fool the cop by generating false data and the cop's role is to detect the lies. The feedback from the discriminator is passed on to the generator so that it can improvise at each iteration. Note that although both networks optimize a different and opposite objective function, the stability and accuracy of the whole system depends on the individual accuracy of both these networks.

Here is the overall objective function of a GAN network:

$$\min_{G}\max_{D}V(D,G) = E_{x \sim p_{data}(x)}[log(D(x))] + E_{z \sim p_z(z)}[log(1 - (D(G(z))))]$$

$$where, \text{G(z) is a mapping from latent space to z,}$$
$$\text{D(x) is a mapping from data space to a probability score which}$$
$$\text{indicates that the input is drawn from true data distribution}$$

The following diagram shows how GANs work:

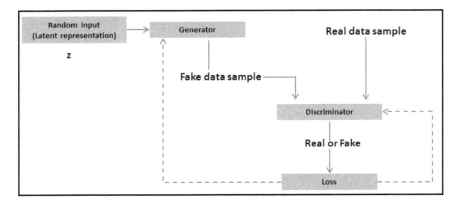

In this recipe, we will implement a GAN model to reconstruct handwritten digits.

Getting ready

We will be using the MNIST dataset of handwritten digits in this example. It consists of 60,000 training and 10,000 test grayscale images that are 28x28 in size.

Let's start by loading the required libraries:

```
library(keras)
library(grid)
library(abind)
```

Now, let's load the data:

```
# Input image dimensions
img_rows <- 28
img_cols <- 28

# The data, shuffled and split between train and test sets
mnist <- dataset_mnist()
x_train <- mnist$train$x
y_train <- mnist$train$y
x_test <- mnist$test$x
y_test <- mnist$test$y
```

Now, we can check the dimensions of the data:

```
dim(x_train)
```

In the following screenshot, you can see that there are 60,000 images in the training data, each of which are 28x28 in size:

```
60000  28  28
```

Now that we've done this, we can redefine the dimensions of the training data from a matrix of 28x28 to a flattened 1D array that's 784 in length:

```
x_train <- array_reshape(x_train, c(nrow(x_train), 784))
```

Next, we normalize the training data and transform the values within the range of 0 and 1:

```
x_train <- x_train/255
```

Let's print one sample image data to see what it looks like:

```
x_train[1,]
```

Now that we are aware of the data, let's move on to the model building part.

How to do it...

There are two components within GANs – the generator and the discriminator. We start by creating individual generator and discriminator networks first, followed by chaining these two networks through a GAN model and training it. Let's get started:

1. Since we are dealing with grayscale images, the number of channels will be 1. We also set the dimension of our random noise vector, which is used as input for the generator network, to 100:

```
channels <- 1
set.seed(10)
latent_dimension <- 100
```

2. Next, we create the generator network. The generator network maps random normal noise vectors of shape `latent_dimension` to a vector of length equal to the flattened input image. The generator network consists of three hidden layers; the activation function is Leaky ReLU:

```
input_generator <- layer_input(shape = c(latent_dimension))

output_generator <- input_generator %>%
 layer_dense(256,input_shape = c(784),kernel_initializer =
initializer_random_normal(mean = 0,    stddev = 0.05, seed = NULL))
%>%
 layer_activation_leaky_relu(0.2) %>%
 layer_dense(512) %>%
 layer_activation_leaky_relu(0.2) %>%
 layer_dense(1024) %>%
 layer_activation_leaky_relu(0.2) %>%
 layer_dense(784,activation = "tanh")

generator <- keras_model(input_generator, output_generator)
```

Let's look at the summary of the generator network:

```
summary(generator)
```

The following screenshot shows the description of the generator model:

```
Layer (type)                    Output Shape            Param #
=================================================================
input_1 (InputLayer)            (None, 100)             0
_____
dense (Dense)                   (None, 256)             25856
_____
leaky_re_lu (LeakyReLU)         (None, 256)             0
_____
dense_1 (Dense)                 (None, 512)             131584
_____
leaky_re_lu_1 (LeakyReLU)       (None, 512)             0
_____
dense_2 (Dense)                 (None, 1024)            525312
_____
leaky_re_lu_2 (LeakyReLU)       (None, 1024)            0
_____
dense_3 (Dense)                 (None, 784)             803600
=================================================================
Total params: 1,486,352
Trainable params: 1,486,352
Non-trainable params: 0
_____
```

3. Now, we can create the discriminator network. This network maps the images that were produced by the generator to a probability of the generated image being real or fake:

```
input_discriminator <- layer_input(shape = c(784))

output_discriminator <- input_discriminator %>%
  layer_dense(units = 1024,input_shape = c(784),kernel_initializer
= initializer_random_normal(mean = 0, stddev = 0.05, seed = NULL))
%>%
  layer_activation_leaky_relu(0.2) %>%
  layer_dropout(0.3)%>%

  layer_dense(units = 512) %>%
  layer_activation_leaky_relu(0.2) %>%
  layer_dropout(0.3)%>%

  layer_dense(units = 256) %>%
  layer_activation_leaky_relu(0.2) %>%
  layer_dropout(0.3)%>%
  layer_dense(1,activation = "sigmoid")

discriminator <- keras_model(input_discriminator,
output_discriminator)
```

Let's take a look at the summary of the discriminator:

```
summary(discriminator)
```

The following screenshot shows the description of the discriminator model:

Layer (type)	Output Shape	Param #
input_1 (InputLayer)	(None, 784)	0
dense (Dense)	(None, 1024)	803840
leaky_re_lu (LeakyReLU)	(None, 1024)	0
dropout (Dropout)	(None, 1024)	0
dense_1 (Dense)	(None, 512)	524800
leaky_re_lu_1 (LeakyReLU)	(None, 512)	0
dropout_1 (Dropout)	(None, 512)	0
dense_2 (Dense)	(None, 256)	131328
leaky_re_lu_2 (LeakyReLU)	(None, 256)	0
dropout_2 (Dropout)	(None, 256)	0
dense_3 (Dense)	(None, 1)	257

```
Total params: 1,460,225
Trainable params: 1,460,225
Non-trainable params: 0
```

After configuring the discriminator network, we need to compile it. We use `adam` as the optimizer and `binary_crossentropy` as the loss function. The learning rate is specified as 0.0002. We use `clipvalue` for gradient clipping, which limits the magnitude of the gradient so that it behaves better in the proximity of steep cliffs:

```
discriminator %>% compile(
  optimizer = optimizer_adam(lr = 0.0002, beta_1 = 0.5,clipvalue =
1),
  loss = "binary_crossentropy"
)
```

4. Next, we freeze the weights of the discriminator before we start training the GAN network. This makes the discriminator non-trainable and its weights don't get updated while training the GAN:

```
freeze_weights(discriminator)
```

5. Let's configure the GAN network and compile it. The GAN network combines the generator and the discriminator networks:

```
gan_input <- layer_input(shape = c(latent_dimension),name =
'gan_input')
gan_output <- discriminator(generator(gan_input))
gan <- keras_model(gan_input, gan_output)

gan %>% compile(
  optimizer = optimizer_adam(lr = 0.0002, beta_1 = 0.5,clipvalue =
1),
  loss = "binary_crossentropy"
)
```

Let's take a look at the summary of the gan model:

```
summary(gan)
```

The following screenshot shows the description of the GAN model:

Layer (type)	Output Shape	Param #
gan_input (InputLayer)	(None, 100)	0
model (Model)	(None, 784)	1486352
model_1 (Model)	(None, 1)	1460225

Total params: 2,946,577
Trainable params: 1,486,352
Non-trainable params: 1,460,225

6. Now, we can start training the GAN network. We train our GAN network for 1,000 iterations, with a batch of 20 new images in each iteration. We create a folder named `gan_images` and store the generated images for various iterations in that folder. We also store the models at different iterations in another folder named `gan_model`:

```
iterations <- 1000
batch_size <- 20

# create directory to store generated images
dir.create("gan_images")
# create directory to store model
dir.create("gan_model")
```

Let's start training the GAN model:

```
start_index <- 1
for (i in 1:iterations) {

# Sample random points in the normally distributed latent
# space of dimension (batch_size * latent_dimension)

 latent_vectors <- matrix(rnorm(batch_size * latent_dimension),
 nrow = batch_size, ncol = latent_dimension)

# Use generator network to decode the above random points to fake
images
 generated_images <- generator %>% predict(latent_vectors)

# Combine the fake images with real images to build the training
data for discriminator
 stop_index <- start_index + batch_size - 1
 real_images <- x_train[start_index:stop_index,]
 rows <- nrow(real_images)
 combined_images <- array(0, dim = c(rows * 2,
dim(real_images)[-1]))
 combined_images[1:rows,] <- generated_images
 combined_images[(rows+1):(rows*2),] <- real_images
 dim(combined_images)

# Provide appropriate labels for real and fake images
 labels <- rbind(matrix(1, nrow = batch_size, ncol = 1),
 matrix(0, nrow = batch_size, ncol = 1))

# Adds random noise to the labels to increase robustness of the
discriminator
 labels <- labels + (0.5 * array(runif(prod(dim(labels))),
```

```r
dim = dim(labels)))

# Train the discriminator using both real and fake images
 discriminator_loss <- discriminator %>%
train_on_batch(combined_images, labels)

# Sample random points in the latent space
 latent_vectors <- matrix(rnorm(batch_size * latent_dimension),
 nrow = batch_size, ncol = latent_dimension)

# Assembles labels that say "all real images"
 misleading_targets <- array(0, dim = c(batch_size, 1))

# Training the generator by using the gan model,note that the
discriminator weights are frozen
 gan_model_loss <- gan %>% train_on_batch(
latent_vectors,
misleading_targets
)
 start_index <- start_index + batch_size
 if (start_index > (nrow(x_train) - batch_size))
 start_index <- 1

 # At few iterations save the model and save generated images
 if(i %in% c(5,10,15,20,40,100,200,500,800,1000)){

 # Save model
 save_model_hdf5(gan,paste0("gan_model/gan_model_",i,".h5"))

 # Save generated images
 generated_images <- generated_images *255
 generated_images = array_reshape(generated_images ,dim =
c(batch_size,28,28,1))
 generated_images = (generated_images -min(generated_images
))/(max(generated_images )-min(generated_images ))
 grid = generated_images [1,,,]
 for(j in seq(2,5)){
 single = generated_images [j,,,]
 grid = abind(grid,single,along = 2)
 }
 png(file=paste0("gan_images/generated_digits_",i,".png"),
width=600, height=350)
 grid.raster(grid, interpolate=FALSE)
 dev.off()
 }
}
```

The generated digits look as follows:

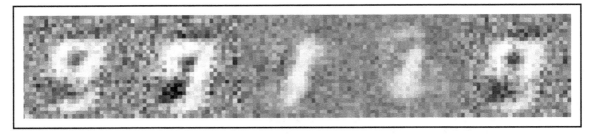

From the preceding image, we can infer that our model is working well. In the next section, you will be given an in-depth explanations of the steps we implemented here.

How it works...

In *step 1*, we defined the shape of the input image and the number of channels. Since the images that we used were grayscale, we specified the channels as 1. We also defined the latent space dimension, which is used as the input for the generator. In *step 2*, we constructed a generator network. The goal of the generator is to produce images from the random normal vectors of the `latent_dim` dimension. It generates an output tensor of 784 dimensions. We used a deep neural network as the generator network in our example. Note that we used `tanh` as the activation function in the last layer of the generator since it performs better than the sigmoid activation function. Also, Leaky ReLU was used as the activation function in the hidden layers because this activation function relaxes sparse gradient constraints by allowing small negative activation values.

 Using a normal distribution to generate points from a latent space rather than a uniform distribution is recommended for better results.

In the next step, we defined and compiled the discriminator network. It mapped a vector of size 784, which was produced by the generator, to a probability that indicates whether the generated image is real or fake. Since our generator network was a deep neural network with three hidden layers, the discriminator is also a deep neural network with the same number of layers. Note that we added dropout layers and random noise to the labels of the discriminator in order to induce randomness and make our GAN model robust. In *step 4*, we froze the weights of the discriminator to make it non-trainable.

Then, in *step 5*, we configured and compiled the GAN network. A GAN network chains both the generator and discriminator. We can represent a GAN network as follows:

$$gan(x) \leftarrow discriminator(generator(x))$$

The GAN network we created, maps the images that were generated by the generator to the discriminator's assessment of real and fake images. In *step 6*, we trained the GAN network. To train GAN, we need to train the discriminator so that it identifies the real and fake images accurately. The generator uses feedback from the discriminator to update its weights. In this way, the discriminator assists in training the generator. We use the gradients of the generator's weights with respect to the loss of the `gan` model to train the generator. This way, at each iteration, we make the weights of the generator move in a direction that makes the discriminator more likely to classify the images that were decoded by the generator as real. The robustness of both the generator and discriminator is essential for the overall network's accuracy. Finally, we saved the models and the generated images for a few batches.

There's more...

Although GANs have become quite a popular deep learning technique, there are several challenges associated with working with GANs. The critical ones are listed here:

- GANs are extremely hard to train. Often, the model parameters destabilize and don't converge.
- Sometimes, the discriminator gets so accurate that the generator's gradient vanishes and learns nothing.
- The imbalance between the generator and the discriminator can cause overfitting.
- GANs are too sensitive to model tuning and hyperparameter selection.

See also

To find out more about other major types of GAN architectures, refer to the following links:

- Conditional GAN: https://arxiv.org/pdf/1411.1784.pdf
- Wasserstein GAN (WGAN): https://arxiv.org/pdf/1904.08994.pdf and https://arxiv.org/pdf/1704.00028.pdf
- Least Squares GAN: https://arxiv.org/pdf/1611.04076.pdf

Implementing DCGANs

Convolutional GANs are a very successful variation of GANs. They contain convolution layers in both the generator and discriminator networks. In this recipe, we will implement a **deep convolutional generative adversarial network (DCGAN)**. This is an improvement over vanilla GANs because of its stable architecture. There are some standard guidelines that, when followed, result in the robust performance of DCGAN.

They are as follows:

- Replace pooling layers with convolutional strides in the discriminator and use transpose convolutions in the generator network.
- Use batch normalization in the generator and discriminator, except for the output layer.
- Do not use fully connected hidden layers.
- Use ReLU in the generator, except for the output layer, which uses tanh.
- Use Leaky ReLU in the discriminator.

Getting ready

In this recipe, we will use a subset of the Flowers Recognition dataset, which is credited to Alexsandr Mamaev. The subset of data that we'll be using in this example contains around 2,500 images of three types of flowers – sunflower, dandelion, and daisy. Each class consists of about 800 photos. The data can be downloaded from Kaggle at `https://www.kaggle.com/alxmamaev/flowers-recognition`.

Let's start by loading the required libraries:

```
library(keras)
library(reticulate)
library(abind)
library(grid)
```

Now, we can load the data into the R environment. We will leverage the `flow_images_from_directory()` function from `keras` to load the data. The data is present in a folder named `flowers`, which contains subfolders, each belonging to a particular class of flower. Since our input images are not uniform in size, while loading the data itself, we specify the target size so that each image is resized accordingly:

```
train_path <- "data/flowers/"

image_width = 32
image_height = 32
target_image_size = c(image_width,image_height)

training_data <- flow_images_from_directory(directory =
train_path,target_size = target_image_size, color_mode = "rgb", class_mode
= NULL, batch_size = 2500)

training_data = as_iterator(training_data)
training_data = iter_next(training_data)
training_data <- training_data/255
dim(training_data)
```

The following screenshot shows the dimensions of the training data:

```
2500  32  32  3
```

Now that we are aware of the data, let's move on to the model building stage.

How to do it...

Let's start by declaring a few variables that will be required for the model's configuration:

1. First, we define the image's size in terms of height, width, and the number of channels. Since we are doing our analysis on colored images, we keep the number of channels to 3, meaning RGB mode. We also define the shape of the latent space vectors:

   ```
   latent_dim <- 32
   height <- 32
   width <- 32
   channels <- 3
   ```

2. Next, we create the generator network. The generator network maps random vectors of shape `latent_dim` to images of the input size, which in our case is (32, 32, 3):

```
input_generator <- layer_input(shape = c(latent_dim))

output_generator <- input_generator %>%
# We transform the input data into a 16x16 128-channels feature map
initially
 layer_dense(units = 128 * 16 * 16) %>%
 layer_activation_leaky_relu() %>%
 layer_reshape(target_shape = c(16, 16, 128)) %>%
# Next ,we add a convolution layer
 layer_conv_2d(filters = 256, kernel_size = 5,
 padding = "same") %>%
 layer_activation_leaky_relu() %>%
# Now we upsample the data to 32x32 dimension using the
layer_conv_2d_transpose()
 layer_conv_2d_transpose(filters = 256, kernel_size = 4,
 strides = 2, padding = "same") %>%
 layer_activation_leaky_relu() %>%
# Now we add more convolutional layers to the network
 layer_conv_2d(filters = 256, kernel_size = 5,
 padding = "same") %>%
 layer_activation_leaky_relu() %>%
 layer_conv_2d(filters = 256, kernel_size = 5,
 padding = "same") %>%
 layer_activation_leaky_relu() %>%
# Produce a 32x32 1-channel feature map
 layer_conv_2d(filters = channels, kernel_size = 7,
 activation = "tanh", padding = "same")

generator <- keras_model(input_generator, output_generator)
```

Let's look at the summary of the generator network:

```
summary(generator)
```

The following screenshot shows the description of the generator model:

```
Layer (type)                        Output Shape              Param #
=====================================================================
input_1 (InputLayer)                (None, 32)                0
_____
dense (Dense)                       (None, 32768)             1081344
_____
leaky_re_lu (LeakyReLU)             (None, 32768)             0
_____
reshape (Reshape)                   (None, 16, 16, 128)       0
_____
conv2d (Conv2D)                     (None, 16, 16, 256)       819456
_____
leaky_re_lu_1 (LeakyReLU)           (None, 16, 16, 256)       0
_____
conv2d_transpose (Conv2DTranspose)  (None, 32, 32, 256)       1048832
_____
leaky_re_lu_2 (LeakyReLU)           (None, 32, 32, 256)       0
_____
conv2d_1 (Conv2D)                   (None, 32, 32, 256)       1638656
_____
leaky_re_lu_3 (LeakyReLU)           (None, 32, 32, 256)       0
_____
conv2d_2 (Conv2D)                   (None, 32, 32, 256)       1638656
_____
leaky_re_lu_4 (LeakyReLU)           (None, 32, 32, 256)       0
_____
conv2d_3 (Conv2D)                   (None, 32, 32, 3)         37635
=====================================================================
Total params: 6,264,579
Trainable params: 6,264,579
Non-trainable params: 0
```

3. Now, we create the discriminator network. This network maps images produced by the generator of shape (32, 32, 3) to a binary value and estimates the probability of the generated image being real or fake:

```
input_discriminator <- layer_input(shape = c(height, width,
channels))

output_discriminator <- input_discriminator %>%
  layer_conv_2d(filters = 128, kernel_size = 3) %>%
  layer_activation_leaky_relu() %>%
  layer_conv_2d(filters = 128, kernel_size = 4, strides = 2) %>%
  layer_activation_leaky_relu() %>%
  layer_conv_2d(filters = 128, kernel_size = 4, strides = 2) %>%
  layer_activation_leaky_relu() %>%
  layer_conv_2d(filters = 128, kernel_size = 4, strides = 2) %>%
  layer_activation_leaky_relu() %>%
  layer_flatten() %>%
  # One dropout layer
  layer_dropout(rate = 0.3) %>%
  # Classification layer
  layer_dense(units = 1, activation = "sigmoid")

discriminator <- keras_model(input_discriminator,
output_discriminator)
```

Let's look at the summary of the discriminator network:

```
summary(discriminator)
```

The following screenshot shows the description of the discriminator model:

```
Layer (type)                   Output Shape              Param #
=================================================================
input_1 (InputLayer)           (None, 32, 32, 3)         0
_____
conv2d (Conv2D)                (None, 30, 30, 128)       3584
_____
leaky_re_lu (LeakyReLU)        (None, 30, 30, 128)       0
_____
conv2d_1 (Conv2D)              (None, 14, 14, 128)       262272
_____
leaky_re_lu_1 (LeakyReLU)      (None, 14, 14, 128)       0
_____
conv2d_2 (Conv2D)              (None, 6, 6, 128)         262272
_____
leaky_re_lu_2 (LeakyReLU)      (None, 6, 6, 128)         0
_____
conv2d_3 (Conv2D)              (None, 2, 2, 128)         262272
_____
leaky_re_lu_3 (LeakyReLU)      (None, 2, 2, 128)         0
_____
flatten (Flatten)              (None, 512)               0
_____
dropout (Dropout)              (None, 512)               0
_____
dense (Dense)                  (None, 1)                 513
=================================================================
Total params: 790,913
Trainable params: 790,913
Non-trainable params: 0
```

After configuring the discriminator network, we compile it. We use `rmsprop` as the optimizer and `binary_crossentropy` as the loss function. The learning rate is specified as 0.0008. We use `clipvalue` for gradient clipping, which limits the magnitude of the gradient so that it behaves better in the proximity of steep cliffs:

```
discriminator %>% compile(
  optimizer = optimizer_rmsprop(lr = 0.0008,clipvalue = 1.0,decay =
1e-8),
  loss = "binary_crossentropy"
)
```

4. Before we start training the GAN network, we freeze the weights of the discriminator to make it non-trainable:

```
freeze_weights(discriminator)
```

5. Let's configure the DCGAN network and compile it. A GAN network combines the generator and the discriminator networks:

```
gan_input <- layer_input(shape = c(latent_dim),name =
'dc_gan_input')
gan_output <- discriminator(generator(gan_input))
gan <- keras_model(gan_input, gan_output)

gan %>% compile(
 optimizer = optimizer_rmsprop(lr = 0.0004,clipvalue = 1.0,decay =
1e-8),
 loss = "binary_crossentropy"
)
```

Let's take a look at the summary of our GAN model:

```
summary(gan)
```

The following screenshot shows the description of the GAN model:

```
Layer (type)                    Output Shape                Param #
=================================================================
dc_gan_input (InputLayer)       (None, 32)                  0
_____
model (Model)                   (None, 32, 32, 3)           6264579
_____
model_1 (Model)                 (None, 1)                   790913
=================================================================
Total params: 7,055,492
Trainable params: 6,264,579
Non-trainable params: 790,913
```

6. Now, let's start training the network. We train our DCGAN network for 2,000 iterations on a batch of 40 new images for each iteration. We create a folder named dcgan_images and store the generated images for various iterations in that folder. We also store the models at different iterations in another folder named dcgan_model:

```
iterations <- 2000
batch_size <- 40
dir.create("dcgan_images")
dir.create("dcgan_model")
```

Now, we train our GAN model:

```
start_index <- 1

for (i in 1:iterations) {

# Sample random points in the normally distributed latent space of
dimension :
# (batch_size *latent_dimension)

 random_latent_vectors <- matrix(rnorm(batch_size * latent_dim),
 nrow = batch_size, ncol = latent_dim)

# Use generator network to decode the above random points to fake
images
 generated_images <- generator %>% predict(random_latent_vectors)

# Combine the fake images with real images to build the training
data for discriminator
 stop_index <- start_index + batch_size - 1
 real_images <- training_data[start_index:stop_index,,,]
 rows <- nrow(real_images)
 combined_images <- array(0, dim = c(rows * 2,
dim(real_images)[-1]))
 combined_images[1:rows,,,] <- generated_images
 combined_images[(rows+1):(rows*2),,,] <- real_images

 # Provide appropriate labels for real and fake images
 labels <- rbind(matrix(1, nrow = batch_size, ncol = 1),
 matrix(0, nrow = batch_size, ncol = 1))

 # Adds random noise to the labels to increase robustness of the
discriminator
 labels <- labels + (0.5 * array(runif(prod(dim(labels))),
 dim = dim(labels)))

 # Train the discriminator using both real and fake images
 discriminator_loss <- discriminator %>%
train_on_batch(combined_images, labels)

 # Sample random points in the latent space
 random_latent_vectors <- matrix(rnorm(batch_size * latent_dim),
 nrow = batch_size, ncol = latent_dim)

 # Assembles labels that say "all real images"
 misleading_targets <- array(0, dim = c(batch_size, 1))

 # Train the generator by using the gan model,note that the
```

```
discriminator weights are frozen.
 gan_model_loss <- gan %>% train_on_batch(
 random_latent_vectors,
 misleading_targets
 )

 start_index <- start_index + batch_size
 if (start_index > (nrow(training_data) - batch_size))
 start_index <- 1

# At few iterations save the model and save generated images
if(i %in% c(5,10,15,20,40,100,200,500,800,1000,1500,2000)){

# Save models
 save_model_hdf5(gan,paste0("dcgan_model/gan_model_",i,".h5"))

# Save generated images
 generated_images <- generated_images *255
 generated_images = array_reshape(generated_images ,dim =
c(batch_size,32,32,3))
 generated_images = (generated_images -min(generated_images
))/(max(generated_images )-min(generated_images ))
 grid = generated_images [1,,,]
 for(j in seq(2,5)){
 single = generated_images [j,,,]
 grid = abind(grid,single,along = 2)
 }
 png(file=paste0("dcgan_images/generated_flowers_",i,".png"),
 width=600, height=350)
 grid.raster(grid, interpolate=FALSE)
 dev.off()
 }
}
```

After 2,000 iterations, the generated images look as follows:

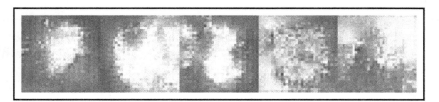

If we wish to enhance the accuracy of the model, we can train it for more iterations.

How it works...

In *step 1*, we defined the shape of the input images and the number of channels. Since the images that were used were colourful, we specified the number of channels as 3, meaning **RGB** mode. We also specified the latent space dimension. In *step 2*, we constructed a generator network. The job of this generator is to map random normal vectors of shape `latent_dim` to images of shape (32, 32, 3).

> Use normal distribution to generate points from latent space rather than a uniform distribution for robust results.

We used a deep convolutional network as the generator network in our example. The `layer_conv_2d_transpose()` function is used to upsample the image data. We used **tanh** as the activation function in the last layer of the generator and **Leaky Relu** as the activation function for the hidden layers.

> It is recommended to use strided convolutions rather than max-pooling while downsampling to avoid the risk of sparse gradients.

In the next step, we defined and compiled the discriminator network. It mapped images of shape (32, 32, 3) that were produced by the generator to a probability that indicates whether the generated image is real or fake. Since our generator network was a **convnet**, the discriminator was also a convolutional network. To induce randomness and make our GAN robust, we added dropout layers and random noise to the labels of the discriminator.

In *step 4*, we froze the weights of the discriminator to make it non-trainable. In step 5, we configured and compiled the GAN network. This GAN network maps the images that have been generated by a generator to the discriminator's assessment of real and fake images. In the last step, we trained the GAN network. When training GANs, we need to train the discriminator so that it identifies the real and fake images accurately. The generator uses feedback from the discriminator to update its weights. We use the gradients of the generator's weights with respect to the loss of the `gan` model to train the generator. Finally, we saved the models and the generated images for a few batches.

There's more...

Despite the stable architecture of DCGANs, convergence is still not guaranteed, and training could be unstable. There are a few architectural features and training procedures that, when applied while training GANs, show a remarkable improvement in their performance. These techniques leverage the heuristic understanding of the non-convergence problem and lead to improved learning performance and sample generation. In fact, in a few cases, the generated data cannot be distinguished from the real data for specific datasets, such as MNIST, CIFAR, and many more.

The following are a few techniques that can be used to achieve the same:

- **Feature matching**: This technique provides a new objective to the generator in order to generate data that matches the statistics of real data rather than directly maximizing the discriminator's output. The discriminator is used to specify the statistics that are worth matching, and the generator is trained to match the expected value of the features on an intermediate layer of the discriminator.
- **Minibatch discrimination**: One of the challenges associated with GANs is the collapse of the generator to one particular parameter setting that makes it always generate similar data always. This happens because the gradients of the discriminator might point to similar directions for many similar points since it processes each batch independently, with no coordination among individual batches. Due to this, the generator doesn't learn to differentiate between batches. Minibatch discrimination allows the discriminator to look at multiple examples in coordination, rather than in isolation, which in turn helps the generator adjust its gradients accordingly.
- **Historical averaging**: In this technique, the average of the past values of each parameter is taken into account while updating the parameters. This kind of learning scales well to long time series. The generator and discriminator's cost values are modified to include the following term:

$$\| \theta - \sum_{i=1}^{t} \theta[i] \|^2$$

where, $\theta[i]$ is the value of the parameters at the past time i.

- **One-sided label smoothing**: This technique replaces the 0 and 1 targets for a classifier with smoothed values, such as .9 or .1, which improves model performance when dealing with adversarial examples.
- **Virtual batch normalization**: Although batch normalization leads to better performance in neural networks, it also causes the output for a training example to be dependent on other training examples from the same batch. Virtual batch normalization avoids this dependency by normalizing the results of each training example with respect to the statistics collected on a reference batch, which is fixed at the start of training. This technique is computationally expensive since forward propagation is run on two mini-batches of data. Hence, this is only used in the generator network.

See also

To find out more about conditional image synthesis with auxiliary classifier GANs, go to `https://arxiv.org/pdf/1610.09585.pdf`.

Implementing variational autoencoders

In `Chapter 4`, *Implementing Autoencoders with Keras*, we learned about autoencoders. We know that an autoencoder learns to represent input data in a latent feature space of reduced dimensions. It learns an arbitrary function to express input data in a compressed latent representation. A **variational autoencoder** (**VAE**), instead of learning an arbitrary function, learns the parameters of the probability distribution of the compressed representation. If we can sample points from this distribution, we can generate new data. A VAE consists of an encoder network and a decoder network.

The structure of a VAE is illustrated in the following diagram:

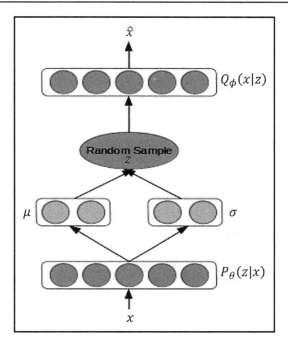

Let's understand the roles of encoder and decoder networks in a VAE:

- **Encoder**: This is a neural network that takes an input, x, and outputs a latent representation, z. The goal of an encoder network is to predict the mean(μ) and standard deviation (σ) of the latent distribution and then sample a random point, z, from this distribution. In essence, an encoder in VAE learns a probability distribution, $P_\theta(z|x)$, where θ is the parameter of the encoder network.
- **Decoder**: The goal of the decoder network is to reconstruct the input data, x, from a randomly sampled point, z (z belongs to a distribution with parameters μ and σ). Its job is to predict a probability distribution, $Q_\phi(x|z)$, where ϕ is the parameter of the decoder network.

In a typical autoencoder, the loss function consists of two parts: reconstruction loss and a regularizer. The loss function of a VAE for one training example is given by the following equation:

$$l(\theta, \phi) = -E_{z \sim P_\theta(z|x)}[\log(Q_\phi(x|z))] + KL(P_\theta(z|x) \mid P(z))$$

The first term of the equation is reconstruction loss; that is, the negative log-likelihood of the data. The second term is the KL divergence between the learned probability distribution, $P_\theta(z|x)$, and the true distribution of the latent variable, $P(z)$. In VAE, we assume that the latent variables come from a standard normal distribution; that is, $P(z)$ follows $N(0, 1)$.

In this recipe, we will implement a variational autoencoder in order to generate images.

Getting ready

In this recipe, we are going to use the fashion MNIST dataset. We used this dataset in `Chapter 2`, *Working with Convolutional Neural Networks*, where we divided it into training and testing datasets. We will use this dataset and flatten each image that's 28x28 in size into an array of 784 values.

Let's start by importing the required libraries:

```
library(keras)
library(abind)
library(grid)
```

Next, we load the dataset and reshape it:

```
mnist <- dataset_fashion_mnist()
x_train <- mnist$train$x/255
x_test <- mnist$test$x/255
x_train <- array_reshape(x_train, c(nrow(x_train), 784), order = "F")
x_test <- array_reshape(x_test, c(nrow(x_test), 784), order = "F")
```

Our data is ready. In the next section, we will build a VAE model.

How to do it...

In this section, we will build a VAE model so that we can reconstruct fashion MNIST images. Let's start by defining the network parameters of our VAE:

1. First, we need to define some variables that will set the network parameters, batch size, input dimension, latent dimension, and the number of epochs:

```
# network parameters
batch_size <- 100L
input_dim <- 784L
```

```
latent_dim <- 2L
epochs <- 10
```

2. Let's define the input layer and the hidden layer of the encoder part of the VAE:

```
# VAE input layer and hidden layer encoder
input <- layer_input(shape = c(input_dim))
x <- input %>% layer_dense(units = 256, activation = "relu")
```

3. Now, we configure the dense layers that represent the mean and log of the standard deviation of the latent distribution:

```
# mean of latent distribution
z_mean <- x %>% layer_dense(units = latent_dim,name = "mean")

# log variance of latent distribution
z_log_sigma <- x %>% layer_dense(units = latent_dim,name = "sigma")
```

4. Next, let's define a sampling function so that we can sample new points from the latent space:

```
# sampling
sampling <- function(arg) {
 z_mean <- arg[, 1:(latent_dim)]
 z_log_var <- arg[, (latent_dim + 1):(2 * latent_dim)]
 epsilon <- k_random_normal(shape = list(k_shape(z_mean)[1],
latent_dim),
 mean = 0, stddev = 1)
 z_mean + k_exp(z_log_sigma) * epsilon
}
```

5. Now, we create a layer that takes the mean and standard deviation of the latent distribution and generates a random sample from it:

```
# random pont from latent distributiom
z <- layer_concatenate(list(z_mean, z_log_sigma)) %>%
layer_lambda(sampling)
```

6. So far, we have defined a layer to extract a random point. Now, we create some hidden layers for the decoder part of the VAE and combine them to create the output layer:

```
# VAE decoder hidden layers
x_1 <- layer_dense(units = 256, activation = "relu")
x_2 <- layer_dense(units = input_dim, activation = "sigmoid")

# decoder output
vae_output <- x_2(x_1(z))
```

7. Next, we build a variational autoencoder and visualize its summary:

```
# variational autoencoder
vae <- keras_model(input, vae_output)
summary(vae)
```

The following screenshot shows the summary of the VAE model:

Layer (type)	Output Shape	Param #	Connected to
input_1 (InputLayer)	(None, 784)	0	
dense (Dense)	(None, 256)	200960	input_1[0][0]
mean (Dense)	(None, 2)	514	dense[0][0]
sigma (Dense)	(None, 2)	514	dense[0][0]
concatenate (Concatenate)	(None, 4)	0	mean[0][0] sigma[0][0]
lambda (Lambda)	(None, 2)	0	concatenate[0][0]
dense_1 (Dense)	(None, 256)	768	lambda[0][0]
dense_2 (Dense)	(None, 784)	201488	dense_1[0][0]

```
Total params: 404,244
Trainable params: 404,244
Non-trainable params: 0
```

8. Now, we create a separate encoder model:

```
# encoder, from inputs to latent space
encoder <- keras_model(input, c(z_mean, z_log_sigma))
summary(encoder)
```

The following screenshot shows the summary of the encoder model:

```
Layer (type)            Output Shape       Param #  Connected to
================================================================================
input_1 (InputLayer)    (None, 784)        0

dense (Dense)           (None, 256)        200960   input_1[0][0]

mean (Dense)            (None, 2)          514      dense[0][0]

sigma (Dense)           (None, 2)          514      dense[0][0]
================================================================================
Total params: 201,988
Trainable params: 201,988
Non-trainable params: 0
```

9. Let's create an independent decoder model as well:

```
# Decoder input
decoder_input <- layer_input(k_int_shape(z)[-1])

# Decoder hidden layers
decoder_output <- x_2(x_1(decoder_input))
# Decoder
decoder <- keras_model(decoder_input,decoder_output)

summary(decoder)
```

The following screenshot shows the summary of the decoder model:

```
Layer (type)              Output Shape          Param #
================================================================================
input_2 (InputLayer)      (None, 2)             0

dense_1 (Dense)           (None, 256)           768

dense_2 (Dense)           (None, 784)           201488
================================================================================
Total params: 202,256
Trainable params: 202,256
Non-trainable params: 0
```

10. Next, we define a custom loss function for the VAE:

```
# loss function
vae_loss <- function(x, decoded_output){
  reconstruction_loss <- (input_dim/1.0)*loss_binary_crossentropy(x,
decoded_output)
  kl_loss <- -0.5*k_mean(1 + z_log_sigma - k_square(z_mean) -
k_exp(z_log_sigma), axis = -1L)
  reconstruction_loss + kl_loss
}
```

11. Then, we compile and train the model:

```
# compile
vae %>% compile(optimizer = "rmsprop", loss = vae_loss)
```

Afterwards, we train the model:

```
# train
vae %>% fit(
  x_train, x_train,
  shuffle = TRUE,
  epochs = epochs,
  batch_size = batch_size,
  validation_data = list(x_test, x_test)
)
```

12. Now, let's have a look at some sample images that have been generated by the model:

```
random_distribution = array(rnorm(n = 20,mean = 0,sd = 4),dim =
c(10,2))
predicted =
array_reshape(predict(decoder,matrix(c(0,0),ncol=2)),dim =
c(28,28))

for(i in seq(1,nrow(random_distribution))){
 one_pred = predict(decoder,matrix(random_distribution[i,],ncol=2))
 predicted = abind(predicted,array_reshape(one_pred,dim =
c(28,28)),along = 2)
}

options(repr.plot.width=10, repr.plot.height=1)
grid.raster(predicted, interpolate=FALSE)
```

The following image shows the images that were generated after the 10th epoch:

In the next section, we'll go through a detailed explanation of the steps we implemented in this section.

How it works...

In *step 1*, we set the values of the network parameters. We set the input dimension equal to 784, which is equal to the dimension of a flattened MNIST fashion image. In *step 2*, we defined an input layer for the VAE and the first hidden layer with 256 neural units and the ReLU activation function. In *step 3*, we created two dense layers, z_mean and z_sigma. These layers have units equal to the dimensions of the latent distribution. In our example, we compressed the input space of 784 dimensions to a two-dimensional latent space. Note that these layers are individually connected to the layers defined previously. These layers represent the mean (μ) and standard deviation (σ) attributes of the latent representation. In *step 4*, we defined a sampling function that produces a random sample from a distribution whose mean and variance is known. It takes a four-dimensional tensor as input, extracts the mean and standard deviation from the tensor, and generates a random point sample from the distribution. The new random sample is generated as per $\mu + \sigma(epsilon)$, where epsilon is a point from a standard normal distribution.

In the next step, we created a layer that concatenates the output tensors of the z_mean and z_sigma layers, and then we stacked a lambda layer. A lambda layer in Keras is a wrapper that wraps arbitrary an expression as a layer. In our example, the lambda layer wraps the sampling function we defined in the previous step. The output of this layer is the input to the decoder section of the VAE. In *step 6*, we built the decoder part of the VAE. We instantiated two layers, x_1 and x_2, with 256 and 784 units, respectively. We combined these layers to create the output layer. In *step 7*, we built the VAE model.

In *steps 8* and *9*, we built an encoder and decoder model, respectively. In *step 10*, we defined the loss function of the VAE model. It is the sum of the reconstruction loss and the Kullback-Leibler divergence between the assumed true probability distribution of the latent variable and the conditional probability distribution of the latent variable over the input, x. In *step 11*, we compiled the VAE model and trained it for ten epochs to minimize the VAE loss using the rmsprop optimizer. In the last step, we generated a sample of new synthetic images.

See also

To find out more about generative models for natural language processing, check out the following links:

- GPT-2: https://openai.com/blog/better-language-models/
- BERT: https://arxiv.org/pdf/1810.04805.pdf

6
Handling Big Data Using Large-Scale Deep Learning

Training a neural network is a computationally intensive process that requires a significant amount of time. As the size of the data increases and the neural network gets deep, training deep learning models become more complex and requires more computing power and memory. To train our models efficiently, we can use a modern system with GPU capabilities. Deep learning libraries in R provide support for training models on multiple GPUs to accelerate the training process. We can also use cloud computing to build deep learning models. Cloud infrastructure scales efficiently and allows users to prototype them faster at a cheaper cost and optimized performance. The pay-per-use model offered by most of the cloud-based solutions makes life much more comfortable as one can quickly scale. This chapter will help you to gain an understanding of how to create a scalable deep learning environment on various cloud platforms. You will also learn how to use MXNet to build different neural networks and accelerate training deep learning models.

In this chapter, we will cover the following recipes:

- Deep learning on Amazon Web Services
- Deep learning on Microsoft Azure
- Deep learning on Google Cloud Platform
- Accelerating with MXNet
- Implementing a deep neural network using MXNet
- Forecasting with MXNet

Deep learning on Amazon Web Services

Amazon Web Services (**AWS**) offers scalable, reliable, and easy to use on-demand cloud computing platforms and APIs on a pay-as-you-go basis. It is a comprehensive platform that provides access to numerous services such as computing, security services, analytics, database, storage, developer tools, and many other **Infrastructures as a Service (IaaS)**, **Platform as a Service (PaaS)**, and **Software as a Service (SaaS)** offerings. With this wide range of services available to individuals, profit and non-profit enterprises, and educational institutions, AWS is considered one of the most successful cloud infrastructure companies, holding the majority of the market share. In this section, we will primarily work with EC2, which is a virtual computing environment. We will also use an **Amazon Machine Image (AMI)** for deep learning using R. AMI has software applications and libraries pre-installed on it.

In AWS, there are three options to rent a virtual machine:

- **On-demand instances:** With this option, users can pay for the compute capacity by the hour or the second depending on the instances they run. There is the flexibility of increasing or decreasing the capacity depending on the demand for the application, and it is suitable for cases that do not require any long term commitment.
- **Spot instances:** With this option, you can bid for the spare unused Amazon EC2 instances. The bid price fluctuates in real time based on demand and supply. Once your bid exceeds the current spot price and the capacity is available, your spot instances run. This option is recommended for applications that have flexible start and end times since, with this option, AWS can terminate your instance at any time.
- **Reserved instances:** This option is almost around 50% cheaper than the on-demand pricing and provides capacity reservation when you commit to renting the machine for a certain amount of time.

You can use any of the preceding options to set up your deep learning instance on AWS based on your needs and convenience.

In this recipe, we will go through the steps of setting up a deep learning environment in AWS for training our models.

Getting ready

Before using the AWS services, first, you need to create an AWS account if you do not have one already. For doing so, you can use this link: `https://portal.aws.amazon.com/billing/signup`. For more details on the pricing model, please refer to this link: `https://aws.amazon.com/pricing/?nc2=h_ql_pr_ln`. We will use a pre-built AWS AMI from RStudio with TensorFlow and the `keras` library installed.

How to do it...

Once you have created an AWS account, follow these steps to launch an EC2 instance with an RStudio AMI:

1. Sign in to the AWS console using your credentials. You will see the following screen:

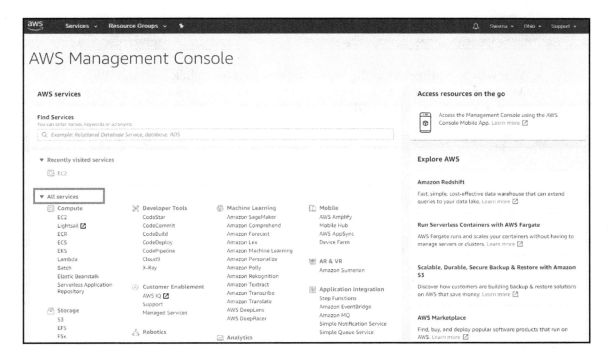

2. From the **All Services** tab, click on **EC2**. This will lead you to the following EC2 console page. Click on **Launch Instance** to launch an EC2 instance:

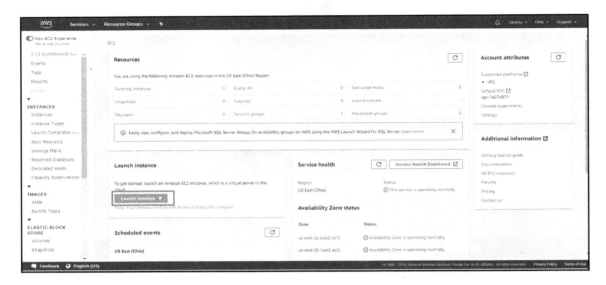

3. You will be redirected to the following screen. Next, click on the **AWS Marketplace** option, as shown in the following screenshot, and type **RStudio Server with Tensorflow-GPU for AWS** in the search box:

4. On selecting the **RStudio Server with Tensorflow-GPU for AWS** AMI, you will be prompted with the following pop-up window. Click **Continue** to proceed further:

RStudio Server with Tensorflow-GPU for AWS

RStudio Server with Tensorflow-GPU for AWS

RStudio Server with Tensorflow-GPU for AWS is an on-demand, open source AGPL-licensed integrated development environment (IDE) for R. It is designed to provide a stable, secure, and high performance execution environment for deep learning applications running on Amazon EC2. The tensorflow, tfestimators, and keras R packages (along with their pre-requisites, including the GPU version of TensorFlow) are installed as part of the image. The software is provided by RStudio at no charge. AWS charges apply.

Show less

View Additional Details in AWS Marketplace

Product Details

By	Rstudio, Inc.
Customer Rating	★★★★★ (1)
Latest Version	1.2.1335-1.aws.1*
Base Operating System	Linux/Unix, Ubuntu V16.04
Delivery Method	64-bit (x86) Amazon Machine Image (AMI)
License Agreement	End User License Agreement
On Marketplace Since	12/19/17
AWS Services Required	Amazon EBS, Amazon EC2

Pricing Details

Hourly Fees

Instance Type	Software	EC2	Total
g3s.xlarge	$0.00	$0.75	$0.75/hr
g3.4xlarge	$0.00	$1.14	$1.14/hr
g3.8xlarge	$0.00	$2.28	$2.28/hr
g3.16xlarge	$0.00	$4.56	$4.56/hr
p2.xlarge	$0.00	$0.90	$0.90/hr
p2.8xlarge	$0.00	$7.20	$7.20/hr
p2.16xlarge	$0.00	$14.40	$14.40/hr
p3.2xlarge	$0.00	$3.06	$3.06/hr
p3.8xlarge	$0.00	$12.24	$12.24/hr
p3.16xlarge	$0.00	$24.48	$24.48/hr

EBS Magnetic volumes
$0.05 per GB-month of provisioned storage
$0.05 per 1 million I/O requests

You will not be charged until you launch this instance.

Cancel   Continue

5. In the next step, you will be asked to choose an instance type. For training complex deep learning models, it is recommended to use an instance with a GPU. To do so, choose **GPU Instances** from the **Filter by** drop-down list and then select `p2.xlarge` from the list. Click on the **Next: Configure Instance Details** button to continue:

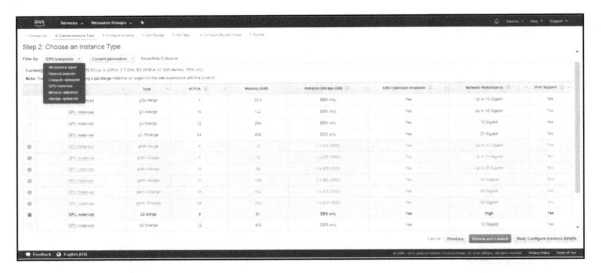

6. In this step, you can configure the instance according to our requirements. In this case, we just go with the default options. Click on **Next: Add Storage** button to move to the next step:

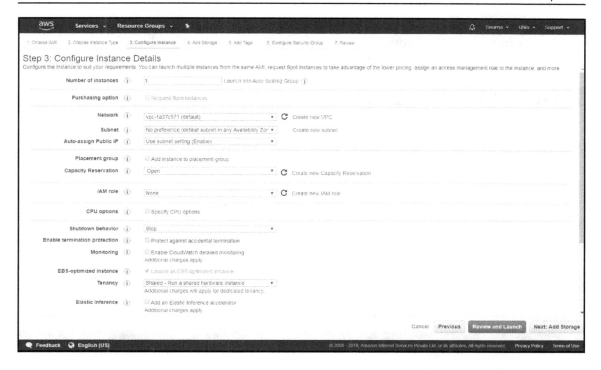

7. In the next step, you are allowed to change the storage options based on the size of your data. To continue to the next step, click on the **Next: Add Tags** button:

8. In AWS, it is possible to assign metadata to the resources in the form of tags. You can add tags that consist of key-value pairs. Once done, click on the **Next: Configure Security Group** button to proceed further:

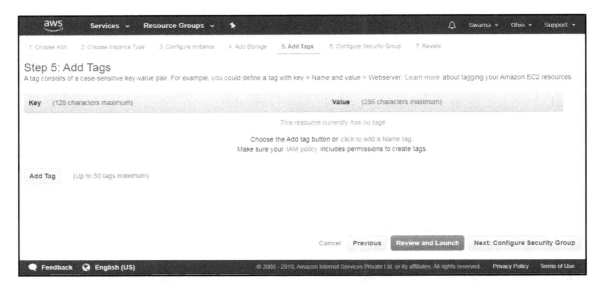

9. In the following screen, you can configure the security options for your instance by adding rules. To proceed to the next step, click on the **Review and Launch** button:

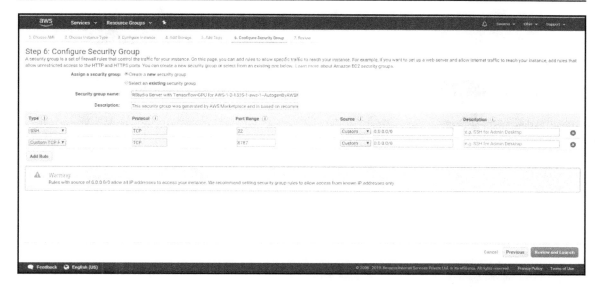

10. This will lead you to the following screen. In the **Boot From General Purpose (SSD)** popup, choose an option according to your requirements and click on **Next**:

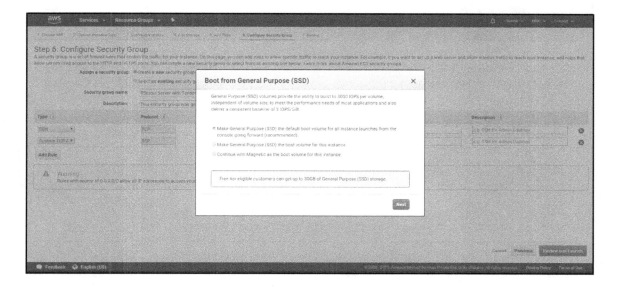

This will lead you to the following screen. There will be certain warning messages that you need to address. Review your instance configuration and click on **Launch**:

If you have not created a key pair already, you are given an option to create one; otherwise, go with an existing one. Download the key pair and click on **Launch Instances**:

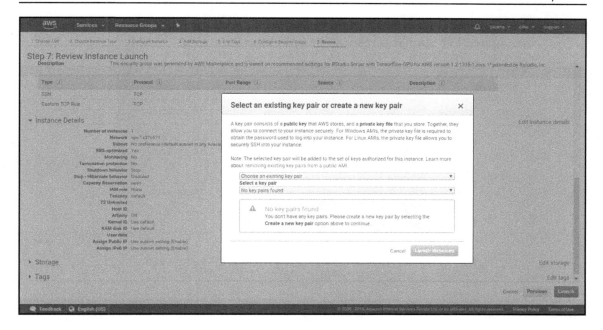

11. Now you can return to your EC2 dashboard where you can see that you have one running instance, as shown in the following screenshot:

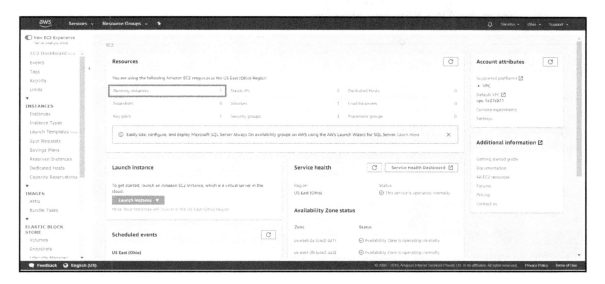

You can click on that for further details about your instance. You will be navigated to a similar screen, as shown in the following:

12. You will be provided with an IP address and a port number to launch the AWS RStudio interface on a web page. For connecting to the interface, use **rstudio-user** as the username and your instance ID as the password. The following screenshot shows the AWS RStudio interface:

In the preceding screenshot, you can see that we have successfully executed the R script to classify handwritten digits.

How it works...

In *steps 1* and *2*, we demonstrated how to launch an EC2 instance, which is a virtual server in AWS. In *steps 3* and *4*, we selected an RStudio server AMI with TensorFlow and Keras support. All of the software configuration details of your instance such as the application server, operating system, and other applications are stored in the AMI template.

In *step 5* we selected a GPU-based instance type. AWS offers a choice of a mix of resources for your application. In *step 6*, we configured our instance as per our requirements. While configuring the instance, it is also possible to launch multiple instances from the same AMI.

Next, we selected the storage options based on the size of the data we were using. You can configure the storage device settings and increase the **Elastic Block Store** (**EBS**) volume if required. An EBS is a flexible block-level storage device that can be attached to an EC2 instance and can be used as primary storage for frequently updated data.

AWS provides four types of EBS volumes based on performance and price:

- General Purpose SSD
- Provisioned IOPS SSD
- Throughput Optimized HDD
- Cold HDD
- Magnetic

We did not define any tags while setting up our instance. Tags are a way to assign metadata to resources such as the purpose of the resource, owner details, and version details.

In the next step, we configured the security group using the default options. A security group is a set of firewall rules to control the traffic to your instance. In *step 10*, we reviewed the instance configuration and launched it. We also created a key pair that consists of a public key stored by AWS and a private key stored by us. This key pair allows us to access our instance securely. This way we created and configured our EC2 instance with RStudio AMI.

Once we finished creating and configuring our instance, in *step 11*, we went back to our EC2 dashboard and clicked on the **Running Instances** option to see the details of our instance. In our case, we were provided with an IP address, which was 18.188.193.201, and the port used was 8787. The instance ID is used as the password for connecting to the RStudio instance. In the last step, we launched the RStudio interface by AWS on another web page using the credentials provided. We executed a classification model for MNIST handwritten digits.

Deep learning on Microsoft Azure

Similar to AWS, Microsoft is another leading cloud services provider for building and managing applications through Microsoft-managed data centers. The name of the cloud service is Microsoft Azure, which offers SaaS, PaaS, and IaaS and supports various tools and frameworks. For running deep learning models in Azure, we can use its deep learning virtual machines that have the necessary deep learning libraries installed. Microsoft Azure is a fast, flexible, scalable, and cheaper platform with 24/7 support. It offers automatic patch management for the virtual machines so that users can focus on building and deploying their applications rather than managing the infrastructure. In this recipe, we will go through the steps of setting up a deep learning environment on Microsoft Azure for training our models.

Getting ready

Before training your models, you need to create an account in Azure and log in to the portal using this link: https://portal.azure.com/. To read about the pricing details of Azure, please refer to this link: https://azure.microsoft.com/en-in/pricing/.

How to do it...

Once you have created your account in Azure, log in to the Azure portal. Follow these steps to create a deep learning virtual environment in it:

1. Click on the **Create a resource** button:

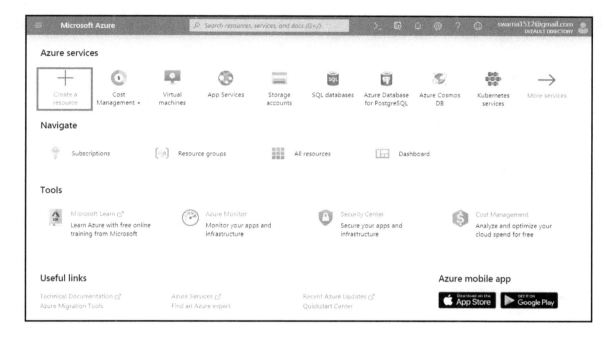

You should see the following screen. Type **Deep learning virtual machine** in the search bar:

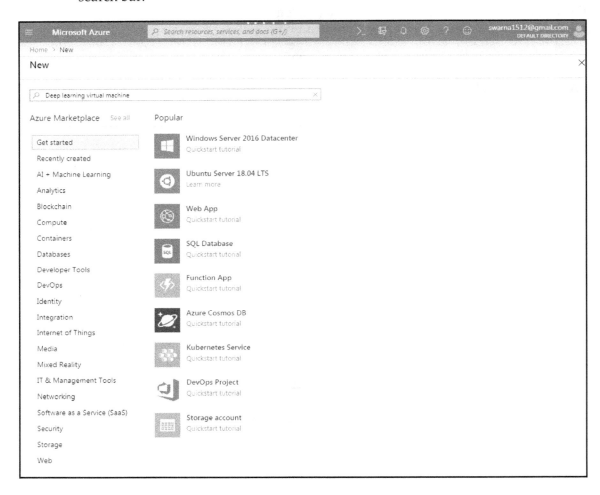

2. You should see the following screen after selecting **Deep Learning Virtual Machine**. Now, click on the **Create** button:

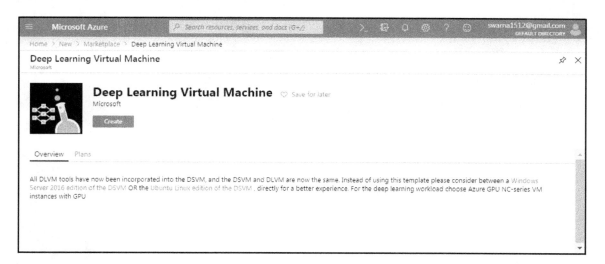

3. Once you click on the **Create** button, you will be navigated to a 4-step configuration window, as shown in the following screenshot. In the **Basics** tab, you can provide the name of your instance and the type of operating system along with the username and password and the subscription you want to be billed. Create a new **Resource group** if you do not have one. In the **Settings** tab, make sure that you choose an appropriate VM size compatible with the GPU. In this example, we choose to go with a VM of a size of **1 x Standard ND6s**. The **Summary** tab summarizes your requirements. Click **OK** to proceed further.

The following screenshot shows the **Basics** tab:

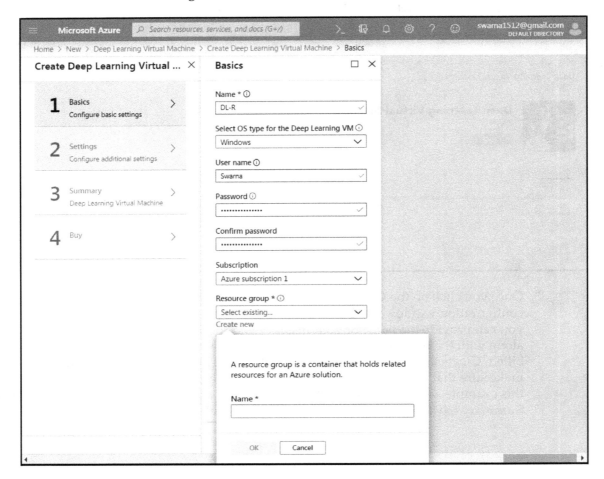

The following screenshot shows the **Settings** tab:

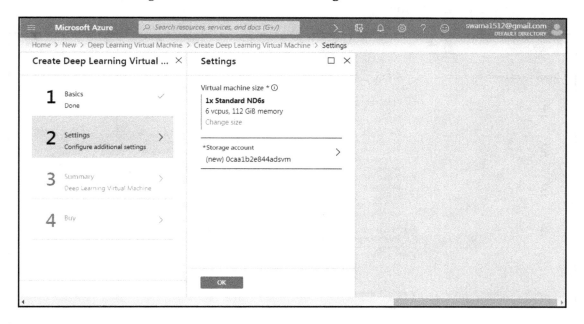

The following screenshot shows the **Summary** tab:

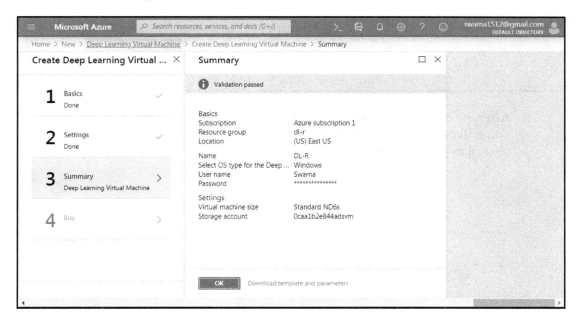

The following screenshot shows the **Buy** tab. Click on the checkbox and then click on the **Create** button:

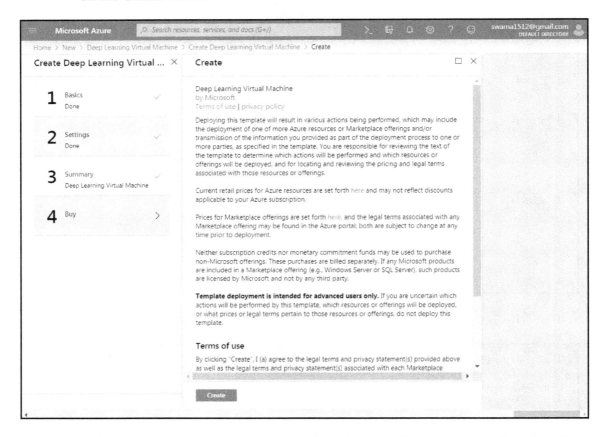

4. After the creation of the resources, select click on **All resources** on the left and you will be directed to the following console window, which shows all of the resources provisioned:

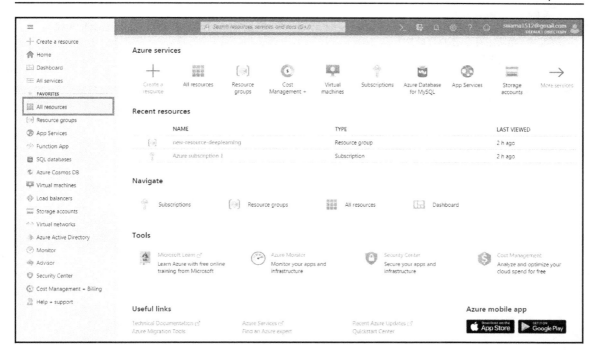

5. Click on that particular resource where the **Type** is **Virtual Machine** and the name matches the resource you created in *step 3*. You will see the following screen. Click on the **Connect** button on the screen:

6. A window appears on the right side of the screen that gives you a button to **Download RDP File**. Click on that button and when the file is downloaded, double-click on it:

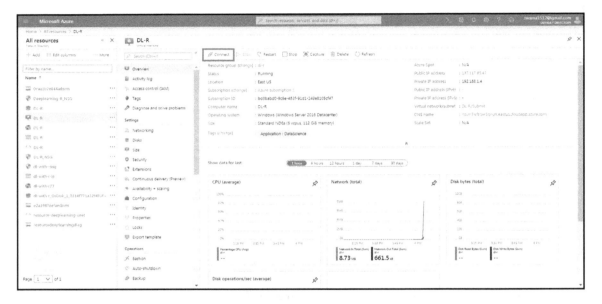

Here is how you can download the RDP file:

7. Now, you will be redirected to a login window to connect to the cloud instance. You need to enter the username and password to connect to the instance. After connecting, you should see a screen similar to the following:

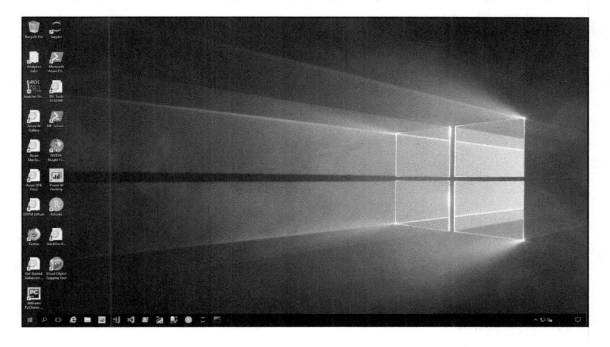

8. Now, you can launch RStudio and since the `keras` library will already be installed, you can run any deep learning code in R:

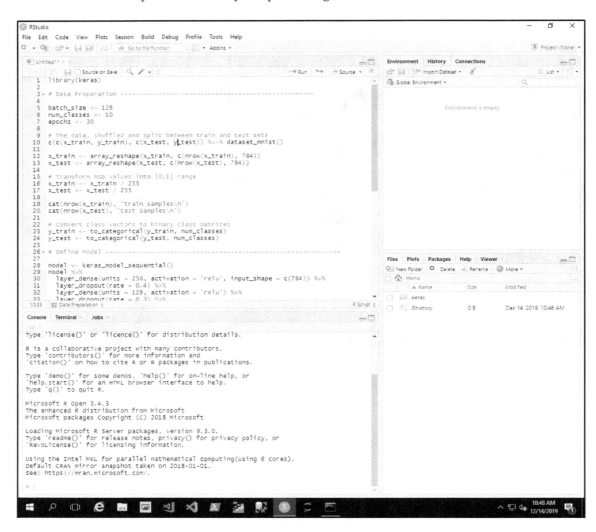

In this way, you can leverage Microsoft Azure's architecture to write deep learning code in R.

How it works...

In *steps 1* and *2*, we created a deep learning virtual machine in Azure. A deep learning virtual machine in Azure is a pre-configured environment to use GPU-based VM instances to train deep learning models. It is supported on either Windows 2016 or Ubuntu operating systems and has many data science tools pre-installed to enable building applications for advanced analytics.

In *step 3*, we configured the VM according to our requirements. In the **Basics** tab, you need to provide the following details:

- **Name**: This is the name of the VM instance.
- **OS type**: This is the type of OS support you need, either Windows or Ubuntu.
- **Username**: This is the username that you will use to log in to the VM.
- **Password**: This is the password you will use to log in to the VM.
- **Subscription**: This is the subscription that you want the VM instance to be billed from and that has proper resource creation privileges.
- **Resource group**: This is a logical container for all of the resources for an Azure solution. You need to create a new group or use an already existing one.
- **Location**: This is the data center location. For faster access, you can choose the center closest to your physical location or the one that has most of your data.

In the **Settings** tab, you choose the size of your VM. ND6s is one of the cheapest ND series GPU-enabled VMs in Azure, designed for AI and deep learning work. ND instances offer good performance and are powered by NVIDIA Tesla P40 GPUs and Intel Xeon E5-2690 v4 (Broadwell) CPUs. The **Summary** tab summarizes your requirements for the validation check.

In *step 4*, we saw a list of all of the resources provisioned in the VM. In *steps 5, 6*, and *7*, we connected to the configured VM via **Remote Desktop Protocol** (**RDP**). Finally, once we connected to the remote desktop machine, we launched an RStudio session and ran a classification model for the identification of handwritten MNIST digits.

There's more...

We all are aware of the fact that R is a single-threaded in-memory application, but there are multiple tools and architectures that allow implementing parallel processing while using R. Microsoft Azure has come up with a package in R, known as **doAzureParallel**, that allows the distributing of parallel computations to a cluster in Azure. This package enables users to leverage Azure Batch service, making it possible to run parallel simulations directly from an R session. This package is a parallel backend for the `foreach` package of R and supports multiple processes across numerous Azure VMs, hence eliminating the need for manually creating and configuring multiple VMs. It is also possible to scale the size of the clusters according to the workload. To read about the installation instructions and prerequisites for `doParallelAzure`, please refer to this link: `https://github.com/Azure/doAzureParallel`.

See also

Azure Batch service supports parallel and high-performance computing batch jobs by managing a pool of compute nodes in Azure. To read more about Azure Batch, please refer to this link: `https://docs.microsoft.com/en-us/azure/batch/batch-technical-overview`.

Deep learning on Google Cloud Platform

In the past few years, cloud computing services have enabled individuals as well as enterprises to develop and deploy solutions on different cloud providers. **Google Cloud Platform** (**GCP**) is a relatively newer suite of cloud computing services offered by Google that supports multiple services such as computing, storage, big data, analytics, and application development. It also supports GPU instances and beats the prices offered by other cloud service providers. Google's robust, scalable, and innovative infrastructure and its streamlined solutions across various capacities allow users to easily build applications on this platform in a secure way. In this recipe, we will learn how to train a deep learning model on GCP.

Getting ready

The first thing you need to do before using CloudML is to create a Google Cloud account. You can create your account from this link: `https://console.cloud.google.com` if you do not have one. To know more about pricing details, please refer to this link: `https://cloud.google.com/pricing/`.

How to do it...

After creating your account on Google, follow these steps to train a deep learning model in GCP:

1. Log in to the Google Cloud portal and select **APIs & Services** from the menu, as shown in the following screenshot:

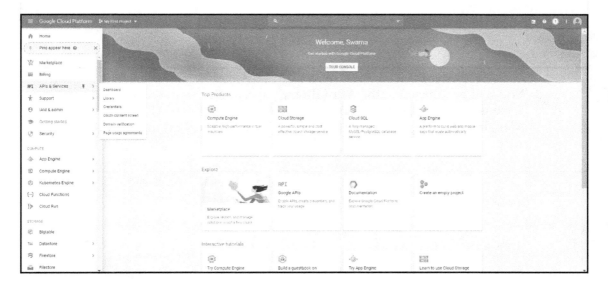

2. Once you click on the **APIs & Services** link, you should be able to see the following screen. Click on the **ENABLE APIs AND SERVICES** option:

3. You will be directed to the **API Library** page, as shown in the following screenshot. These APIs are organized in groups; click on **VIEW ALL** for the **Machine learning** group and then select **AI Platform Training and Prediction API**:

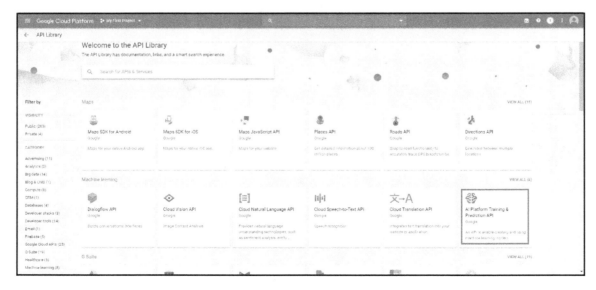

4. Next, you will be able to see the following page. Click on the **ENABLE** button:

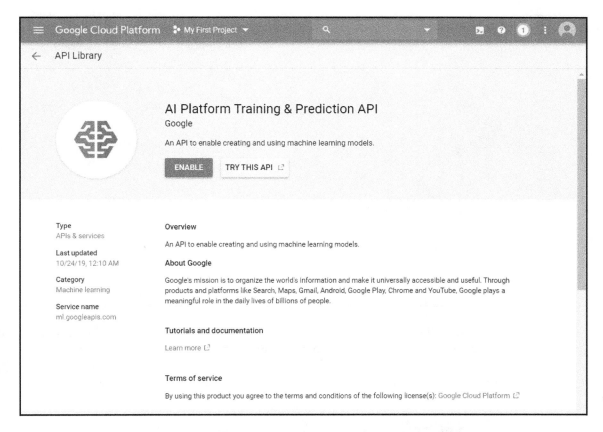

5. Once this API is enabled, go to RStudio and execute the following code to install the `cloudml` library and the Google Cloud SDK:

```
install.packages("cloudml")
library(cloudml)
gcloud_install()
```

The following screenshot shows the **Google Cloud SDK Setup** window:

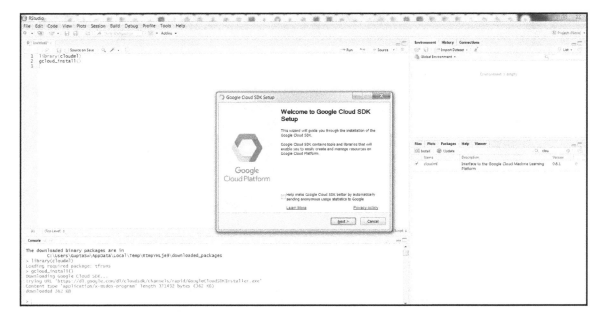

6. After the installation of the Google Cloud SDK, you will be asked to log in with your credentials. You will then be prompted with a series of options in the Terminal window, as shown in the following screenshot. Select an already existing project and your Google account will be linked to the Google SDK:

7. Now, you can submit jobs to execute deep learning codes using the machine learning APIs of Google. In this example, we will train a multi-layer deep neural network for classifying digits using the MNIST handwritten digits dataset:

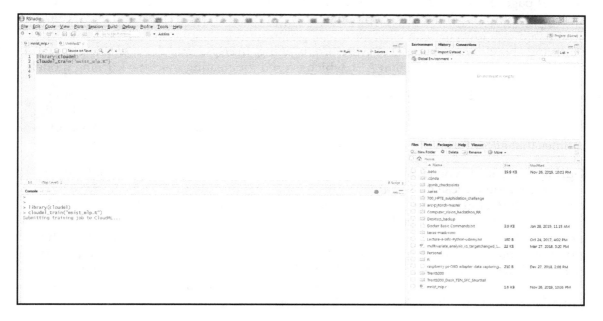

8. Once you submit your job, you can monitor it using the **Jobs** option under the **AI Platform** menu:

The preceding screenshot shows the status of a deep learning job on GCP.

How it works...

In *steps 1* and *2*, we logged in to the Google Cloud portal and navigated to the APIs and services page. These APIs provide user-friendly interfaces for accessing any service from storage to computation and the deployment of applications. Using these APIs, you can automate workflows using a wide variety of programming languages and tools without worrying about hardware and software provisioning. In *steps 3* and *4*, we enabled the AI Platform Training and Prediction API, which is used for creating machine learning models.

This API enables data enthusiasts to build, deploy, and monitor their machine learning applications seamlessly in a portable and cost-effective manner. In *step 5*, we installed the cloudML package in R using RStudio and the Google Cloud SDK. This SDK consists of utilities that allow us to interact with our Google Cloud account from within R.

During installation, you need to specify the default account, project, and compute region for Google Cloud; these details are then used for all of your CloudML jobs. In *step 6*, we provided the Google account details that needed to be linked with the Google Cloud SDK. In *step 7*, we submitted a deep learning job to perform training on the cloud. A good practice is to first run the scripts locally with smaller data and then submit the job in the cloud once outputs come as expected. In this example, we ran a classification model using the MNIST handwritten digits dataset. To do this, we created an R script with the name mnist_mlp.R and then saved it in the current working directory. The R script is provided in the GitHub repository of this chapter.

Then, in a new R script, we executed the following code to submit the job to GCP:

```
library(cloudml)
cloudml_train("mnist_mlp.R")
```

In the last step, we went to the Google Cloud portal to monitor the job submitted in *step 7*.

There's more...

Google's **Cloud Machine Learning** (**CloudML**) Engine also provides an automated tool for model hyperparameter tuning. It allows us to test different hyperparameter configurations when training a model. To submit a hyperparameter tuning job, we need to pass a CloudML training configuration file to the cloudml_train() function. We discussed hyperparameter tuning using Keras in the *There's more...* section of the *Training your first deep neural network* recipe in Chapter 1, *Understanding Neural Networks and Deep Neural Networks*, where we showcased how to tune model parameters. We first defined flags for parameters that we want to optimize and then used these flags in the definition of our model.

In the same way, we define the flags and model to execute a hyperparameter tuning job using CloudML. In the following code block, we show how to write a configuration file for the model defined in the *There's more...* section of the *Training your first deep neural network* recipe in `Chapter 1`, *Understanding Neural Networks and Deep Neural Networks*:

```
trainingInput:
  scaleTier: CUSTOM
  masterType: standard_gpu
  hyperparameters:
    goal: MAXIMIZE
    hyperparameterMetricTag: acc
    maxTrials: 10
    maxParallelTrials: 2
    params:
      - parameterName: dense_units1
        type: INTEGER
        minValue: 8
        maxValue: 16
        scaleType: UNIT_LINEAR_SCALE
      - parameterName: dropout1
        type: DOUBLE
        minValue: 0.2
        maxValue: 0.4
        scaleType: UNIT_LINEAR_SCALE
      - parameterName: dense_units2
        type: INTEGER
        minValue: 8
        maxValue: 16
        scaleType: UNIT_LINEAR_SCALE
      - parameterName: dropout2
        type: DOUBLE
        minValue: 0.2
        maxValue: 0.4
        scaleType: UNIT_LINEAR_SCALE
```

In the preceding configuration file, the goal represents the objective function and `hyperparameterMetricTag` represents the metric to be optimized. The `maxTrials` argument specifies the number of trials that need to be attempted to optimize the parameter.

In our example, the goal was to maximize accuracy. The `params` argument represents the set of parameters to be tuned. The parameters can be of the integer, double, or categorical type and can be specified using the argument `type`. `minValue` and `maxValue` represent the range of values for optimizing the parameter defined if the parameters are of the integer or double type. For categorical parameters, these fields should be left unset. `scaleType` defines the method to scale the parameter. For more details about the configuration file, please refer to this link: `https://cloud.google.com/ml-engine/reference/rest/v1/projects.jobs#HyperparameterSpec`.

Before submitting the tuning job, we need to save the contents of the preceding code block in a `cloudml_tuning.yml` file and then pass the name of the config file to the `cloudml_train()` function:

```
cloudml_train("hyperparameter_tuning_model.R", config =
"cloudml_tuning.yml")
```

The preceding code demonstrates how to pass the `.yml` file while training the model.

Accelerating with MXNet

MXNet stands for mix and maximize. It is a flexible and scalable deep learning framework that is used to develop and deploy deep learning models. It is capable of running on various heterogeneous systems in a memory-efficient way. MXNet is also supported by various cloud providers such as Amazon Web Services and Microsoft Azure. Developers have the flexibility to go for both imperative and symbolic programming, making it easier for debugging and hyperparameter tuning while maximizing efficiency. Another advantage that MXNet offers is that it supports multiple languages such as Python, R, Scala, Clojure, Julia, Perl, MATLAB, and JavaScript. In this recipe, we will demonstrate how to set up MXNet in Windows and Linux systems.

Getting ready

MXNet accelerates performance by distributing training across multiple CPUs/GPUs. For utilizing GPU capabilities, your system needs an NVIDIA GPU, and you need to install the CUDA Toolkit and cuDNN. Instructions to install the CUDA Toolkit and cuDNN can be found at `https://developer.nvidia.com/cuda-downloads` and `https://docs.nvidia.com/deeplearning/sdk/cudnn-install/index.html` respectively.

How to do it...

Let's now install MXNet on your system. Depending on the operating system, you can choose a suitable method:

1. To install the CPU version on a Windows operating system, use the following:

```
cran <- getOption("repos")
cran["dmlc"] <-
"https://apache-mxnet.s3-accelerate.dualstack.amazonaws.com/R/CRAN/
"
options(repos = cran)
install.packages("mxnet")
```

Please note that MXNet requires R 3.5. At the time of writing this book, support for 3.6 was not available.

2. To install the GPU version on the Windows operating system, use the following:

```
cran <- getOption("repos")
cran["dmlc"] <-
"https://apache-mxnet.s3-accelerate.dualstack.amazonaws.com/R/CRAN/
GPU/cu100"
options(repos = cran)
install.packages("mxnet")
```

Change the second line of the preceding code block to `cu92` or `cu101` for a different version of CUDA.

3. To install the GPU/CPU version in Linux, do the following:

You need Ubuntu 16.4 for installing MXNet. The later versions are not yet supported. Before installing, you need to install Git, OpenBLAS, and OpenCV. To install these dependencies, execute the following commands in the Terminal:

```
apt-get install -y build-essential git
apt-get install -y libopenblas-dev liblapack-dev
apt-get install -y libopencv-dev
```

To install MXNet on the Linux platform, we need an R version greater than 3.4.4 and we need GCC 4.8 or later to compile C++ 11. 2. GNU Make.

After installing the dependencies, clone the repository from GitHub:

```
git clone --recursive https://github.com/apache/incubator-mxnet
cd incubator-mxnet
```

Then, update the config file to set compilation options:

```
echo "USE_OPENCV = 1" >> ./config.mk
echo "USE_BLAS = openblas" >> ./config.mk
```

Execute the following commands to compile and build MXNet:

```
make -j $(nproc)
make rpkg
```

To install the GPU version, you need to set the following options before building MXnet:

```
echo "USE_CUDA=1" >>config.mk
echo "USE_CUDA_PATH=/usr/local/cuda" >>config.mk
echo "USE_CUDNN=1" >>config.mk
```

In this section, we saw how to install MXNet on various operating systems

How it works...

With the Windows installation, we installed MXNet using pre-built binary packages. We use the `getOption()` function to get a variety of global options in R. The `repos` parameter is used to extract the URL of the repositories from where R fetches libraries. To install MXNet, we added a new URL to fetch the pre-built `mxnet` R package. We used the `options()` function to add the new URL. Note that the only difference between installing a CPU and a GPU version is the URL that we added. We can also build the `mxnet` library from the source. Instructions to build are available on the following web page: `https://mxnet.apache.org/get_started/windows_setup.html#install-mxnet-package-for-r`.

With the Linux installation, we installed all of the dependencies to install MXNet and then cloned the MXNet source code. We then set compilation options and built the library.

There's more...

Until now, we saw how to set up MXNet in a local system. MXNet is also supported by various cloud platforms such as AWS, Microsoft Azure, and GCP.

For working with MXNet using AWS, we can use Amazon SageMaker, which provides a fully-fledged platform to build, train, and deploy deep learning models in a scalable manner. You can also leverage the AWS deep learning AMIs like the NVIDIA deep learning AMIs, which are pre-configured environments to prototype deep learning applications quickly. In AWS, it is also possible to build our own customized deep learning environments for using MXNet.

GCP provides the NVIDIA GPU Cloud Image that offers an optimized environment to run GPU optimized containers for running deep learning applications using MXNet.

Microsoft Azure offers the NVIDIA NGC image for Deep Learning and HPC, which is an optimized environment for running the GPU-accelerated containers from the NGC container registry, which includes frameworks such as MXNet, CNTK, and Theano.

Implementing a deep neural network using MXNet

In the previous recipe, *Accelerating with MXNet*, we introduced MXNet and demonstrated how to install the package. In this recipe, we will implement a neural network to predict the median price of homes in different locations in the Boston suburb. We will use the Boston Housing Prices dataset. This dataset contains information regarding attributes of houses at different locations such as the average number of rooms, crime rate, and property tax rate.

You can read about the attributes of the data at `https://www.cs.toronto.edu/~delve/data/boston/bostonDetail.html`.

Getting ready

The Boston Housing Prices dataset can be accessed directly from the keras library. It has 404 training examples and 102 test examples.

Let's load the required libraries:

```
library(mxnet)
library(keras)
```

We load the dataset and split it into training and testing sets:

```
boston = dataset_boston_housing()
train_x = boston$train$x
train_y = boston$train$y
test_x = boston$test$x
test_y = boston$test$y
```

Let's now scale the dataset:

```
# normalize train set
train_x <- scale(train_x)

# normalize test set
train_means <- attr(train_x, "scaled:center")
train_stddevs <- attr(train_x, "scaled:scale")
test_x <- scale(test_x, center = train_means, scale = train_stddevs)
```

This completes the data preprocessing part.

How to do it...

We are now familiar with the dataset. Let's now move on to building and training the neural network:

1. Let's create a neural network. The first line of the following code block creates a symbol variable and the next lines add hidden layers:

```
in_layer <- mx.symbol.Variable("data")
layer1 =
mx.symbol.FullyConnected(in_layer,name="dense1",num_hidden=64)
activation1 <- mx.symbol.Activation(layer1, name="relu1",
act_type="relu")
layer2 =
mx.symbol.FullyConnected(activation1,name="dense2",num_hidden=64)
activation2 <- mx.symbol.Activation(layer2, name="relu2",
act_type="relu")
layer3 =
mx.symbol.FullyConnected(activation2,name="dense3",num_hidden=1)
out = mx.symbol.LinearRegressionOutput(layer3)
```

2. We set the device to use, for training the model:

```
devices <- mx.cpu()
```

3. We proceed to set the seed and define the number of epochs. Then, we train the model:

```
mx.set.seed(0)
epochs = 100
model = mx.model.FeedForward.create(symbol =out,X =train_x,y =
train_y,ctx = devices,num.round = epochs,optimizer =
"rmsprop",array.batch.size = 50,learning.rate=0.001,eval.metric =
mx.metric.rmse)
```

4. Let's visualize the model:

```
graph.viz(model$symbol)
```

The following screenshot shows the visualization of the model:

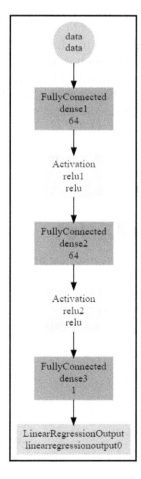

5. We evaluate model's performance on the test dataset:

```
predicted <- predict(model,test_x)
paste("Test error:",sqrt(mean((predicted-as.numeric(test_y))^2)))
```

The following screenshot shows the test error:

'Test error: 3.54900451270231'

From the preceding screenshot, we can see that we got a test error of around 3.54.

How it works...

In *step 1*, we created a variable of type symbol. We used this variable to configure the network. The `mx.symbol.Variable("data")` function uses data to represent the input data, that is, the input layer. We added the hidden layers using the `mx.symbol.FullyConnected` function; its parameters are data with the type as `symbol`, the name of the layer, and the number of neurons in the layer. We applied activation layers using the `mx.symbol.Activation()` function. At the end of the network, we added a regression output layer. In *step 2*, we selected the device to train the network. We can also use the `mx.gpu()` function for training on GPUs.

In the next step, we trained the model. In *step 4*, we visualized our network. In the last step, we evaluated the model's performance.

Forecasting with MXNet

Time-series forecasting is one of the most popular applications in deep learning. MXNet enables machine learning enthusiasts to utilize its deep learning framework for various applications including time series forecasting. In this recipe, we will implement a one-to-one forecasting solution using an LSTM network to predict shampoo sales. At the time of writing this book, MXNet supported only two variants of the sequence prediction problem, one-to-one and many-to-one.

Getting ready

In this recipe, we will use the shampoo sales dataset that contains the monthly sales of shampoo over a 3-year period. The original dataset is credited to Makridakis, Wheelwright, and Hyndman (1998). It is also available in the GitHub repository of this chapter in the folder named `data`. Download the `shampoo_sales.txt` file and copy it to a folder named `data` in your working directory.

Let's load the required library and read the dataset:

```
library("mxnet")
sales_data <- read.table("data/shampoo_sales.txt",sep = ",",header = TRUE)

# We require only one column from the dataset
sales_data <- as.data.frame(sales_data[,2])
```

Next, we normalize the data within a range of 0 to 1 using min-max normalization:

```
min_max_scaler <- function(x) {
  (x - min(x))/(max(x) - min(x))
}

norm_sales_data <- min_max_scaler(sales_data)
t_sales_data <- t(norm_sales_data)
```

To train a one-to-one sequence prediction model using MXNet-R, we need to transform the training data into a suitable form. The training feature set should be of the form (n_dim x seq_len * num_samples) and the training labels should be of the form (seq_len x num_samples). Since we have one-dimensional data, n_dim is equal to 1.

The following code block converts data into the required structure:

```
n_dim <- 1
seq_len <- 4
num_samples <- 7

# extract only required data from dataset
x_data <- t_sales_data[1, 1:(seq_len * num_samples)]
dim(x_data) <- c(n_dim, seq_len, num_samples)

y_data <- t_sales_data[1, 2:(1+(seq_len * num_samples))]
dim(y_data) <- c(seq_len, num_samples)
```

In the next section, we will build the forecasting model using RNN with MXNet.

How to do it...

Let's move on to create a neural network using symbolic programming:

1. We start with sampling data into training and validation datasets and creating respective iterators:

```
batch_size <- 3
train_ids <- 1:4
val_ids <- 5:6

## create data iterators
train_data <- mx.io.arrayiter(data = x_data[,,train_ids, drop =
F],label = y_data[, train_ids], batch.size = batch_size,shuffle =
TRUE)
val_data <- mx.io.arrayiter(data = x_data[,,val_ids, drop = F],
label = y_data[, val_ids], batch.size = batch_size, shuffle =
FALSE)
```

2. Now, let's create an RNN symbol with a one-to-one model configuration:

```
symbol <- rnn.graph(num_rnn_layer = 2,
 num_hidden = 30,
 input_size = NULL,
 num_embed = NULL,
 num_decode = 1,
 masking = F,
 loss_output = "linear",
 ignore_label = -1,
 cell_type = "lstm",
 output_last_state = T,
 config = "one-to-one")
```

3. Next, we define our loss function:

```
seq_metric_mse <- mx.metric.custom("MSE", function(label, pred) {
 label = mx.nd.reshape(label, shape = -1)
 pred = mx.nd.reshape(pred, shape = -1)
 res <- mx.nd.mean(mx.nd.square(label - pred))
 return(as.array(res))
})
```

4. We set the device to use for training the model. Then, we define weight initialization and configure the optimizer:

```
ctx <- mx.cpu()
initializer <- mx.init.Xavier(rnd_type = "gaussian",
 factor_type = "avg",
```

```
  magnitude = 1)
optimizer <- mx.opt.create("adadelta",
 rho = 0.9,
 eps = 1e-06,
 wd = 1e-06,
 clip_gradient = 1,
 rescale.grad = 1/batch_size)
```

5. Let's now train the network for 50 epochs with bucket support:

```
model <- mx.model.buckets(symbol = symbol,
 train.data = train_data,
 eval.data = val_data,
 num.round = 50,
 ctx = ctx,
 verbose = TRUE,
 metric = seq_metric_mse,
 initializer = initializer,
 optimizer = optimizer)
```

6. After training the network, we extract the state symbols from the trained model:

```
internals <- model$symbol$get.internals()
sym_state <- internals$get.output(which(internals$outputs %in%
"RNN_state"))
sym_state_cell <- internals$get.output(which(internals$outputs %in%
"RNN_state_cell"))
sym_output <- internals$get.output(which(internals$outputs %in%
"loss_output"))
symbol <- mx.symbol.Group(sym_output, sym_state, sym_state_cell)
```

7. We use the symbol created in *step 6* to create an inference of the RNN model. We also use the sixth data sample to get the initial values for RNN states, which will be used to initiate the prediction of future timestamps.

   Note that the label is required only to create the iterator and will not be used in the inference:

```
data <- mx.nd.array(x_data[, , 6, drop = F])
label <- mx.nd.array(y_data[, 6, drop = F])

inference_data <- mx.io.arrayiter(data = data,
 label = label,
 batch.size = 1,
 shuffle = FALSE)
infer <- mx.infer.rnn.one(infer.data = inference_data,
 symbol = symbol,
 arg.params = model$arg.params,
```

```
aux.params = model$aux.params,
input.params = NULL,
ctx = ctx)
```

8. Now, we iterate over timesteps to generate predictions for three timesteps of our seventh sample. For predicting a timestep, we use the RNN states information generated from the actual values of the previous timestep and not the predicted one:

```
pred_length <- 3
predicted <- numeric()

for (i in 1:pred_length) {
 data <- mx.nd.array(x_data[, i, 7, drop = F])
 label <- mx.nd.array(y_data[i, 7, drop = F])
 infer.data <- mx.io.arrayiter(data = data,
 label = label,
 batch.size = 1,
 shuffle = FALSE)
 ## use previous RNN state values
 infer <- mx.infer.rnn.one(infer.data = infer.data,
 symbol = symbol,
 ctx = ctx,
 arg.params = model$arg.params,
 aux.params = model$aux.params,
 input.params =
 list(rnn.state=infer[[2]],
 rnn.state.cell = infer[[3]]))
 pred <- infer[[1]]
 predicted <- c(predicted, as.numeric(as.array(pred)))
}

predicted
```

Next, we will understand the steps carried out in this section.

How it works...

In *step 1*, we divided the input data into training and validation and created data iterators for each. These data iterators are iterator objects that allow fetching batches of data sequentially by calling next, each batch containing some training examples and their respective labels.In *step 2*, we created an RNN symbol. We specified the number of layers as two and the number of hidden units as 30. We configured the type of RNN cell to `lstm` and set the config parameter to one-to-one. In the next step, we defined the loss function. In *step 4*, we used the `mx.opt.create()` function to create an optimizer by name and parameters. We created an `adadelta` optimizer and configured its parameters. The `wd` parameter is an L2 regularization coefficient and the `clip_gradient` argument clips the gradient by projecting onto the box, [`-clip_gradient,clip_gradient`]. We used Xavier weight initialization for our model. In this type of weight initialization, the variance remains the same with each passing layer, hence preventing the network from vanishing or exploding gradient problems.

 To read more about this technique, please refer to this paper: `http://proceedings.mlr.press/v9/glorot10a/glorot10a.pdf`.

In *step 5*, we trained the network for 50 epochs using buckets. Bucketing is a technique used to train multiple networks with different but similar architectures that share the same set of parameters. In the next step, we extracted the state symbols from the trained model to use it for inference. In *step 7*, we created an inference model. Finally, in the last step, we predicted the values for the first test sample.

Working with Text and Audio for NLP

7

Natural language processing (NLP) is a rapidly advancing field whose overarching goal is to bridge the gap between how computers and humans understand and communicate. With the recent advancements in NLP-related technologies and applications, nowadays, computers can understand text, speech, and sentiments and analyze them without any bias in order to generate meaning. The nature of the human language and its rules makes NLP one of the most challenging branches of computer science. NLP works primarily by breaking down a language into small elements and trying to understand the relationship between them so that they make sense. This chapter will make you familiar with some of the popular NLP applications of deep learning while using R.

In this chapter, we will cover the following recipes:

- Neural machine translation
- Summarizing text using deep learning
- Speech recognition

Neural machine translation

Neural machine translation gained popularity when tech giants such as Google came up with this service. However, this concept has been around for years and is considered one of the most challenging tasks that deals with very sophisticated linguistic models. In this recipe, we will implement an end-to-end encoder-decoder **long short-term memory (LSTM)** model for translating German phrases into English. This encoder-decoder LSTM architecture is the state of the art approach of addressing **sequence-to-sequence (Seq2Seq)** problems such as language translation, word prediction, and so on, and is widely used in various industrial translation applications.

Sequence prediction is often framed as an architecture that involves forecasting the next value or set of values in a real-valued sequence or predicting a class label for an input sequence. In this recipe, the objective of Seq2Seq learning will be to convert sequences from one language into another; that is, German into English.

Getting ready

The dataset that we'll be using in this recipe is comprised of thousands of German phrases with English translations. It is available at http://www.manythings.org/anki/deu-eng.zip. The examples have been taken from the Tatoeba Project.

Let's start by loading the required libraries:

```
library(keras)
library(stringr)
library(reshape2)
library(purrr)
library(ggplot2)
library(readr)
library(stringi)
```

The data is in the form of a tab-delimited text file. We will be using the first 10,000 phrases. Let's load the dataset and have a look at the sample data:

```
lines <- readLines("data/deu.txt", n = 10000)
sentences <- str_split(lines, "\t")
sentences[1:10]
```

The following screenshot shows a few records from the data. It contains German phrases and their translations in English:

```
 1. 'Hi.'    'Hallo!'
 2. 'Hi.'    'Grüß Gott!'
 3. 'Run!'   'Lauf!'
 4. 'Wow!'   'Potzdonner!'
 5. 'Wow!'   'Donnerwetter!'
 6. 'Fire!'  'Feuer!'
 7. 'Help!'  'Hilfe!'
 8. 'Help!'  'Zu Hülf!'
 9. 'Stop!'  'Stopp!'
10. 'Wait!'  'Warte!'
```

We will use the preceding dataset to build our neural machine translation model.

How to do it...

Before moving on to the model-building part, we need to preprocess the input data. Let's get started:

1. We start by cleaning the data by removing any punctuation and non-alphanumeric characters, normalizing all the Unicode characters to ASCII, and converting all the data into lowercase:

```
data_cleaning <- function(sentence) {
  sentence = gsub('[[:punct:] ]+',' ',sentence)
  sentence = gsub("[^[:alnum:]\\-\\.\\s]", " ", sentence)
  sentence = stringi::stri_trans_general(sentence, "latin-ascii")
  sentence = tolower(sentence)
  sentence
}


sentences <- map(sentences,data_cleaning)
```

2. Next, we create two separate lists of German and English phrases and capture the maximum length of statements in each of these. We will use these lengths to pad the sentences:

```
english_sentences = list()
german_sentences = list()
for(i in 1:length(sentences)){
  current_sentence <- sentences[i]%>%unlist()%>%str_split('\t')
  english_sentences <- append(english_sentences,current_sentence[1])
  german_sentences <- append(german_sentences,current_sentence[2])
}
```

Then, we convert the data into a DataFrame so that it can be manipulated easily:

```
data <- do.call(rbind, Map(data.frame,
"German"=german_sentences,"English"=english_sentences))
head(data,10)
```

The following screenshot shows the input data in the form of a DataFrame:

German	English
hallo	hi
gra a gott	hi
lauf	run
potzdonner	wow
donnerwetter	wow
feuer	fire
hilfe	help
zu ha lf	help
stopp	stop
warte	wait

Now, we can see the maximum number of words in all the sentences in German and English phrases:

```
german_length = max(sapply(strsplit(as.character(data[,"German"] ),
" "), length))
print(paste0("Maximum length of a sentence in German
data:",german_length))

eng_length = max(sapply(strsplit(as.character(data[,"English"] ), "
"), length))
print(paste0("Maximum length of a sentence in English data:",
eng_length))
```

From the following screenshot, we can infer that the maximum length of a sentence in German is 10, whereas for English, it is 6:

```
[1] "Maximum length of a sentence in German data:10"
[1] "Maximum length of a sentence in English data:6"
```

3. Now, we build a function for tokenization and use it to tokenize the German and English phrases:

```
tokenization <- function(lines){
 tokenizer = text_tokenizer()
 tokenizer = fit_text_tokenizer(tokenizer,lines)
 return(tokenizer)
}
```

Here, we prepare the German tokenizer:

```
german_tokenizer = tokenization(data[,"German"])
german_vocab_size = length(german_tokenizer$word_index) + 1

print(paste0('German Vocabulary Size:',german_vocab_size))
```

From the following screenshot, we can see that the German vocabulary size is 3,542:

```
[1] "German Vocabulary Size:3542"
```

Now, we prepare the English tokenizer:

```
eng_tokenizer = tokenization(data[,"English"])
eng_vocab_size = length(eng_tokenizer$word_index) + 1

print(paste0('English Vocabulary Size:',eng_vocab_size))
```

From the following screenshot, we can see that the English vocabulary size is 2,189:

```
[1] "English Vocabulary Size:2189"
```

4. Next, we create a function that will encode the phrases into a sequence of integers and pad the sequences to make each phrase uniform in length:

```
# Function to encode and pad sequences
encode_pad_sequences <- function(tokenizer, length, lines){
 # Encoding text to integers
 seq = texts_to_sequences(tokenizer,lines)
 # Padding text to maximum length sentence
 seq = pad_sequences(seq, maxlen=length, padding='post')
 return(seq)
}
```

5. Next, we divide the data into training and testing datasets and apply the encode_pad_sequences() function we defined in *step 4* to these datasets:

```
train_data <- data[1:9000,]
test_data <- data[9001:10000,]
```

We prepare the training and test data:

```
x_train <-
encode_pad_sequences(german_tokenizer,german_length,train_data[,"Ge
rman"])
y_train <-
encode_pad_sequences(eng_tokenizer,eng_length,train_data[,"English"
])
y_train <- to_categorical(y_train,num_classes = eng_vocab_size)

x_test <-
encode_pad_sequences(german_tokenizer,german_length,test_data[,"Ger
man"])
y_test <-
encode_pad_sequences(eng_tokenizer,eng_length,test_data[,"English"]
)
y_test <- to_categorical(y_test,num_classes = eng_vocab_size)
```

6. Now, we define the model. We initialize a few parameters that will be fed into the model's configuration:

```
in_vocab = german_vocab_size
out_vocab = eng_vocab_size
in_timesteps = german_length
out_timesteps = eng_length
units = 512
epochs = 70
batch_size = 200
```

Here, we configure the layers of the model:

```
model <- keras_model_sequential()
model %>%
  layer_embedding(in_vocab,units, input_length=in_timesteps,
mask_zero=TRUE) %>%
  layer_lstm(units = units) %>%
  layer_repeat_vector(out_timesteps)%>%
  layer_lstm(units,return_sequences = TRUE)%>%
  time_distributed(layer_dense(units = out_vocab,
activation='softmax'))
```

Let's have a look at the summary of the model:

```
summary(model)
```

The following screenshot shows the summary of the translation model:

```
Layer (type)                        Output Shape          Param #
=================================================================
embedding (Embedding)               (None, 10, 512)        1813504
_____
lstm (LSTM)                         (None, 512)            2099200
_____
repeat_vector (RepeatVector)        (None, 6, 512)         0
_____
lstm_1 (LSTM)                       (None, 6, 512)         2099200
_____
time_distributed (TimeDistributed)  (None, 6, 2189)        1122957
=================================================================
Total params: 7,134,861
Trainable params: 7,134,861
Non-trainable params: 0
_____
```

7. Now, we compile the model and train it:

```
model %>% compile(optimizer = "adam",loss =
'categorical_crossentropy')
```

Then, we define the callbacks and checkpoints:

```
model_name <- "model_nmt"

checkpoint_dir <- "checkpoints_nmt"
 dir.create(checkpoint_dir)
 filepath <- file.path(checkpoint_dir,
paste0(model_name,"weights.{epoch:02d}-
{val_loss:.2f}.hdf5",sep=""))

cp_callback <- list(callback_model_checkpoint(mode = "min",
 filepath = filepath,
 save_best_only = TRUE,
 verbose = 1))
```

Next, we fit the training data to the model:

```
model %>% fit(x_train,y_train,epochs = epochs,batch_size =
batch_size,validation_split = 0.2,callbacks = cp_callback,verbose =
2)
```

8. In this step, we generate predictions for test data:

```
predicted = model %>% predict_classes(x_test)
```

Let's create a function that will create a reversed list of key-value pairs of the word index. We will use this to decode the phrases in German and English:

```
reverse_word_index <- function(tokenizer){
 reverse_word_index <- names(tokenizer$word_index)
 names(reverse_word_index) <- tokenizer$word_index
 return(reverse_word_index)
}

german_reverse_word_index <- reverse_word_index(german_tokenizer)
eng_reverse_word_index <- reverse_word_index(eng_tokenizer)
```

Let's decode a sample phrase from the test data in German and look at its prediction in English:

```
index_to_word <- function(data_sample,word_index_dict){
 phrase = list()
 for(i in 1:length(data_sample)){
 index = data_sample[[i]]
 word = word_index_dict[index]
# word = if(!is.null(word)) word else "?"
 phrase = paste0(phrase," ",word)
 }
 return(phrase)
}
```

Now, we can print some sample German sentences and their original and predicted translations in English:

```
cat(paste0("The german sample phrase is -
->",index_to_word(x_test[90,],german_reverse_word_index)))
cat('\n')
cat(paste0("The actual translation in english is -
->",as.character(test_data[90,"English"])))
cat('\n')
cat(paste0("The predicted translation in english is -
->",index_to_word(predicted[90,],eng_reverse_word_index)))
```

The following screenshot shows one example of translation being done by our model. We can see that our model did a great job:

```
The german sample phrase is --> du kannst nicht verlieren
The actual translation in english is -->you can t lose
The predicted translation in english is --> you can t lose
```

Let's have a look at one more translation, as shown in the following code:

```
cat(paste0("The german sample phrase is -
->",index_to_word(x_test[6,],german_reverse_word_index)))
cat('\n')
cat(paste0("The actual translation in english is -
->",as.character(test_data[6,"English"])))
cat('\n')
cat(paste0("The predicted translation in english is -
->",index_to_word(predicted[6,],eng_reverse_word_index)))
```

The following screenshot shows another accurate translation that was done by our model:

```
The german sample phrase is --> wer hat das kaputtgemacht
The actual translation in english is -->who broke this
The predicted translation in english is --> who broke this
```

Now, let's move on to the nitty-gritty of the model and look at a detailed explanation of how it works.

How it works...

In *step 1*, we preprocessed the raw data by removing any punctuation and non-alphanumeric characters, normalizing all the Unicode characters to ASCII, and converting all the data into lowercase. We created lists of German and English phrases and combined them into a DataFrame for easy data manipulation.

In a sequence-to-sequence model, both the input and output phrases need to be converted into integer sequences of a fixed length. Thus, in *step 2*, we calculated the number of words in the lengthiest statements from each of these lists, which will be used to pad the sentences in their respective languages in the upcoming steps.

Next, in *step 3*, we created tokenizers for both the German and English phrases. For working with language models, we broke the input text into tokens. Tokenization provides us with an indexed list that consists of words that have been indexed by their overall frequency in the dataset.

The `num_words` argument of `text_tokenizer()` can be used to define the maximum number of words to keep, based on the word frequency in the word index list.

In *Step 4*, we created a function to map the text, both in German and English, to a specific sequence of integer values by using the `texts_to_sequences()` function. Each integer represents a particular word in the dictionaries we created in the preceding step. The function also pads these sequences with zeros to make all the sequences of a uniform length, which is essentially the maximum sentence length in that language. Note that the `padding='post'` argument in the `pad_sequences()` function pads zeros at the end of each sequence. Next, in *Step 5*, we split the data into training and testing datasets and encoded them into sequences by applying the custom `encode_pad_sequences` function that we created in the preceding step.

In *Step 6*, we defined the sequence-to-sequence model's configuration. We used an encoder-decoder LSTM model, where the input sequence was encoded by an encoder model, followed by a decoder that then decoded the text word by word. The encoder consisted of an embedding layer and an LSTM layer, whereas the decoder model consisted of another LSTM layer followed by a dense layer. The embedding layer in the encoder transformed the input feature space into a latent feature with *n* dimensions; in our example, it transforms it into 512 latent features. In this architecture, the encoder produced a two-dimensional matrix of outputs, the length of which is equal to the number of memory units in the layer. The decoder expects a 3D input to produce a decoded sequence. For this issue, we used `layer_repeat_vector()`, which repeats the provided 2D input multiple times to create a 3D output, as expected by the decoder.

In the next step, we compiled the model and trained it using the training data. For model compilation, we used RMSprop as the optimizer and `categorical_crossentropy` as the loss function. To train the model, we used an 80:20 split for the training and validation datasets, respectively. We trained the model for 50 epochs, with a batch size of 500. Then, we plotted the training loss and validation loss.

In the last step, we predicted the translation in English for a sample German phrase from our test dataset. We created a custom `reverse_word_index` function in order to create a key-value pair of indexes and words for both German and English. Then, we utilized this function to map the integer sequences' outputs to words.

There's more...

Evaluating the quality of generated text works similarly to evaluating labels. The **Bilingual Evaluation Understudy** (**BLEU**) score is a popular metric for comparing a generated translation of a piece of text to a reference translation and varies from 0 to 1. The closer the generated text is to the original text, the higher the score, with 1 being the score of a perfect match. Through the BLEU score metric, the n-grams of the candidate text are compared with the n-grams of the reference translation, along with the number of matches; these matches are also position-independent. Also, the n-grams matching is modified in such a way that it does not reward any such translation that generates only a few reasonable words. This technique is referred to as modified n-gram precision.

For example, let's say we have the following reference text and generated text:

- **Reference text**: I am feeling very enthusiastic.
- **Generated text 1**: I am feeling very very enthusiastic enthusiastic.
- **Generated text 2**: I feel enthusiastic.

In this example, we can see that candidate text 2 has a better prediction of the reference text, although the precision of candidate text 1 might be more. Modified n-gram precision solves this issue for us. The BLEU score is fast and easy to calculate.

However, there are a few challenges with this metric. For example, it considers neither the meaning of the sentences nor their structures and so it doesn't map well to human judgment.

There are a few other metrics that we can use to evaluate the quality of generated translation compared to one or more reference translations, such as **Recall Oriented Understudy for Gisting Evaluation** (**ROGUE**) and **Metric for Evaluation for Translation with Explicit Ordering** (**METEOR**).

See also

For more available resources:

- *Learning Phrase Representations using an RNN Encoder-Decoder for Statistical Machine Translation*: https://arxiv.org/pdf/1406.1078.pdf.
- *Neural Machine Translation by Jointly Learning to Align and Translate*: https://arxiv.org/pdf/1409.0473.pdf.

Summarizing text using deep learning

With the evolution of the internet, we have been flooded with a lot of voluminous data from various sources such as news articles, social media platforms, blogs, and so on. Text summarization in the field of natural language processing is the technique of creating a concise and accurate summary of textual data, capturing the essential details that are coherent with the source text.

Text summarization can be of two types, which are as follows:

- **Extractive summarization**: This method extracts key sentences or phrases from the original source text without modifying them. This approach is simpler.
- **Abstractive summarization**: This method, on the other hand, works on a complex mapping between the context of the source text and the summary rather than merely copying words from the input to the output. A significant challenge with this approach is that it requires a lot of data for training the model so that the machine-generated summaries are equivalent to human-generated summaries.

The encoder-decoder LSTM architecture has been proven to work efficiently for addressing sequence-to-sequence problems and is capable of working with multiple inputs and outputs. In this recipe, we will slightly modify the standard one-hot encoder-decoder architecture that we used in the previous recipe by inducing a technique known as teacher forcing. Teacher forcing is a strategy that's often used for training recursive networks and uses the model output from a prior time step as the input in the next time step. In this architecture, the encoder takes the input text and converts it into an internal representation of a fixed length, capturing the context of the input text appropriately. The decoder uses the internal representation generated by the encoder, as well as the sequence of words or phrases that have already been generated, as a summary. Thus, in this architecture, the decoder has the flexibility to utilize the distributed representation of all the words that have been generated so far as an input to predict the next word.

Getting ready

In this recipe, we will work with the famous Amazon Fine Food Reviews dataset from Kaggle, which can be downloaded from `https://www.kaggle.com/snap/amazon-fine-food-reviews`. This data consists of fine food reviews from Amazon and spans more than 10 years. We will only use the review texts and their summaries in our analysis.

Let's start by loading the required libraries:

```
pckgs <- c("textclean","keras","stringr","tm","qdap")
lapply(pckgs, library, character.only = TRUE ,quietly = T)
```

Now, we read two columns, **Text** and **Summary**, from the data. We will only use the first 10,000 reviews:

```
reviews <- read.csv("data/Reviews.csv", nrows = 10000)[,c('Text',
'Summary')]
head(reviews)
```

The following screenshot shows a few records from the input data:

Text	Summary
I have bought several of the Vitality canned dog food products and have found them all to be of good quality. The product looks more like a stew than a processed meat and it smells better. My Labrador is finicky and she appreciates this product better than most.	Good Quality Dog Food
Product arrived labeled as Jumbo Salted Peanuts...the peanuts were actually small sized unsalted. Not sure if this was an error or if the vendor intended to represent the product as "Jumbo".	Not as Advertised
This is a confection that has been around a few centuries. It is a light, pillowy citrus gelatin with nuts - in this case Filberts. And it is cut into tiny squares and then liberally coated with powdered sugar. And it is a tiny mouthful of heaven. Not too chewy, and very flavorful. I highly recommend this yummy treat. If you are familiar with the story of C.S. Lewis' "The Lion, The Witch, and The Wardrobe" - this is the treat that seduces Edmund into selling out his Brother and Sisters to the Witch.	"Delight" says it all
If you are looking for the secret ingredient in Robitussin I believe I have found it. I got this in addition to the Root Beer Extract I ordered (which was good) and made some cherry soda. The flavor is very medicinal.	Cough Medicine
Great taffy at a great price. There was a wide assortment of yummy taffy. Delivery was very quick. If your a taffy lover, this is a deal.	Great taffy
I got a wild hair for taffy and ordered this five pound bag. The taffy was all very enjoyable with many flavors: watermelon, root beer, melon, peppermint, grape, etc. My only complaint is there was a bit too much red/black licorice-flavored pieces (just not my particular favorites). Between me, my kids, and my husband, this lasted only two weeks! I would recommend this brand of taffy -- it was a delightful treat.	Nice Taffy

We are only interested in keeping those rows that have both text and summary information in the data:

```
reviews <- reviews[complete.cases(reviews),]
rownames(reviews) <- 1:nrow(reviews)
```

In the next section, we will preprocess the input data and build a model for text summarization.

How to do it...

Before jumping to the model-building part, let's clean the input data:

1. First, we need to create a custom function, `clean_data()`, in order to convert the messy data into a cleaned dataset. We will apply this function to both the reviews and the associated summaries and then put the cleaned versions into a DataFrame for easy data manipulation:

```
clean_data <- function(data,remove_stopwords = TRUE){
 data <- tolower(data)
 data = replace_contraction(data)
 data = gsub('<br />', '', data)
 data = gsub('[[:punct:] ]+',' ',data)
 data = gsub("[^[:alnum:]\\-\\.\\s]", " ", data)
 data = gsub('&amp;', '', data)
 data = if(remove_stopwords ==
"TRUE"){paste0(unlist(rm_stopwords(data,tm::stopwords("english"))),
collapse = " ")}else{data}
 data = gsub('\\.', "", data)
 data = gsub('\\s+', " ", data)
 return(data)
}

cleaned_text <-
unlist(lapply(reviews$Text,clean_data,remove_stopwords = TRUE))
cleaned_summary <-
unlist(lapply(reviews$Summary,clean_data,remove_stopwords = FALSE))

# Adding cleaned reviews and their summaries in a dataframe
cleaned_reviews <- data.frame("Cleaned_Text"=
cleaned_text,"Cleaned_Summary"= cleaned_summary)

# Converting the Text and Summary columns to character datatypes
cleaned_reviews$Cleaned_Text <-
as.character(cleaned_reviews$Cleaned_Text)
cleaned_reviews$Cleaned_Summary <-
as.character(cleaned_reviews$Cleaned_Summary)
head(cleaned_reviews)
```

The following screenshot displays a few sample records from the cleaned data:

Cleaned_Text	Cleaned_Summary
bought several vitality canned dog food products found good quality product looks like stew processed meat smells better labrador finicky appreciates product better	Good quality dog food
product arrived labeled jumbo salted peanuts peanuts actually small sized unsalted sure error vendor intended represent product jumbo	Not as advertised
confection around centuries light pillowy citrus gelatin nuts case filberts cut tiny squares liberally coated powdered sugar tiny mouthful heaven chewy flavorful highly recommend yummy treat familiar story c s lewis lion witch wardrobe treat seduces edmund selling brother sisters witch	Delight says it all
looking secret ingredient robitussin believe found got addition root beer extract ordered good made cherry soda flavor medicinal	Cough medicine
great taffy great price wide assortment yummy taffy delivery quick taffy lover deal	Great taffy
got wild hair taffy ordered five pound bag taffy enjoyable many flavors watermelon root beer melon peppermint grape etc complaint bit much red black licorice flavored pieces just particular favorites kids husband lasted two weeks recommend brand taffy delightful treat	Nice taffy

2. Now, we use start and end tokens to signal the start and end of the sequences in the summary, respectively:

```
cleaned_reviews[,"Cleaned_Summary"] <- sapply(X =
cleaned_reviews[,2],FUN = function(X){paste0("<start> ",X,"
<end>")})
```

3. Now, we decide on and fix the maximum length of the reviews and summary sequences:

```
max_length_text = 110
max_length_summary = 10
```

4. Next, we build a function for tokenization and use it to tokenize the text and summary information:

```
tokenization <- function(lines){
 tokenizer = text_tokenizer()
 tokenizer = fit_text_tokenizer(tokenizer, lines)
 return(tokenizer)
}
```

We prepare a tokenizer on the text data and calculate the vocabulary size of the text data:

```
x_tokenizer <- tokenization(cleaned_reviews$Cleaned_Text)
x_tokenizer$word_index
x_voc_size = length(x_tokenizer$word_index) +1
print(paste0('Xtrain vocabulary size:', x_voc_size))
```

The following screenshot shows a sample of words from the tokenized text data:

```
$like
1
$coffee
2
$good
3
$can
4
$will
5

[1] "Xtrain vocabulary size:19347"
```

Then, we prepare a tokenizer on the summary data and calculate the vocabulary size of the summary data:

```
y_tokenizer <- tokenization(cleaned_reviews$Cleaned_Summary)
y_tokenizer$word_index[1:5]
y_voc_size = length(y_tokenizer$word_index) +1
print(paste0('Ytrain data vocabulary size:', y_voc_size))
```

The following screenshot shows a sample of words from the tokenized summary data:

```
$start
1
$end
2
$great
3
$good
4
$the
5

[1] "Ytrain data vocabulary size:4565"
```

5. Now, we need to create another custom function, `encode_pad_sequences()`, in order to encode the text and summary data into a sequence of integers and pad these sequences to make each sentence uniform in length. We will divide the data into training and test datasets and apply the `encode_pad_sequences` function to them:

```
encode_pad_sequences <- function(tokenizer, length, lines){
 # Encoding text to integers
 seq = texts_to_sequences(tokenizer,lines)
 # Padding text to maximum length sentence
 seq = pad_sequences(seq, maxlen=length, padding='post')
 return(seq)
}
```

We split the data into training and validation datasets:

```
sample_size <- floor(0.80 * nrow(cleaned_reviews))

## Setting the seed to make the partition reproducible
set.seed(0)
train_indices <- sample(seq_len(nrow(cleaned_reviews)), size =
sample_size)

x_train <- cleaned_reviews[train_indices,"Cleaned_Text"]
y_train <- cleaned_reviews[train_indices,"Cleaned_Summary"]

x_val <- cleaned_reviews[-train_indices,"Cleaned_Text"]
y_val <- cleaned_reviews[-train_indices,"Cleaned_Summary"]
```

Now, we encode the training and validation datasets into integer sequences and pad these sequences to their respective maximum lengths:

```
num_train_examples = length(x_train)
num_val_examples = length(x_val)

x <- encode_pad_sequences(x_tokenizer,max_length_text,x_train)
x_val <- encode_pad_sequences(x_tokenizer,max_length_text,x_val)

y_encoded <-
encode_pad_sequences(y_tokenizer,max_length_summary,y_train)
y1 <-
encode_pad_sequences(y_tokenizer,max_length_summary,y_train)[,-
max_length_summary]
y2 <-
encode_pad_sequences(y_tokenizer,max_length_summary,y_train)[,-1]
y2 <- array_reshape(x =
y2,c(num_train_examples,(max_length_summary-1),1))
```

```
y_val_encoded <-
encode_pad_sequences(y_tokenizer,max_length_summary,y_val)
y_val1 <-
encode_pad_sequences(y_tokenizer,max_length_summary,y_val)[,-
max_length_summary]
y_val2 <-
encode_pad_sequences(y_tokenizer,max_length_summary,y_val)[,-1]
y_val2 <- array_reshape(x =
y_val2,c(num_val_examples,(max_length_summary-1),1))
```

6. Let's start building the model. First, we initialize a few parameters that will be fed into the model's configuration:

```
latent_dim = 500
batch_size = 200
epochs = 100
```

Here, we configure the layers of the encoder and decoder part of the model. We are using a stacked LSTM configuration, with three layers of LSTM stacked on top of each other.

Let's configure the encoder part of the network:

```
# Defining and processing the input sequence
encoder_inputs <- layer_input(shape=c(max_length_text),name =
"encoder_inputs")

# Adding an embedding layer to encoder
embedding_encoder <- encoder_inputs %>% layer_embedding(input_dim =
x_voc_size, output_dim = latent_dim,trainable = TRUE,name =
"encoder_embedding")

# Adding first LSTM layer to encoder
encoder_lstm1 <- layer_lstm(units=latent_dim, return_sequences =
TRUE, return_state=TRUE, name = "encoder_lstm1")
encoder_results1 <- encoder_lstm1(embedding_encoder)
encoder_output1 <- encoder_results1[1]
state_h1 <- encoder_results1[2]
state_c1 <- encoder_results1[3]

# Adding second LSTM layer to encoder
encoder_lstm2 <- layer_lstm(units=latent_dim, return_sequences =
TRUE, return_state=TRUE,name = "encoder_lstm2")
encoder_results2 <- encoder_lstm2(encoder_output1)
encoder_output2 <- encoder_results2[1]
state_h2 <- encoder_results2[2]
state_c2 <- encoder_results2[3]
```

```
# Adding third LSTM layer to encoder
encoder_lstm3 <- layer_lstm(units=latent_dim, return_sequences =
TRUE, return_state=TRUE, name = "encoder_lstm3")
encoder_results3 <- encoder_lstm3(encoder_output2)
encoder_outputs <- encoder_results3[1]
state_h <- encoder_results3[2]
state_c <- encoder_results3[3]
encoder_states <- encoder_results3[2:3]
```

Let's configure the decoder part of the network:

```
# Setting up the decoder
decoder_inputs <- layer_input(shape=list(NULL),name =
"decoder_inputs")

# Adding embedding layer to decoder
embedding_layer_decoder <- layer_embedding(input_dim =
y_voc_size,output_dim = latent_dim,trainable = TRUE,name =
"decoder_embedding")
embedding_decoder <- embedding_layer_decoder(decoder_inputs)

# Adding lstm layer to decoder
decoder_lstm <- layer_lstm(units=latent_dim,
return_sequences=TRUE,return_state=TRUE,name="decoder_lstm")
decoder_results <- decoder_lstm(embedding_decoder,
initial_state=encoder_states)
decoder_outputs <- decoder_results[1]
decoder_fwd_state <- decoder_results[2]
decoder_back_state <- decoder_results[3]

decoder_dense <- time_distributed(layer = layer_dense(units =
y_voc_size, activation='softmax'))
decoder_outputs <- decoder_dense(decoder_outputs[[1]])
```

Now, we need to combine the encoder and decoder into a single model:

```
model <- keras_model(inputs = c(encoder_inputs,
decoder_inputs),outputs = decoder_outputs)
```

Let's have a look at the summary of the model:

```
summary(model)
```

The following screenshot shows the summary of the combined model:

```
Layer (type)                Output Shape       Param #  Connected to
=================================================================================
encoder_inputs (InputLaye  (None, 110)         0

encoder_embedding (Embedd  (None, 110, 500)   9673500  encoder_inputs[0][0]

encoder_lstm1 (LSTM)       [(None, 110, 500)  2002000  encoder_embedding[0][0]

decoder_inputs (InputLaye  (None, None)        0

encoder_lstm2 (LSTM)       [(None, 110, 500)  2002000  encoder_lstm1[0][0]

decoder_embedding (Embedd  (None, None, 500)  2282500  decoder_inputs[0][0]

encoder_lstm3 (LSTM)       [(None, 110, 500)  2002000  encoder_lstm2[0][0]

decoder_lstm (LSTM)        [(None, None, 500  2002000  decoder_embedding[0][0]
                                                        encoder_lstm3[0][1]
                                                        encoder_lstm3[0][2]

time_distributed_3 (TimeD  (None, None, 4565  2287065  decoder_lstm[0][0]
=================================================================================
Total params: 22,251,065
Trainable params: 22,251,065
Non-trainable params: 0
```

7. Now, we compile the model using the RMSprop optimizer and use `sparse_categorical_crossentropy` as the loss function. Then, we fit the training data into the model in order to train it:

```
model %>% compile(optimizer = "rmsprop",loss =
'sparse_categorical_crossentropy')
```

Let's define the callbacks and checkpoints for our model:

```
model_name <- "model_TextSummarization"

# Checkpoints
checkpoint_dir <- "checkpoints_text_summarization"
dir.create(checkpoint_dir)
filepath <- file.path(checkpoint_dir,
paste0(model_name,"weights.{epoch:02d}-
{val_loss:.2f}.hdf5",sep=""))
```

```
# Callback
ts_callback <- list(callback_model_checkpoint(mode = "min",
 filepath = filepath,
 save_best_only = TRUE,
 verbose = 1,
 callback_early_stopping(patience = 100)))
```

Now, we can train the model:

```
model %>% fit(x = list(x,y1),y = y2,epochs = epochs,batch_size =
batch_size,validation_data =
list(list(x_val,y_val1),y_val2),callbacks = ts_callback,verbose =
2)
```

8. Now, we need to generate some predictions for the holdout sample data using the model we built in the preceding step. For this, we create an encoder and a decoder inference model in order to decode unknown input sequences.

Let's begin by creating a function that will generate a reversed list of key-value pairs of the word index. We will use this to decode the content in the text and summary as this reverse word index will map the integer sequences back to words and make the content readable:

```
reverse_word_index <- function(tokenizer){
 reverse_word_index <- names(tokenizer$word_index)
 names(reverse_word_index) <- tokenizer$word_index
 return(reverse_word_index)
}

x_reverse_word_index <- reverse_word_index(x_tokenizer)
y_reverse_word_index <- reverse_word_index(y_tokenizer)

# Reverse-lookup token index to decode sequences back to meaningful
sentences or phrases
reverse_target_word_index=y_reverse_word_index
reverse_source_word_index=x_reverse_word_index
target_word_index= y_tokenizer$word_index
```

The following code block shows the inference mode for decoding the sentences:

```
# Defining sampling models
encoder_model <- keras_model(inputs = encoder_inputs, outputs =
encoder_results3)

decoder_state_input_h <- layer_input(shape=latent_dim)
decoder_state_input_c <- layer_input(shape=latent_dim)
decoder_hidden_state_input <- layer_input(shape =
c(max_length_text,latent_dim))
```

```
decoder_embedding2 <- embedding_layer_decoder(decoder_inputs)
decoder_results2 <- decoder_lstm(decoder_embedding2,initial_state =
c(decoder_state_input_h,decoder_state_input_c))
decoder_outputs2 <- decoder_results2[1]
state_h2 <- decoder_results2[2]
state_c2 <- decoder_results2[3]

decoder_outputs2 <- decoder_dense(decoder_outputs2[[1]])
inp =
c(decoder_hidden_state_input,decoder_state_input_h,decoder_state_in
put_c)
dec_states = c(state_h2,state_c2)
decoder_model <- keras_model(inputs = c(decoder_inputs,inp),outputs
= c(decoder_outputs2,dec_states))
```

Here, we define a function called `decode_sequence()`, which is the implementation of the inference process. This function encodes the input sequence and retrieves the encoder state. Then, it runs one step of the decoder, with the encoder states as the initial states and the start of sequence token as the target. The output is the next target token. This way, the summary is built up by recursively calling the model with the previously generated word appended to it:

```
decode_sequence <- function(input_seq) {
    # Encoding the input as state vectors
    encoder_predict <- predict(encoder_model, input_seq)
    e_out = encoder_predict[[1]]
    e_h = encoder_predict[[2]]
    e_c = encoder_predict[[3]]

    # Generating empty target sequence of length 1
    target_seq <- array(0,dim = c(1,1))

    # Populating the first character of target sequence with the
start character.
    target_seq[1,1] <- target_word_index[['start']]

    stop_condition = FALSE
    decoded_sentence = ''
    niter = 1
    while (stop_condition==FALSE) {

        decoder_predict <- predict(decoder_model, list(target_seq,
e_out,e_h,e_c))
        output_tokens <- decoder_predict[[1]]
        h <- decoder_predict[[2]]
        c <- decoder_predict[[3]]
```

```
                 ## Sampling a token
                 sampled_token_index <- which.max(output_tokens[1, 1, ])
                 sampled_token <-
reverse_target_word_index[sampled_token_index]

             if (sampled_token != 'end'){
                 decoded_sentence = paste0(decoded_sentence,
sampled_token," ")
                 if(sapply(strsplit(decoded_sentence, " "), length) >=
max_length_summary){
                     stop_condition = TRUE
                 }
             }

             target_seq <- array(0,dim = c(1,1))
             target_seq[ 1,1] <- sampled_token_index

             e_h = h
             e_c = c

    }
     return(decoded_sentence)
     }
```

Now, we need to define a few functions in order to convert an integer sequence
into a word sequence for the reviews and the summaries:

```
seq2summary<- function(input_seq){
 newString=''
 for(i in input_seq){
 if((i!=0 & i!=target_word_index[['start']]) &
i!=target_word_index[['end']]){
 newString=paste0(newString,reverse_target_word_index[[i]],' ')
 }
 }
 return(newString)
}

seq2text <- function(input_seq){
newString=''
for(i in input_seq){
if(i!=0){
newString=paste0(newString,reverse_source_word_index[[i]],' ')
}
}
return(newString)
}
```

The following code shows how you can decode sample reviews and look at their summary predictions:

```
for(i in 1:dim(x_val)[1]){
 print(paste0("Review:",seq2text(x_val[i,])))
 print(paste0("Original summary:",seq2summary(y_val_encoded[i,])))
 print(paste0("Predicted
summary:",decode_sequence(array_reshape(x_val[i,],dim=
c(1,max_length_text)))))
 print("\n")
 }
```

Let's take a look at a sample translation for one of the reviews:

```
[1] "Review:these backyard bbq kettle chips were a great deal with the promo code it was nice to have a larger size bag some
kettle chips in the grocery store are only about 5 ounces and we polish them off in one family lunch they arrived fresh and
were not in crumbles as some other chips from amazon grocery have been great flavor and all natural "
[1] "Original summary:great deal "
[1] "Predicted summary:and tasty for best for buy great great great great "
```

By doing this, we've learned how to implement an abstractive text summarization using the encoder-decoder model.

How it works...

In *Step 1*, we preprocessed the raw data in the text and summary by converting all the data into lowercase and replacing contractions such as "don't", "I'm", to, "do not", and "I am", respectively. Then, we removed any punctuation, non-alphanumeric characters, and stopwords such as "I", "me", "you", "for", and so on.

Note that we didn't remove any stopwords from the summary because doing so can lead to changes in the meaning of the summary. For example, a summary that says "not that great" will become "great" after removing any stopwords.

In *Step 2*, we put special start and end tokens in the summary, which in this case is the target text. The prediction of the first word of the target sequence happens when the model is provided with the start token. The end token signals the end of the sentence.

In the next step, we fixed the length of the source and target sentences that will be used to pad the sequences in the upcoming steps to make them uniform in length. Note that we had decided on the maximum length based on the distribution of the majority of the reviews. Next, in *Step 4*, we created tokenizers for the source and target phrases. Tokenization provides us with an indexed list that consists of words that have been indexed by their overall frequency in the dataset.

In *Step 5*, we created a custom function called `encode_pad_sequences()` to map the reviews and the associated summaries to a specific sequence of integer values. Each integer represents a particular word in the indexed lists that were created in the preceding step. This function also padded the sequences with zeros to make all the sequences of uniform length, which is essentially the maximum length that we had fixed for the source and target texts in *Step 3*. The `padding='post'` argument in the `pad_sequences()` function pads zeros at the end of each sequence. We split the data into training and testing datasets and applied the `encode_pad_sequences()` function to them. Note that in this step, we created additional input data from the already generated summaries, labelled as `y1`, to train the model. The target data, `y2`, is one step ahead of the input data and will not include the start token. The same was done for the validation data.

In *Step 6*, we configured a stacked LSTM encoder-decoder model architecture. First, we created the encoder network, followed by the decoder network. The encoder LSTM network converts the input reviews into its two state vectors: the hidden state and the cell state. We discarded the output of the encoder and only retained the state information. The decoder LSTM was configured to learn to convert the target sequences, that is, the internal representation of the summary information, into the same sequence but offset by one time step in the future. This type of training is known as teacher forcing. The initial states of the decoder LSTM are the state vectors from the encoder. This is done in order to make the decoder learn to generate targets at time *t+1*, given the targets at time *t*, conditioned on the input sequence.

In *Step 7*, we compiled the model and trained it while using RMSprop as the optimizer and `sparse_categorical_crossentropy` as the loss function. This loss function converts the integer sequence into a one-hot vector on the fly and overcomes memory issues. We trained the model for 100 epochs, with a batch size of 200.

In *Step 8*, we created an inference model that generates summaries of unknown input sequences. In this inference mode, we encoded the input sequences and got the state vectors. Then, we generated a target sequence of size 1, which is essentially the start of the sequence character (start). Next, this target sequence, along with the state vectors, was fed to the decoder to predict the next word. The predicted sample word was appended to the target sequence. The same procedure took place recursively until either we got the end-of-sequence word (end) or we hit the sequence limit. This model architecture gave the decoder an opportunity to leverage previously generated words, along with the source text, as the context to generate the next word. Finally, we predicted the summaries for a few sample reviews.

There's more...

A lot of popular models that have been proposed for neural machine translation across various domains belong to the encoder-decoder architecture family. However, this architecture restricts the encoder to encoding the input sequence to a fixed-length representation, which results in deteriorated performance for lengthy input sequences. One of the ways to overcome this bottleneck in performance is to use the attention mechanism within the sequences, which makes the network learn to pay selective attention to the inputs that are relevant for predicting a target output. Most importantly, attention allows the network to encode the input sequence into a sequence of vectors and choose among these vectors while decoding, thus freeing the network to encode all the information in one fixed-length vector. Although the idea of the attention mechanism originated from the context of neural machine translation, it can be extended to a wide range of problems, such as image captioning and descriptions, speech recognition, and text summarization.

See also

To find out more about the attention mechanism, please refer to the following paper: https://arxiv.org/pdf/1706.03762.pdf.

Speech recognition

In the past few decades, there has been a tremendous amount of research on leveraging deep learning for speech-related applications. Speech recognition has become a part of many day-to-day applications, such as our phones, smartwatches, homes, games, and many more.

It's being implemented as a salient feature in many voice search applications such as Siri and Alexa by tech giants such as Apple and Amazon, respectively. Sound waves are time-domain signals, which means that when we plot a sound wave, one of the axes is time (independent variable) and the other is the amplitude of the wave (dependent variable).

To create a digital recording of the sound wave, we convert the analog sound signal into a digital form by performing sampling. Sampling converts the analog audio signal into a digital signal by taking measurements of the dependent variable at a regular time interval called the sampling interval. A small sampling interval results in a better quality sound. To describe the quality of a recorded sound, we often use a term sampling rate as opposed to the sampling interval. The sampling rate defines the number of samples that are taken per second from an analog sound wave.

The sampling rate can be expressed as follows:

$$sampling\ rate = \frac{1}{sampling\ interval}$$

The time-domain representation of sound is not always the best. The most distinguished information is hidden in the frequency spectrum of the signal. Mathematical transformations such as **Fourier Transform** (**FT**) are used to transform a sound wave into its frequency domain. When we apply a Fourier Transform to a signal in a time domain, we obtain its frequency-amplitude representation. Since the digital recording of sound is a discrete process in time, we use **Discrete Fourier Transform** (**DFT**) to transform it into its frequency domain. **Fast Fourier Transform** (**FFT**) is an algorithm that's used to compute the FT quickly. Computing FFT on the entire sound is not informative enough. To extract more information, we need to use the **Short-Time Fourier Transform** (**STFT**). In STFT, we slide a window across the signal and compute a DFT at each sliding window to calculate the magnitude of the frequency spectrum.

Getting ready

In this recipe, we will train a neural network that learns to classify sound waves based on the frequency spectrum. We will work with the Google speech commands dataset for this. It was created by the TensorFlow and AIY teams to showcase a speech recognition example using the TensorFlow API. It contains recordings of many spoken words, and each recording is sampled at 16 kHz. It can be downloaded from `https://storage.cloud.google.com/download.tensorflow.org/data/speech_commands_v0.01.tar.gz`. We will use the `tuneR` package to read the WAV files and the `seewave` package to perform STFT on the audio signal.

Let's start by importing the required libraries:

```
library(seewave)
library(stringr)
library(keras)
library(tuneR)
library(splitstackshape)
```

We now load one sample and look at the wave object:

```
# read file
wav_file =
readWave("data/data_speech_commands_v0.01/no/012c8314_nohash_0.wav")
wav_file
```

In the following screenshot, we can see that the wave object has 16,000 data points, a 16 kHz sampling rate, and that its duration is 1 second:

```
Wave Object
        Number of Samples:      16000
        Duration (seconds):     1
        Samplingrate (Hertz):   16000
        Channels (Mono/Stereo): Mono
        PCM (integer format):   TRUE
        Bit (8/16/24/32/64):    16
```

Now, let's access these attributes:

```
# sample
head(wav_file@left)
# sampling rate
paste("Sampling rate of the audio:", wav_file@samp.rate)
# num of samples
paste("Number of samples in the audio:",length(wav_file@left))
# duration of audio
paste("Duration of audio
is:",length(wav_file@left)/wav_file@samp.rate,"second")
```

The following screenshot shows the attributes of the wave object:

```
236   200   181   191   198   198

'Sampling rate of the audio: 16000'

'Number of samples in the audio: 16000'

'Duration of audio is: 1 second'

We can plot the oscillogram of the sond wave using oscillo() function from seewave.
```

Let's save these wave attributes into some variables:

```
# wave data
wave_data = wav_file@left
# Number of data samples
num_samples = length(wav_file@left)
# sampling rate of the wave
sampling_rate = wav_file@samp.rate
```

We can plot the oscillogram of the sound wave using the `oscillo()` function from the `seewave` package:

```
# plot oscillogram
oscillo(wave = wav_file,f = sampling_rate)
```

The following plot shows the oscillogram for our wave data:

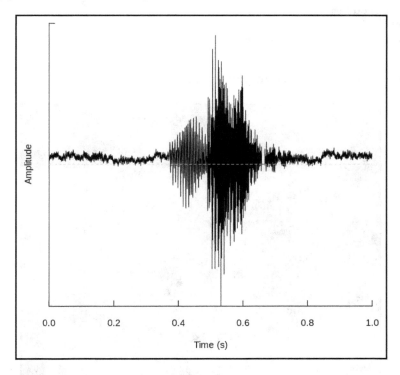

Now, we can plot the spectrogram of the wave. A spectrogram is a visual representation of the spectrum of frequencies of a signal as it varies with time. The following plot is a 2D spectrogram and an oscillogram combined.

In the following code block, we're setting the parameters for the spectrogram and producing the plot. The definition of the three parameters in the following code block are:

- `window length`: This is the length of the sliding window over the wave. It is a numeric value that represents the number of samples in the window.
- `overlap`: This defines the overlap between two successive windows in the form of a percentage.
- `window type`: This defines the shape of the window.

We use the `spectro()` function from the `seewave` package to plot the spectrogram:

```
window_length = 512
overlap = 40
window_type = "hanning"

# plot spectrogram
spectro(wav_file, f=sampling_rate, wl=512, ovlp=40,
osc=TRUE, colgrid="white", colwave="white", colaxis="white", collab="white",
colbg="black")
```

The following plot shows the spectrogram of the wave:

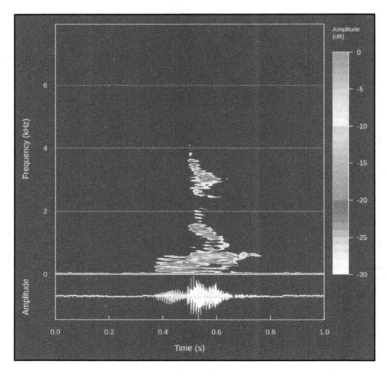

The `spectro()` function also returns statistics based on STFT time, frequency, and amplitude contours. If the `complex` argument is set to true, it provides us with complex values:

```
stft_wave = spectro(wave_data,f = sampling_rate,wl = window_length,ovlp =
overlap,wn = window_type,complex = T,plot = F,dB = NULL,norm = F)
str(stft_wave)
```

The following screenshot shows the structure of the values that are returned by the `spectro()` function:

```
List of 3
 $ time: num [1:51] 0 0.02 0.04 0.06 0.08 0.1 0.12 0.14 0.16 0.18 ...
 $ freq: num [1:256] 0 0.0312 0.0625 0.0938 0.125 ...
 $ amp : cplx [1:256, 1:51] 148.8+0i -74.65+6.57i -0.74-4.15i ...
```

Now, let's look at the dimension of the amplitude contour:

```
dim(stft_wave$amp)
```

The number of rows in the amplitude contour represent the number of frequencies (256) for which we obtained amplitudes in a window. Each column is a Fourier transform of `window_length/2`. Let's store it in a variable:

```
# fft size
fft_size = window_length/2
```

The number of columns in the amplitude contour represents the number of FFT windows. The following code block implements the formula to extract the same:

```
# number of fft window
num_fft_windows = length(seq(1, num_samples + 1 - window_length,
window_length - (overlap * window_length/100)))
```

So far, we've learned how to extract the properties of a sound wave and we became familiar with wave transforms. Now, let's preprocess the wave data in order to build a speech recognition system.

How to do it...

The speech commands dataset contains ~65,000 WAV files. It contains sub-folders with the label names, where each file is a recording of one of 30 words, spoken by different speakers. In the *Getting ready* section of this recipe, we learned how to read a WAV file and obtain its frequency-amplitude representation by applying STFT. In this section, we'll extend the same idea in order to write a generator and then train a neural network to recognize the spoken word.

Let's begin by preparing a dataset for the generator:

1. First, we list all the files inside the `data_speech_commands_v0.01` folder and create a DataFrame:

```
files = list.files("data/data_speech_commands_v0.01",all.files =
T,full.names = F,recursive = T)
paste("Number audio files in dataset: ",length(files)

file_df = as.data.frame(files)
head(file_df)
```

The following screenshot shows a few records from the data:

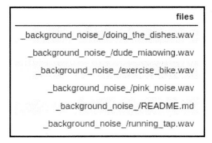

files
_background_noise_/doing_the_dishes.wav
_background_noise_/dude_miaowing.wav
_background_noise_/exercise_bike.wav
_background_noise_/pink_noise.wav
_background_noise_/README.md
_background_noise_/running_tap.wav

Here, we can see that all the files have their label names prefixed. Now, let's create a DataFrame that contains all the filenames and their respective class labels. We will work with three classes, that is, `bird`, `no`, and `off`:

```
file_df$class = str_split_fixed(file_df$files,pattern = "/",n = 2)[,1]
file_df <- file_df[sample(nrow(file_df)),]
rownames(file_df) <- NULL
file_df = file_df[file_df$class %in% c("bird","no","off"),]
file_df$files <- as.character(file_df$files)
file_df$class <- as.numeric(as.factor(file_df$class)) -1
rownames(file_df) <- NULL
head(file_df)
```

The following screenshot shows a sample of the DataFrame we created in the preceding code block:

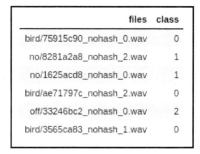

files	class
bird/75915c90_nohash_0.wav	0
no/8281a2a8_nohash_2.wav	1
no/1625acd8_nohash_0.wav	1
bird/ae71797c_nohash_2.wav	0
off/33246bc2_nohash_0.wav	2
bird/3565ca83_nohash_1.wav	0

Let's create a variable that represents the number of unique labels:

```
num_speech_labels = length(unique(file_df$class))
```

2. Now, we split our data into train, test, and validation sets. We use the `stratified()` function from the `splitstackshape` library to do this:

```
# split data into train, test and validation
set.seed(200)
train_index = stratified(file_df,group = "class",.80,keep.rownames
= T)$rn
test_index = setdiff(row.names(file_df),train_index)
val_index = stratified(file_df[train_index,],group =
"class",.20,keep.rownames = T)$rn

train_data = file_df[setdiff(train_index,val_index),]
test_data = file_df[test_index,]
val_data = file_df[val_index,]
```

Now, let's shuffle the train and test data:

```
# shuffle train and test data
test_data = test_data[sample(nrow(test_data)),]
train_data = train_data[sample(nrow(train_data)),]
```

3. Next, let's build a sequential `keras` model to classify the audio and compile it:

```
model <- keras_model_sequential()
model %>%
  layer_conv_2d(input_shape = c(fft_size, num_fft_windows,1),
                filters = 32, kernel_size = c(3,3), activation =
'relu') %>%
  layer_max_pooling_2d(pool_size = c(2, 2)) %>%
```

```
layer_conv_2d(filters = 64, kernel_size = c(3,3), activation =
'relu') %>%
    layer_max_pooling_2d(pool_size = c(2, 2)) %>%
    layer_dropout(rate = 0.25) %>%
    layer_flatten() %>%
    layer_dense(units = 128, activation = 'tanh') %>%
    layer_dense(units = num_speech_labels, activation = 'softmax')
```

After building the model, we need to compile and visualize its summary:

```
# compile model
model %>% compile(
  loss = "categorical_crossentropy",
  optimizer = "rmsprop",
  metrics = c('accuracy')
)

summary(model)
```

The following screenshot shows the summary of the model:

```
Model: "sequential"
_____
Layer (type)                    Output Shape              Param #
=================================================================
conv2d (Conv2D)                 (None, 254, 49, 32)       320
_____
max_pooling2d (MaxPooling2D)    (None, 127, 24, 32)       0
_____
conv2d_1 (Conv2D)               (None, 125, 22, 64)       18496
_____
max_pooling2d_1 (MaxPooling2D)  (None, 62, 11, 64)        0
_____
dropout (Dropout)               (None, 62, 11, 64)        0
_____
flatten (Flatten)               (None, 43648)             0
_____
dense (Dense)                   (None, 128)               5587072
_____
dense_1 (Dense)                 (None, 3)                 387
=================================================================
Total params: 5,606,275
Trainable params: 5,606,275
Non-trainable params: 0
_____
```

4. Next, we need to build a data generator:

```
data_generator <-
function(data,windowlen,overlap,numfftwindows,fftsize,windowtype,nu
m_classes,batchsize) {
    function(){
        indexes <- sample(1:nrow(data), batchsize, replace = TRUE)
        x <- array(0, dim = c(length(indexes),fftsize,
```

```
numfftwindows,1))
        y <- array(0, dim = c(length(indexes)))
        for (j in 1:length(indexes)){
            wav_file_name = data[indexes[j],"files"] %>%
as.character()
            wav_file =
readWave(paste0("data/data_speech_commands_v0.01/",wav_file_name))
            # wave attributes
            wave_data = wav_file@left
            num_samples = length(wav_file@left)
            sampling_rate = wav_file@samp.rate
            # accomodating varying input lengths
            if(num_samples < 16000){
                zero_pad = rep(0,16000 - length(wave_data))
                wave_data = c(wave_data,zero_pad)
            }else if(num_samples > 16000){
                wave_data = wave_data[1:16000]
            }
            # spectrogram representaion
            spectrogram_data = spectro(wave_data,f = sampling_rate
,wl = windowlen,ovlp = overlap,wn = windowtype,complex = T,plot =
F,dB = NULL,norm = F)
            spectrogram_data = spectrogram_data$amp
            spectrogram_data = Mod(spectrogram_data)
            # imputing NaN and Inf
            if((sum(is.nan(spectrogram_data))> 0)){
                spectrogram_data[which(is.nan(spectrogram_data))] =
log(0.01)
            }else if((sum(is.infinite(spectrogram_data)) >0)){
spectrogram_data[which(is.infinite(spectrogram_data))] = log(0.01)
            }else if((sum(is.infinite(spectrogram_data)) >0)){
                spectrogram_data[which(is.na(spectrogram_data))] =
log(0.01)
            }
            spectrogram_data = array_reshape(spectrogram_data,dim =
c(fftsize,numfftwindows,1))
            x[j,,,] = spectrogram_data
            y[j] = data[indexes[j],c("class")] %>% as.matrix()
        }
        list(x, to_categorical(y,num_classes = num_classes))
    }
  }
```

Let's set the batch size and the number of epochs and then create the train and validation generators:

```
batch_size = 20
epochs = 2

# train and validation generator
train_generator = data_generator(data = train_data,windowlen =
window_length,overlap = overlap,numfftwindows =
num_fft_windows,fftsize = fft_size, windowtype =
window_type,num_classes = num_speech_labels,batchsize = batch_size)

val_generator = data_generator(data = val_data,windowlen =
window_length,overlap = overlap,numfftwindows =
num_fft_windows,fftsize = fft_size, windowtype =
window_type,num_classes = num_speech_labels,batchsize = batch_size)
```

5. Now, we define our model callbacks:

```
# model callbacks
model_name = "speech_rec_"

checkpoint_dir <- "checkpoints_speech_recognition"
dir.create(checkpoint_dir)

filepath <- file.path(checkpoint_dir,
paste0(model_name,"weights.{epoch:02d}-
{val_loss:.2f}.hdf5",sep=""))

cp_callback <- list(callback_model_checkpoint(mode = "auto",
 filepath = filepath,
 save_best_only = TRUE,
 verbose = 1),
 callback_early_stopping(min_delta = 0.05,patience = 10))
```

6. Finally, we train our model and test it on a sample:

```
# train model
model %>% fit_generator(generator = train_generator,
                        epochs = epochs,
                        steps_per_epoch =
nrow(train_data)/batch_size,
                        validation_data = val_generator ,
                        validation_steps =
nrow(val_data)/batch_size,
                        callbacks = cp_callback
                        )
```

```
# test sample
test =
readWave("data/data_speech_commands_v0.01/no/0132a06d_nohash_2.wav"
)
# matrix corresponding to the amplitude values
test = spectro(test,wl = window_length,ovlp = overlap,wn =
"hanning",complex = T,plot = F,dB = NULL,norm = F)
test = test$amp
test = array_reshape(test,dim = c(fft_size,num_fft_windows,1))
# predict label of test sample.
model %>% predict_classes( array_reshape(test,dim =
c(1,fft_size,num_fft_windows,1)))
```

Great! The model recognizes the spoken word correctly.

How it works...

In *Step 1*, we prepared a dataset for the generator. We created a DataFrame that contains the file path and the class label of the audio file. In the next step, we created stratified samples and split the DataFrame into train, test, and validation sets. In *Step 3*, we created our convolutional neural network and compiled it.

In *Step 4*, we built a data generator and created training and validation generators. The generator function reads the audio files from disk, transforms each signal into its frequency-amplitude representation, and outputs the data in batches. We know that the speech commands dataset is sampled at 16 kHz; that is, for a 1-second recording, there are 16,000 samples. The dataset also contains a few audio files that are shorter or longer than 1 second. To accommodate recordings of varying lengths, we padded/truncated the audio data to an array that's 16,000 in length and applied STFT. In the *Getting ready* section of this recipe, we observed that the STFT of the 1-second recording sampled at 16 kHz results in an array that's 256x51 in size (`fft_size * num_fft_windows`). This is the reason we defined an input shape of `fft_size * num_fft_windows` for the first convolutional layer of our model.

In *Step 5*, we defined the model callbacks. In the last step, we trained our model and tested its prediction on a test sample.

There's more...

In the *Getting ready* section of this recipe, we used STFT to transform a sound wave into its frequency-amplitude representation. Further transformations can be applied to the wave spectrogram in order to compute the **Mel-Frequency Cepstral Coefficients** (**MFCC**). The **Mel-Frequency Cepstrum** (**MFC**) is used to represent sound in a short-term power spectrum. **Mel-Frequency Cepstral Coefficients** (**MFCCs**) make up an MFC that represents the spectral energy distribution of an audio signal. MFCC works on similar frequencies that can be captured by the human ear.

This is how MFCCs are calculated:

1. An input signal is segmented into several frames, usually in the range of 20-40 ms.
2. Then, for each frame, the power spectrum is calculated by the periodogram estimate. A periodogram estimate identifies which frequencies are present in each frame.
3. Human ears cannot differentiate between two closely spaced frequencies, and this becomes prominent when the frequencies increase. This is why certain periodogram bins are grouped and summed, so that we can get an idea of energy distribution in each frequency region.
4. Humans can't hear loudness on a linear scale; hence, once we get the energy distribution of different frequencies, we take the logarithm of them.
5. The last step involves computing the **discrete cosine transform** (**DCT**) of the logarithmic energy distributions. DCT converts the logarithmic Mel spectrum into the time domain. Higher DCT coefficients indicate fast changes in the energies of the frequency regions and are responsible for low performance; hence, we drop them.

The `tuneR` package in R provides the `melfcc()` function so that we can calculate MFCCs. We can use the following code to obtain MFCCs:

```
melfcc(wav_file)
```

You can also build a speech recognition system using MFCC.

8
Deep Learning for Computer Vision

Computer vision is an exciting field of computer science where the overarching goal is to draw inferences from digital media. The objective is to develop techniques that can train computers to understand the content of digital images and videos and replicate the capability of human vision. With the advent of **deep learning** (**DL**) algorithms and the availability of high-performance computation mechanisms, there has been a significant increase in the use of computer vision in a variety of industries, such as healthcare, retail, autonomous vehicles, robotics, facial recognition, and many more. In this chapter, we will demonstrate some interesting and commonly used applications of DL in the field of computer vision.

In this chapter, we will cover the following recipes:

- Object localization
- Face recognition

Object localization

Object localization is a widespread application of deep learning and has gained a lot of traction in the field of autonomous vehicles, facial detection, object tracking, and many more. Localizing an object is the identification of an area of interest in an image and encapsulating it with a bounding box. In Chapter 1, *Understanding Neural Networks and Deep Neural Networks*, and Chapter 2, *Working with Convolutional Neural Networks*, we worked on image classification, where the output of the network is the probability of each class. For this problem, we will use networks that are similar to the ones we used for image classification, except with a different set of target variables.

In object localization, we predict the output variables that represent the position of the object of interest in the entire input image. Using these, we draw bounding boxes on images. When object localization is accompanied by object classification, the technique is usually called **object recognition**. In this recipe, we are going to follow a simple generic method to localize a single object category in an image.

Getting ready

In this recipe, we will use `raccoon_dataset`, which contains 217 images of varying widths and height. This dataset is credited to Dat Tran and can be downloaded from his GitHub repository: `https://github.com/datitran/raccoon_dataset`.

We downloaded all of the images from the `images` folder of the aforementioned GitHub repository and copied them to the `chapter8 - Deep learning for computer vision/data/raccoon_dataset/images` path. We also downloaded the `raccoon_labels.csv` file from the `data` folder of the preceding GitHub repository and copied it to `chapter8 - Deep learning for computer vision/data/raccoon_dataset`. The `raccoon_labels.csv` file contains the coordinates of the bounding box encapsulating the raccoon in each image.

In this recipe, we will build a single object localization model; that is, we will only locate one area of interest in the entire image. Let's ensure that we have loaded all of the required libraries:

```
library(keras)
library(imager)
library(graphics)
```

Let's load the data and see how it looks:

```
labels <- read.csv('data/raccoon_dataset/raccoon_labels.csv')
# Displaying first 5 rows of data
head(labels)
```

The following screenshot shows a few records from the data:

filename	width	height	class	xmin	ymin	xmax	ymax
raccoon-1.jpg	650	417	raccoon	81	88	522	408
raccoon-10.jpg	450	495	raccoon	130	2	446	488
raccoon-100.jpg	960	576	raccoon	548	10	954	520
raccoon-101.jpg	640	426	raccoon	86	53	400	356
raccoon-102.jpg	259	194	raccoon	1	1	118	152
raccoon-103.jpg	480	640	raccoon	92	54	460	545

Using the following code, we can plot one example image and draw a bounding box from the given coordinates:

```
# Load image
im <- load.image('data/raccoon_dataset/images/raccoon-1.jpg')
# Image information
im_info = labels[labels$filename == 'raccoon-1.jpg' ,]
print(im_info)
plot(im)
rect(xleft = im_info$xmin ,ybottom = im_info$ymin,xright =
im_info$xmax,ytop = im_info$ymax,border = "red",lwd = 1)
```

The following screenshot is a sample from the input data:

The bounding box in the preceding screenshot shows the area of interest.

How to do it...

Let's preprocess the raccoon dataset and build an object localization model:

1. Our dataset contains images of different sizes. Let's fix the image's width and height and initialize a few other parameters:

```
image_channels = 3
batch_size = 15
image_width_resized = 96
image_height_resized = 96
model_name = "raccoon_1_"
```

2. Now, we rescale the coordinates of the bounding box according to the new image dimensions:

```
labels$x_min_resized = (labels[,'xmin']/(labels[,'width']) *
image_width_resized)%>% round()
labels$y_min_resized = (labels[,'ymin']/(labels[,'height']) *
image_height_resized)%>% round()
labels$x_max_resized = (labels[,'xmax']/(labels[,'width']) *
image_width_resized)%>% round()
labels$y_max_resized = (labels[,'ymax']/(labels[,'height']) *
image_height_resized)%>% round()
```

Let's display the resized version of the same example we plotted earlier in the *Getting ready* section of this recipe:

```
x <-labels[labels$filename == 'raccoon-1.jpg',]
im_resized <- resize(im = im,size_x = image_width_resized,size_y =
image_height_resized)
plot(im_resized)
rect(xleft = x$x_min_resized,ybottom = x$y_min_resized,xright =
x$x_max_resized ,ytop = x$y_max_resized,border = "red",lwd = 1)
```

The following screenshot shows the resized version of the same sample image that we plotted in the *Getting ready* section of this recipe:

3. Now, we split the data into training, validation, and test datasets:

```
X_train <- labels[1:150,]
X_val <- labels[151:200,]
X_test <- labels[201:nrow(labels),]
```

4. Let's define a function for calculating the custom metric for our model – **intersection over union** (**IoU**). This is the ratio of the intersection over the union of the two bounding boxes, one is the actual bounding box, while the other is the predicted one:

```
metric_iou <- function(y_true, y_pred) {

  intersection_x_min_resized <- k_maximum(y_true[ ,1], y_pred[ ,1])
  intersection_y_min_resized <- k_maximum(y_true[ ,2], y_pred[,2])
  intersection_x_max_resized <- k_minimum(y_true[ ,3], y_pred[ ,3])
  intersection_y_max_resized <- k_minimum(y_true[ ,4], y_pred[ ,4])

  area_intersection <- (intersection_x_max_resized -
intersection_x_min_resized) *
  (intersection_y_max_resized - intersection_x_max_resized)
  area_y <- (y_true[ ,3] - y_true[ ,1]) * (y_true[ ,4] - y_true[
,2])
```

```
area_yhat <- (y_pred[ ,3] - y_pred[ ,1]) * (y_pred[ ,4] - y_pred[
,2])
area_union <- area_y + area_yhat - area_intersection

iou <- area_intersection/area_union
k_mean(iou)
# c(area_y,area_yhat,area_intersection,area_union,iou)
}
```

5. Next, we define our model and compile it. Let's instantiate a VGG16 model with the `imagenet` weights. We will use this as a feature extractor for our model:

```
feature_extractor <- application_vgg16(include_top = FALSE,
 weights = "imagenet",
 input_shape = c(image_width_resized,
image_height_resized,image_channels)
)
```

Now, we add some layers to VGG16 and build the model:

```
output <- feature_extractor$output %>%
layer_conv_2d(filters = 4,kernel_size = 3) %>%
layer_reshape(c(4))

model <- keras_model(inputs = feature_extractor$input, outputs =
output)
```

Let's have a look at the summary of the model:

```
summary(model)
```

The following screenshot shows the description of the model:

```
Layer (type)                    Output Shape              Param #
=================================================================
input_3 (InputLayer)            (None, 96, 96, 3)         0
_____
block1_conv1 (Conv2D)           (None, 96, 96, 64)        1792
_____
block1_conv2 (Conv2D)           (None, 96, 96, 64)        36928
_____
block1_pool (MaxPooling2D)      (None, 48, 48, 64)        0
_____
block2_conv1 (Conv2D)           (None, 48, 48, 128)       73856
_____
block2_conv2 (Conv2D)           (None, 48, 48, 128)       147584
_____
block2_pool (MaxPooling2D)      (None, 24, 24, 128)       0
_____
block3_conv1 (Conv2D)           (None, 24, 24, 256)       295168
_____
block3_conv2 (Conv2D)           (None, 24, 24, 256)       590080
_____
block3_conv3 (Conv2D)           (None, 24, 24, 256)       590080
_____
block3_pool (MaxPooling2D)      (None, 12, 12, 256)       0
_____
block4_conv1 (Conv2D)           (None, 12, 12, 512)       1180160
_____
block4_conv2 (Conv2D)           (None, 12, 12, 512)       2359808
_____
block4_conv3 (Conv2D)           (None, 12, 12, 512)       2359808
_____
block4_pool (MaxPooling2D)      (None, 6, 6, 512)         0
_____
block5_conv1 (Conv2D)           (None, 6, 6, 512)         2359808
_____
block5_conv2 (Conv2D)           (None, 6, 6, 512)         2359808
_____
block5_conv3 (Conv2D)           (None, 6, 6, 512)         2359808
_____
block5_pool (MaxPooling2D)      (None, 3, 3, 512)         0
_____
conv2d_4 (Conv2D)               (None, 1, 1, 4)           18436
_____
reshape (Reshape)               (None, 4)                 0
=================================================================
Total params: 14,733,124
Trainable params: 14,733,124
Non-trainable params: 0
_____
```

Let's freeze the feature extractor part of the neural network. We will only fine-tune the last layer of our model:

```
freeze_weights(feature_extractor)
```

Now, we compile the model by using adam as the optimizer, mse as the loss function, and metric_iou, which we defined in *step 3*, as the custom metric:

```
model %>% compile(
optimizer = "adam",
loss = "mae",
metrics = list(custom_metric("iou", metric_iou))
)
```

6. Now, we create a custom generator function to get batches of image data and the corresponding resized bounding box coordinates on the fly during the training process:

```
localization_generator <-
function(data,target_height,target_width,batch_size) {

function(){
indexes <- sample(1:nrow(data), batch_size, replace = TRUE)
y <- array(0, dim = c(length(indexes), 4))
x <- array(0, dim = c(length(indexes), target_height,
target_width, 3))
for (j in 1:length(indexes)){
im_name = data[indexes[j],"filename"] %>% as.character()
im = load.image(file
=paste0('data/raccoon_dataset/images/',im_name,sep = ""))
im = resize(im = im,size_x = target_width,size_y = target_height)
im = im[,,,]
x[j,,,] <- as.array(im)
y[j, ] <- data[indexes[j],
c("x_min_resized","y_min_resized","x_max_resized","y_max_resized")]
%>% as.matrix()
}
list(x, y)
}
}
```

Now, we create a generator for the training data by using the
`localization_generator()` function that we created in the preceding code
block:

```
train_generator = localization_generator(data =
X_train,target_height = image_height_resized,target_width
=image_width_resized,batch_size = batch_size )
```

We also create a generator for the validation data in a similar way:

```
validation_generator = localization_generator(data =
X_val,target_height = image_height_resized,target_width
=image_width_resized,batch_size = batch_size )
```

7. Next, we start training the model. We specify the number of epochs that we want
   to run the training process for:

```
epoch = 100
```

Then, we create some checkpoints so that we can save the state of the training
process at certain intervals:

```
checkpoint_dir <- "checkpoints_raccoon"
dir.create(checkpoint_dir)
filepath <- file.path(checkpoint_dir,
paste0(model_name,"weights.{epoch:02d}-{val_loss:.2f}-
val_iou{val_iou:.2f}-iou{iou:.2f}.hdf5",sep=""))
```

We will use callbacks to view the internal states and statistics of the model during
training. To make sure that our model doesn't overfit on the training data, we also
use EarlyStopping:

```
cp_callback <- list(callback_model_checkpoint(mode = "auto"
 filepath = filepath,
 save_best_only = TRUE,
 verbose = 1),
 callback_early_stopping(patience = 100))
```

Now, we fit the training data to the model and start the training process:

```
model %>% fit_generator(
 train_generator,
 validation_data = validation_generator,
 epochs = epoch,
 steps_per_epoch = nrow(X_train) / batch_size,
 validation_steps = nrow(X_val) / batch_size,
 callbacks = cp_callback
)
```

Let's save the final model:

```
model %>%
save_model_hdf5(paste0(model_name,"obj_dect_raccoon.h5",sep=""))
```

8. Now, we do similar data treatment for a sample test image, as we did for the training data images. Then, we predict the bounding box coordinates.
First, we load a sample test image:

```
test <- X_test[1,]
test_img <- load.image(paste(file =
'data/raccoon_dataset/images/',test$filename,sep = ""))
```

Then, we resize the sample test image:

```
test_img_resized <- resize(test_img,size_x =
image_width_resized,size_y = image_width_resized)
test_img_resized_mat = test_img_resized[,,,]
```

Next, we convert the resized image into an array:

```
test_img_resized_mat <- as.array(test_img_resized_mat)
```

Then, we reshape the array to the required dimension:

```
test_img_resized_mat <- array_reshape(test_img_resized_mat,dim =
c(1,image_width_resized,image_width_resized,image_channels))
```

Here, we predict the coordinates of the bounding box for the test sample:

```
predicted_cord <- model %>% predict(test_img_resized_mat)
predicted_cord = abs(ceiling(predicted_cord))
predicted_cord
```

Next, we plot the test image with both the actual bounding box and the predicted bounding box:

```
plot(test_img_resized)
rect(xleft = x$x_min_resized,ybottom = x$y_min_resized,xright =
x$x_max_resized ,ytop = x$y_max_resized,border = "red",lwd = 1)
rect(xleft = predicted_cord[1] ,ybottom = predicted_cord[2] ,xright
= predicted_cord[3] + predicted_cord[1] ,ytop = predicted_cord[4]
,border = "green",lwd = 1)
```

The following screenshot shows the actual (dark gray) and predicted (light gray) bounding boxes:

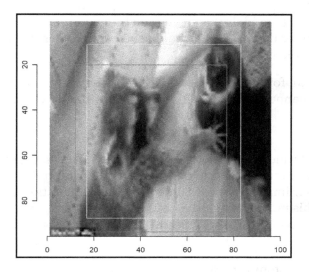

By training the model for 100 epochs, we achieved an IOU of 0.10.

How it works...

In *step 1*, we initialized a few parameters that will be used in the upcoming steps. All our input images are of varying sizes and need to be resized uniformly before they're fed into the model.

In the next step, we rescaled the bounding box coordinates according to the new dimensions. Then, we plotted a sample image to display the resized version of the image. In *step 3*, we split the data into training, validation, and testing datasets based on the indexes. In *step 4*, we defined a custom metric known as the **intersection of union** to evaluate the goodness of fit of our model. A metric function is like a loss function, but the results from evaluating a metric are not used when training the model. This metric is passed during model compilation, needs `y_true` and `y_pred` as arguments, and returns a single tensor value. IoU is a commonly used metric to measure the performance of object localization models in computer vision problems. It allows us to evaluate how close our predicted bounding box is to the ground truth bounding box and is calculated as the ratio of the area of overlap between the two boxes with the combined area of the two boxes. If the predicted and actual bounding boxes overlap completely, then the IoU will be 1 since the area of intersection would be equal to the area of union. By convention, IoU values greater than 0.5 are considered to show decent performance.

In the next step, we configured our model and compiled it. We leveraged the VGG16 model, which is a pre-trained model and achieves 92.7% (top-five) test accuracy in the ImageNet dataset. This approach is prevalent in deep learning and is known as transfer learning. In this approach, models that have been trained for one task are reused as a starting point for another model. This technique also overcomes the limitation of data availability for the problem in hand.

 Note that, for the VGG model, the input shape should have exactly three input channels, and the width and height should be no smaller than 32.

At the end of the pre-trained network, we placed custom layers, depending on the output that we expect from our model. Since we were doing regression to predict the bounding box coordinates for our images, we used a dense layer with units equal to 4 as the last layer. Then, we compiled this model using adam as the optimizer and mse (the mean absolute error) as the loss function. We also specified a custom metric, metric_iou, in the compilation process.

In *step 6*, we created a custom generator function, localization_generator(), to get batches of resized image data and the corresponding scaled bounding box coordinates. We used this function to create generators for the training and validation data. The localization_generator() function takes data, the image's target height and width, and the batch size as arguments.

In the next step, we defined the parameters for model training. We also created checkpoints and specified callbacks while training the model. A checkpoint contains all of the information that we need to save the current state so that we can resume training from this point. **Checkpointing** is a fault tolerance mechanism for processes that take too long to run and allows us to capture the state of the system in case of failure. If we encounter any issues or failures while training the model, checkpoints allow us to continue back from the state we left off by saving the model weights at that particular state. We used callbacks to define where to checkpoint the model weights. Callbacks are used to define a set of functions that need to be applied at given stages of the training procedure. We used early stopping so that the training is stopped once the model's performance improves on the validation dataset. Once we specified all of the model's configuration details, we fit the training data to the model and saved the model's results in a variable.

Once we had trained the model, in the last step, we predicted the bounding box coordinates for a sample test image after preprocessing it.

There's more...

In this recipe, we showcased a general approach to object localization. However, many other techniques can be leveraged for robust object localization and classification in an image with reduced computation time and cost. These techniques can be used to locate and classify multiple objects in one image. Some of these techniques are as follows:

- **Regions Convolutional Neural Network (RCNN)**: This technique uses a selective search algorithm to generate around 2,000 regions for each input image and converts these regions into a fixed size. Each region is then fed into a CNN, which acts as a feature extractor. The extracted features are provided to an SVM, which is usually the last layer of the CNN network and is used to classify whether there is an object in a particular region and also determine the category of the object. Having found the object in the region, the next step in an RCNN is to use a linear regression model to predict the coordinates of the bounding box for the object that was detected in that particular region. A significant challenge with RCNN is that it is very slow and computationally heavy since each region is passed to the CNN network separately.

- **Fast RCNN**: Unlike RCNNs, in this technique, we pass the entire image to several convolutional and pooling layers to produce a feature map rather than passing multiple regions that are generated on top of the original image. Then, by using region proposal methods, we generate **regions of interest** (**ROIs**). For each region, an ROI pooling layer is used to extract a fixed-length feature vector from the feature map. ROI max-pooling divides the h × w ROI window into an H × W grid of sub-windows, each with an approximate size of h/H × w/W. Then, we apply max-pooling to each sub-window. These feature vectors are then passed to fully connected layers that are used for object classification by predicting the softmax probability for each output class and the coordinates of the bounding boxes.

- **Faster RCNN**: Faster RCNNs takes the least amount of computation time compared to RCNNs and Fast RCNNs. In Faster RCNNs, objects are detected in one pass with a single neural network. Instead of using selection search algorithms, Faster RCNN uses a **region proposal network** (**RPN**) to generate region proposals from the feature maps. RPNs rank the region boxes, also known as anchors, and propose the regions that are highly likely to contain objects. The rest of the procedure, that is, detecting the class of the object and predicting the bounding boxes for each object, is the same as it is for Fast RCNNs.

See also

- Deep learning for image segmentation, classification, and detection: `https://arxiv.org/ftp/arxiv/papers/1605/1605.09612.pdf`
- Regression-based object detection techniques (YOLO): `https://pjreddie.com/media/files/papers/yolo.pdf`

Face recognition

Face recognition is one of the most innovative applications of computer vision and has gone through numerous breakthroughs in recent years. There are a plethora of real-world applications where facial detection and recognition are leveraged, such as Facebook, where it is used for image tagging. There are numerous ways to do facial detection, such as by using Haar cascade, **Histogram of oriented gradients** (**HOG**), and CNN-based algorithms. Human facial recognition is an amalgamation of two basic steps: the first is facial detection, that is, locating a human face in an image, while the other is identifying the human face.

In this recipe, we will use the `image.libfacedetection` package in R, which provides a convolutional neural network-based implementation for face detection, and then build a classifier/recognizer for face recognition. The steps for installing the package can be found at `https://github.com/bnosac/image`. For face recognition, we will use a pre-trained model known as **FaceNet**, which is a face recognition system that was developed by Google in 2015. FaceNet is capable of extracting high-quality features from faces, also known as face embeddings, which in turn can be used to train any face recognition system. In this recipe, we will use the pre-trained Keras FaceNet model provided by Hiroki Taniai.

The following screenshot shows the intermediate steps of the face recognition system being implemented in this recipe. First, we detect a face in the image. Using the detected face coordinates, we draw a bounding box around the face. The region inside the box is passed to a recognition algorithm. The recognition model identifies the personality, and then we tag the face in the given image. Note that the recognition model is trained on the cropped face, as shown in the following screenshot:

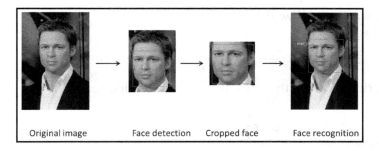

Image Source - Pixabay

Let's start building a deep learning model so that we can recognize the faces of celebrities.

Getting ready

In this application, we will build a custom face recognition system to identify three celebrities: Brad Pitt, Morgan Freeman, and Jason Statham. We have used a few solo images of each personality from Google image's search results to train our model.

Let's start by importing the required libraries:

```
library(magick)
library(image.libfacedetection)
library(keras)
```

In the next section, we will do the required data manipulation in order to build a classifier that leverages FaceNet.

How to do it...

Our dataset contains images of varying sizes. Now, we will preprocess our data and build a facial recognition model:

1. Let's load a sample input image and resize it:

```
width_resized = 500
height_resized = 500
test_img =
image_read("data/face_recognition/brad_pitt/brad_pitt_21.jpg")
test_img <-
image_scale(test_img,paste0(width_resized,"x",height_resized,sep
=""))
```

2. Now, we can localize the face in the image using the `image_detect_faces()` function:

```
faces <- image_detect_faces(test_img)
```

Let's print and save the attributes of the face's locale:

```
faces$detections[,1:4]
face_width = faces$detections$width
face_height = faces$detections$height
face_x = faces$detections$x
face_y = faces$detections$y
```

3. Now that we have localized the face in our image, we can draw a bounding box around it:

```
test_img <- image_draw(test_img)
rect(xleft = face_x,ybottom = face_y,xright = face_x+
face_width,ytop = face_y+ face_height,lwd = 2,border = "red")
dev.off()
plot(test_img)
```

4. Now, let's prepare the training data for our classifier. This will identify a face in a given image. We resize the pictures and then localize each face in it. After that, we crop the faces from the image and store them in a folder named after each celebrity inside a folder called `faces`:

```
# Path to input mages
fold = list.dirs('data/face_recognition',full.names = FALSE,
recursive = FALSE)
fold = grep(paste0("face", collapse = "|"), fold, invert = TRUE,
value = TRUE)
# Create training data path
train_data_dir = "data/face_recognition/faces/"
dir.create(train_data_dir)
# Generating training images.
for (i in fold){
    files = list.files(path =
paste0("data/face_recognition/",i),full.names = FALSE)
  for (face_file in files){
      img =
image_read(paste0("data/face_recognition/",i,"/",face_file,sep=
""))
      img <-
image_scale(img,paste0(width_resized,"x",height_resized,sep =""))
      # Detecting face
      faces <- image_detect_faces(img)
```

```
        face_width = faces$detections$width
        face_height = faces$detections$height
        face_x = faces$detections$x
        face_y = faces$detections$y
        face_dim=
paste0(face_width,"x",face_height,"+",face_x,"+",face_y)
        face_cropped = image_crop(img,face_dim)
        face_cropped = image_crop(img,face_dim)
        if(nchar(face_dim)<= 3){
            print(paste("empty face in:",face_file))
            print(face_file)
        }else{
            fold_name = paste0(train_data_dir,"/",i,"_face")
            dir.create(fold_name)
image_write(face_cropped,paste0(fold_name,"/",face_file))
        }
    }
}
```

5. The cropped face images are of different sizes. Let's set the size of these training images and build a generator:

```
# path of training images
train_path = "data/face_recognition/faces/"
# setting image width height, width and channels
img_size = c(160,160)
img_channels = 3
# class labels
class_label = list.dirs('data/face_recognition/faces', full.names =
FALSE, recursive = TRUE)[-1]
# Data generator with image augmentation
train_data_generator <- image_data_generator(
                         rotation_range = 10,shear_range =
.2,rescale = 1/255,
                         width_shift_range = 0.1,
                         height_shift_range = 0.1,
                         fill_mode = "nearest")
train_data <- flow_images_from_directory(
            directory = train_path,shuffle = T,
            generator = train_data_generator,
            target_size = img_size,
            color_mode = "rgb",
            class_mode = "categorical",
            classes = class_label,
            batch_size = 10)
```

6. Next, we load the FaceNet model. It can be downloaded from `https://drive.`
`google.com/drive/folders/1pwQ3H4aJ8a6yyJHZkTwtjcL4wYWQb7bn`:

```
facenet <- load_model_hdf5("facenet_keras.h5")
print(facenet$input)
print(facenet$output)
```

The following screenshot shows the configuration of the input and output layers of FaceNet:

```
Tensor("input_1:0", shape=(?, 160, 160, 3), dtype=float32)
Tensor("Bottleneck_BatchNorm/batchnorm/add_1:0", shape=(?, 128), dtype=float32)
```

In the preceding screenshot, we can see that the FaceNet model expects square color images that are 160×160 in size as input and produces an output tensor of 128 elements.

7. Now, let's build our face recognition model:

```
facenet_out <- facenet$output %>%
layer_dense(units = 128,activation = "relu") %>%
layer_dense(units = 3,activation = "softmax")
facenet_model <- keras_model(inputs = facenet$input, outputs =
facenet_out)
```

Since we will be using pre-realized ImageNet weights in the model, let us freeze its weights:

```
freeze_weights(facenet)
```

8. After defining the model, we compile and train it:

```
facenet_model %>% compile(optimizer = 'rmsprop', loss =
'categorical_crossentropy',metrics = c('accuracy'))

facenet_model %>% fit_generator(generator =
train_data,steps_per_epoch = 2,
 epochs = 5)
```

9. Now, we start to recognize the face in a sample image:

```
# image path
test_img =
image_read("data/face_recognition/brad_pitt/brad_pitt_21.jpg")
# scaling input image
test_img <-
image_scale(test_img,paste0(width_resized,"x",height_resized,sep
=""))
# detecting faces in the image
faces <- image_detect_faces(test_img)

# extracting attribute of the detected face
face_width = faces$detections$width
face_height = faces$detections$height
face_x = faces$detections$x
face_y = faces$detections$y

# cropping detected face
face_dim= paste0(face_width,"x",face_height,"+",face_x,"+",face_y)
face_cropped = image_crop(test_img,face_dim)

# resizing cropped face
face_cropped = image_resize(image =
face_cropped,paste0(img_size[1],"x",img_size[2]))

# converting  cropped face image to array
face_cropped_arr <- as.integer(face_cropped[[1]])/255
face_cropped_arr <- array_reshape(face_cropped_arr,dim =
c(1,img_size,img_channels))

# Recognizing face
pred <- facenet_model %>% predict(face_cropped_arr)
pred_class <- class_label[which.max(pred)]

# Drawing bounding box around the face and putting name to the face
test_img <- image_draw(test_img)
rect(xleft = face_x,ybottom = face_y,xright = face_x+
face_width,ytop = face_y+ face_height,lwd = 2,border = "red")
text(face_x,face_y,pred_class,offset = 1,pos = 2,cex = 1.5,col =
"pink")
dev.off()
plot(test_img)
```

In the following screenshot, we can see that our model recognizes Brad Pitt:

Image source - Pixabay

You can also test the model for other images of Brad Pitt and Morgan Freeman. By adding new faces to your training data, you can extend this model's ability to recognize faces even further.

How it works...

In *step 1*, we loaded a sample image and resized its height and width to `height_resized` and `width_resized`, respectively. In *step 2*, we localized a face in the image by using the `image_detect_faces()` function from the `image.libfacedetection` library. It returns the left x,y coordinates of the detected face and its width and height. Then, in *step 3*, we drew a bounding box around the face. The `rect()` function draws a rectangle onto an image using pixel coordinates. In the previous three steps, we implemented face localization in an image. In *step 4*, we utilized this face localization technique to prepare a dataset that we will use to train our face recognizer/classifier model.

In *step 5*, we built a generator with data augmentation. In *step 6*, we loaded the FaceNet model and inspected its input and output layers. In *step 7*, we built our face recognition model. We added a dense layer with 128 units. The last layer consisted of three units with a softmax activation function. The last layer of the model has three units because we had three class labels. We defined the loss function and IOU metric of our model and then compiled and trained it. In *step 8*, we tested our face recognition system on a sample image.

There's more...

We discussed region-based techniques for object detection in the *There's more...* section of the previous recipe, *Object localization*, of this chapter. However, numerous techniques are widely used specifically for human face localization.

Let's look at how some of these techniques work:

- **HOG** and **SVM**: They are used as a descriptor for image detection and work seamlessly with varying illumination backgrounds and pose changes. In this technique, the image is divided into 8×8 cells, and then the distribution of magnitudes and the directions of local intensity gradients over the pixels are obtained. Pixels with a large negative change in gradient will be black, pixels with large positive change will be white, and pixels with little or no change will be gray. Each cell is divided into angular bins that correspond to the gradient's direction (0 - 180 degrees for unsigned gradients and 0 - 360 degrees for signed gradients), thus condensing the vectors of size 64(8×8) to just 9 values (in the case of 0-180 degrees) associated with the respective bins. HOG uses a sliding window to compute HOG descriptors for each cell in the image and takes care of scaling issues via image pyramiding. These HOG features, combined with SVM classifiers, are then used for the recognition of human faces.

- **Haar cascade classifiers**: Haar cascades work pretty well when it comes to detecting one particular type of object in an image, such as a face in an image, eyes in an image, and so on. However, they can be used in parallel to detect faces, eyes, and mouths. The algorithm is trained on lots of positive images (images that contain faces) and negative images (images that do not contain faces) and then features are extracted from them over a given base window size (24×24 in the case of the Viola-Jones algorithm). Haar features are like convolution kernels since they detect the presence of that particular feature in a given image, and each feature represents a part of the human face. Each feature result is used to calculate a value by subtracting the sum of pixels under a white rectangle from the sum of pixels under a black rectangle. There are thousands of features that are calculated during this process; however, not all of them may be useful for face detection.

A new image representation approach, known as the integral image, is used to reduce this number of features. The AdaBoost algorithm is then used to get rid of redundant features and select only the relevant ones. Then, a weighted combination of all these features is used to decide whether a given window has a face or not. Instead of using all the selected features to slide over an image, the idea of cascading is used, where all the relevant features are sampled into different cascades in a linear manner. If cascade *i* is able to detect a face in a window, then the image is passed on to the next cascade, *i+1*; otherwise, it is discarded. Cascading classifiers reduces a lot of computation complexity and time. With this approach, we can use any supervised learning technique on top and train for facial recognition.

The following screenshot shows a few Haar cascade features:

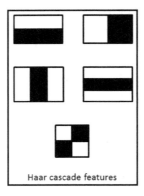

Haar cascade features

- **Maximum margin of detection (MMOD)**: With the non-maximum suppression technique, sometimes, the overlapping windows get rejected and lead to false alarms. The maximum margin of detection works by replacing this technique with a new objective function. Unlike other classifiers, MMOD does not perform any sub-sampling; instead, it optimizes the overall sub-windows of an image. In this technique, a maximum margin approach is taken, which requires the label for each training sample to be predicted correctly with a large margin.

See also

- To find out more about the FaceNet model, go to https://arxiv.org/pdf/1503.03832.pdf.
- To find out more about MMOD, go to https://arxiv.org/pdf/1502.00046.pdf.

Implementing Reinforcement Learning

9

Reinforcement learning (**RL**) has gained considerable traction recently. It is a different approach to machine intelligence from traditional machine learning and deep learning techniques. It has achieved human-level performance in learning complex games such as Go and Dota. RL is an artificial intelligence framework where an agent performs learning through trial and error. It is a learning process that mimics the fundamental way humans learn. The overarching goal of this chapter is to make you conversant with the components of RL. You will learn how to implement RL using various packages in R.

In this chapter, we will cover the following recipes:

- Model-based RL using MDPtoolbox
- Model-free RL
- Cliff walking using RL

Model-based RL using MDPtoolbox

RL is a general-purpose framework for artificial intelligence. It is used to solve sequential decision-making problems. In RL, the computer is given a goal to achieve and it learns how to accomplish that goal by learning from interactions with its environment. A typical RL setup consists of five components, known as the **Agent**, **Environment**, **Action**, **State**, and **Reward**.

In RL, an agent interacts with the environment using an action from a set of **Actions** (**A**). Based on the action taken by the agent, the environment transitions from an initial state to a new state, where each state belongs to a set of **States** within the environment. The transition generates a feedback **Reward** signal (a scalar quantity) from the environment. The reward is an estimate of the agent's performance, and the reward value depends on the current state and the action that's performed. This process of an agent making choices about actions and the environment responding with new states and a reward associated with it continues until the agent learns an optimal behavior to reach the terminal state from any initial state, maximizing the cumulative reward, G_t.

The following diagram is an illustration of an RL setup:

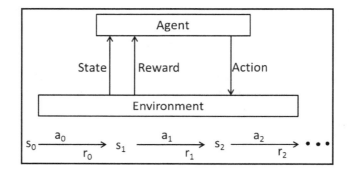

G_t can be expressed as follows:

$$G_t = \sum_{t=0}^{T} \gamma^t r_t$$

Here, G_t is the cumulative reward,
γ is the discount factor,
and t is the timestep

The RL setup follows particular assumptions. First, the agent interacts with the environment sequentially; then, second, the time-space is discrete; finally, the transitions follow the Markov property; that is, the environment's future state, s', depends only on the current state, s. A Markov process is a memoryless random process; that is, it's a sequence of random states with the Markov property. It is a framework for modeling the decision-making process. The **Markov decision process** (**MDP**) specifies a mathematical structure to find a solution to an RL problem.

It is a tuple of five components—(S, A, P, R,γ):

- **S**: Set of states, $s \in S$.
- **A**: Set of actions, $a \in A$.
- **P**: Transition probability, $T^a_{s's}$, which is the probability of reaching s' after taking action a in state s.
- **R**: Reward function, $R^a_{ss'}$, which is the expected reward when moving from s to s' using action a.
- γ: The discount factor. z

Using MDP, we can find a policy, $\pi(s)$, that maximizes the expected long-term reward, $E[G_t]$, with discount factor, γ (it defines an applicable discount for the future rewards). A policy defines the best action that an agent should take based on the current state. It maps actions to states. The function that estimates the long-term reward for an agent starting from a state, s, and following a policy, $\pi(s)$, is known as a value function.

There are two types of value functions:

- The **state-value** function, $V_\pi(s)$: For an MDP, it is the expected return for an agent beginning from state s and following the policy, $\pi(s)$:

$$V_\pi(s) = E[G_t] \; \forall s \in S$$

- The **action-value** function, $Q_\pi(s, a)$: For an MDP, it is the expected return for an agent beginning from state s, taking an action, a, and then following the policy, $\pi(s)$:

$$Q_\pi(s, a) = E[G_t] \; \forall s \in S$$

Among all the possible value functions, an **optimal value function** $V^*(s)$ exists, which yields the highest expected reward for all states. The policy that corresponds to the optimal value function is known as the **optimal policy**.

$V^*(s)$ and $Q^*(s)$ can be expressed as follows:

$$V^*(s) = \max_\pi V_\pi(s) \forall s \in S \text{ optimal state value function}$$

$$Q^*(s) = \max_\pi Q_\pi(s, a) \forall s \in S \text{ optimal action value function}$$

An optimal policy can be found by maximizing over $Q^*(s, a)$. An optimal policy can be described as follows:

$$\pi^* = arg\max_a Q^*(s, a)$$

Using the Bellman equation, we can find the optimal value function. The **Bellman expectation equation** defines a value function as the sum of the immediate reward that's received for transitioning from the current state, s, using action, a, and the expected reward from the next state, s':

$$V_\pi(s) = E_\pi[R^a_{ss'} + \gamma V(s')]$$
$$Q_\pi(s, a) = E_\pi[R^a_{ss'} + \gamma Q(s', a')]$$

The **Bellman optimality equations** for $Q*$ and $V*$ is given as follows:

$$Q^*(s, a) = R^a_{ss'} + \gamma \sum_{s' \in S} T^a_{ss'} V^*(s')$$

$$V^*(s) = \max_a R^a_{ss'} + \gamma \sum_{s' \in S} T^a_{ss'} V^*(s')$$

Also, the optimal state-value and action-value functions are recursively related by the Bellman optimality equations, as per the following equation:

$$V^*(s) = \max_a Q^*(s, a)$$

From this, we get the following:

$$Q^* = R^a_{ss'} + \gamma \sum_{s' \in S} T^a_{ss'} \max_{a'} Q^*(s', a')$$

There are many ways to solve Bellman optimality equations, such as value iteration, policy iteration, SARSA, and Q-learning. RL techniques can be categorized into model-based and model-free approaches. Model-based algorithms depend on explicit models of the environment that provide the state transition probabilities, as well as the representation of the environment in the form of MDPs. These MDPs can be solved by various algorithms, such as value iteration and policy iteration.

On the other hand, model-free algorithms do not rely on any explicit knowledge about the environment representing the problem. Instead, they try to learn an optimal policy based on the dynamic interaction of the agent with the environment. In this recipe, we will solve an RL problem using a model-based policy iteration algorithm.

Getting ready

In this recipe, we will solve a grid navigation problem. The following image is a pictorial representation of the navigation grid. It represents a navigation matrix, where each state has been assigned a label. Each cell in the matrix represents a state, leading to a total of four states. The agent should navigate from any random starting state to the final goal state, 4. The agent can only move between states through the openings in the grid and cannot move off the grid walls. At each state, the agent can perform any action from the available set of actions; that is, they can move up, down, left, or right. When entering the goal state, the agent earns a reward of 100, and every other additional step costs a penalty of -1.

In the following image, the possible states are {1,2,3,4} and the possible set of actions are {UP,DOWN,LEFT,RIGHT}:

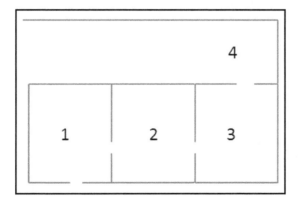

For model-based RL implementation, we will use the MDPtoolbox library.

Let's import the MDPtoolbox library:

```
library(MDPtoolbox)
```

The MDPtoolbox library contains a number of functions related to the resolution of discrete-time MDPs.

How to do it...

In the *Getting ready* section, we defined our RL problem. We know that to solve a model-based RL problem, we need a transition probability matrix and a reward matrix:

1. Let's start by defining the transition probability matrices. We start off by defining the probabilities for all the actions at each state. The sum of the probabilities in each row sums up to 1:

```
# Up
up=matrix(c( 0.9, 0.1, 0, 0,
 0.2, 0.7, 0.1, 0,
 0, 0, 0.1, 0.9,
 0, 0, 0, 1),
 nrow=4,ncol=4,byrow=TRUE)

# Down
down=matrix(c(0.1, 0, 0, 0.9,
 0, 0.8, 0.2, 0,
 0, 0.2, 0.8, 0,
 0, 0, 0.8, 0.2),
 nrow=4,ncol=4,byrow=TRUE)

# Left
left=matrix(c(1, 0, 0, 0,
 0.9, 0.1, 0, 0,
 0, 0.8, 0.2, 0,
 0, 0, 0, 1),
 nrow=4,ncol=4,byrow=TRUE)

# Right
right=matrix(c(0.1, 0.9, 0, 0,
 0.1, 0.2, 0.7, 0,
 0, 0, 0.9, 0.1,
 0, 0, 0, 1),
 nrow=4,ncol=4,byrow=TRUE)
```

Now, let's put all the actions into one single list:

```
actions = list(up=up, down=down, left=left, right=right)
actions
```

The following screenshot displays the state action matrix for each action:

```
$up
   0.9  0.1  0.0  0.0
   0.2  0.7  0.1  0.0
   0.0  0.0  0.1  0.9
   0.0  0.0  0.0  1.0
$down
   0.1  0.0  0.0  0.9
   0.0  0.8  0.2  0.0
   0.0  0.2  0.8  0.0
   0.0  0.0  0.8  0.2
$left
   1.0  0.0  0.0  0
   0.9  0.1  0.0  0
   0.0  0.8  0.2  0
   0.0  0.0  0.0  1
$right
   0.1  0.9  0.0  0.0
   0.1  0.2  0.7  0.0
   0.0  0.0  0.9  0.1
   0.0  0.0  0.0  1.0
```

2. Now, let's define the rewards and penalties. The only reward is on entering state 4; every other step incurs a penalty of -1:

```
rewards=matrix(c( -1, -1, -1, -1,
 -1, -1, -1, -1,
 -1, -1, -1, -1,
 100, 100, 100, 100),
 nrow=4,ncol=4,byrow=TRUE)

rewards
```

The following screenshot shows the reward matrix:

```
  -1    -1    -1    -1
  -1    -1    -1    -1
  -1    -1    -1    -1
 100   100   100   100
```

3. Now, we can solve the problem using the `mdp_policy_iteration()` function. This function takes the transition probability and the rewards matrices as inputs, along with a discount factor:

```
solved_MDP=mdp_policy_iteration(P=actions, R=rewards, discount =
0.2)
solved_MDP
```

The following screenshot shows the result of solving the problem:

```
$V
[1]  21.938776   3.009163  21.938776 125.000000

$policy
[1] 2 3 1 1

$iter
[1] 3

$time
Time difference of 0.1538157 secs
```

Let's have a look at the policy given by the policy iteration algorithm:

```
solved_MDP$policy
names(actions)[solved_MDP$policy]
```

The following screenshot shows the policy for our problem:

```
2  3  1  1

'down'  'left'  'up'  'up'
```

The policy depicted in the previous screenshot lets us take the best action in respective states 1,2,3,4. For example the best action in state 1 is down, in state 2 is left, in state 3 is up and state 4 is up. We can get the values at each step using the following code:

```
solved_MDP$V
```

The following screenshot shows the values at each step of our policy:

```
21.9387755102041  3.009162848813  21.9387755102041  125
```

Here, we can see that at the last step, the value of our policy is **125**.

How it works...

In *step 1*, we defined action probability matrices for each action. We can interpret this as the probability of transitioning from a current state to the next state using an action. Let's say that if the agent is in state **2** and tries to go **LEFT**, there is a 90% probability that the agent will transition to state 1.

The following image represents the transition probability matrix for the **LEFT** action:

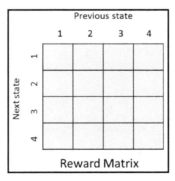

Transition probability matrix for action LEFT

In *step 2*, we defined a reward matrix; that is, a scalar reward that's given to an agent for transitioning from the current state to the next one.

The following image represents the reward matrix:

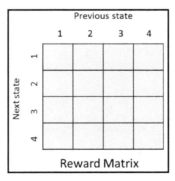

Reward Matrix

In the last step, we solved the RL problem by applying the policy iteration algorithm to solve the discounted MDP. The `mdp_policy_iteration()` function returns **V**, which is the **optimal value function**; the policy, which is the optimal policy; `iter`, which is the number of iterations; and `time`, which is the CPU time taken by the program. The policy iteration algorithm stops when two successive policies are identical. We can also specify the number of iterations by passing a value to the `max_iter` argument.

There's more...

The `MDPtoolbox` package also provides an implementation of the **value iteration** algorithm so that we can solve an MDP. The following code block demonstrates the same:

```
mdp_value_iteration(P=actions, R=rewards, discount = 0.2)
```

The following screenshot displays the optimal policy details:

```
[1] "MDP Toolbox: iterations stopped, epsilon-optimal policy found"

$V
[1]  21.738792    2.809776  21.738792 124.800000

$policy
[1] 2 3 1 1

$iter
[1] 4

$time
Time difference of 0.01425719 secs

$epsilon
[1] 0.01

$discount
[1] 0.2
```

The optimal policy that's given by the value iteration method is {2,3,1,1}. The value at the last step is close to what we got in the policy iteration method.

Model-free RL

In the previous recipe, *Model-based RL using MDPtoolbox*, we followed a model-based approach to solve an RL problem. Model-based approaches become impractical as the state and action space grows. On the other hand, model-free reinforcement algorithms rely on trial-and-error interaction of the agent with the environment representing the problem in hand. In this recipe, we will use a model-free approach to implement RL using the `ReinforcementLearning` package in R. This package utilizes a popular model-free algorithm known as **Q-learning**. It is an off-policy algorithm due to the fact that it explores the environment and exploits the current knowledge at the same time.

Q-learning guarantees to converge to an optimal policy, but to achieve so, it relies on continuous interactions between an agent and its environment, which makes it computationally heavy. This algorithm looks forward to the next state and observes the maximum possible reward for all the possible actions in that state. Then, it utilizes this knowledge to update the action-value information of the respective actions in the current state with a specific learning rate, α. The algorithm tries to learn an optimal evaluation function known as the Q-function, which maps each state and action pair to a value. It is denoted as Q: S × A => V, where V is the value of future rewards for an action, $a \in A$, which is executed in the state, $s \in S$.

The following is the pseudocode for the Q-learning algorithm:

1. Initialize the value as 0 for all state-action pairs (s,a) in the table, $Q(s, a)$.
2. Observe the current state, s.
3. Repeat until convergence:

    * Choose an action, a, and apply it.
    * Get the immediate reward, $R_{ss'}^a$.
    * Move to the new state, s'.
    * Update the table entry for $Q(s, a)$ according to the following formula:

$$Q(s, a) \leftarrow Q(s, a) + \alpha[R_{ss'}^a + \gamma \max_{a'} Q(s', a') - Q(s, a)]$$

    * Move to the next state, s'. Now, s' becomes the current state, s.

Getting ready

In this recipe, we will use the `ReinforcementLearning` package, which performs model-free RL.

Let's import the `ReinforcementLearning` package:

```
library(ReinforcementLearning)
```

In this recipe, we will work on the same navigation example that we used in the previous section, *Model-based RL using MDPtoolbox*. In this case, we won't have any predetermined input data, and we will solve the problem using a model-free approach. The agent will interact dynamically with an environment representing the problem and generate state-action transition tuples. The structure of the environment is specific to the problem at hand. An **environment** is typically a stochastic finite state machine that represents the rules of operating in any specific problem. It provides feedback to the agent about its actions in terms of rewards and penalties.

The following is some generic pseudocode for an environment:

```
environment <- function(state, action) {
  ...
  return(list("NextState" = newState,"Reward" = reward))
  }
```

In the next section, we will create an environment of the navigation grid and train an agent to navigate through the grid using model-free RL.

How to do it...

Let's programmatically create an environment for our problem:

1. We start by defining the states and set of actions:

```
states <- c("1", "2", "3", "4")
actions <- c("up", "down", "left", "right")
cat("The states are:",states)
cat('\n')
cat("The actions are:",actions)
```

2. Next, we create a function that will define a custom environment for our example:

```
gridExampleEnvironment <- function(state, action) {
  next_state <- state
```

```
  if (state == state("1") && action == "down") next_state <-
state("4")
  if (state == state("1") && action == "right") next_state <-
state("2")
  if (state == state("2") && action == "left") next_state <-
state("1")
  if (state == state("2") && action == "right") next_state <-
state("3")
  if (state == state("3") && action == "left") next_state <-
state("2")
  if (state == state("3") && action == "up") next_state <-
state("4")
  if (next_state == state("4") && state != state("4")) {
  reward <- 100
  } else {
  reward <- -1
  }
out <- list("NextState" = next_state, "Reward" = reward)
return(out)
}

print(gridExampleEnvironment)
```

The following screenshot provides a description of the environment:

```
function(state, action) {
  next_state <- state
  if (state == state("1") && action == "down") next_state <- state("4")
  if (state == state("1") && action == "right") next_state <- state("2")
  if (state == state("2") && action == "left") next_state <- state("1")
  if (state == state("2") && action == "right") next_state <- state("3")
  if (state == state("3") && action == "left") next_state <- state("2")
  if (state == state("3") && action == "up") next_state <- state("4")
  if (next_state == state("4") && state != state("4")) {
    reward <- 100
  } else {
    reward <- -1
  }

  out <- list("NextState" = next_state, "Reward" = reward)
  return(out)
}
```

3. Now, we generate some sample experience data in the form of state transition tuples using the `sampleExperience()` function. This function takes states, actions, iterations, and the environment as input arguments:

```
# Let us generate 1000 iterations
sequences <- sampleExperience(N = 1000, env =
gridExampleEnvironment, states = states, actions = actions)
head(sequences,6)
```

The following screenshot shows the first few records of the sample data:

State	Action	Reward	NextState
2	up	-1	2
4	right	-1	4
3	left	-1	2
4	up	-1	4
4	left	-1	4
1	up	-1	1

4. Using the sample experience data we generated in the previous step, we can solve our problem using the `ReinforcementLearning()` function:

```
solver_rl <- ReinforcementLearning(sequences, s = "State", a =
"Action", r = "Reward", s_new = "NextState")

print(solver_rl)
```

The following screenshot shows the state action table, along with the policy and overall reward for our problem. **X1,X2,X3,X4** represents the states 1,2,3,4 respectively:

```
State-Action function Q
         right          up       down        left
X1 -0.1346275  8.8664569  99.7125910   8.8115487
X2  8.8556876 -0.1296954  -0.1346798   8.7847591
X3  8.9162933 99.7623845   8.9042606  -0.1348055
X4 -1.1064408 -1.1080549  -1.0974611  -1.1062077

Policy
     X1       X2        X3        X4
 "down"  "right"     "up"    "down"

Reward (last iteration)
[1] 11423
```

Here, we can see that our overall reward at the last iteration is `11423`.

How it works...

In *step 1*, we defined the possible set of states and actions for this problem. To work with a model-free RL, we need to create a function that mimics the behavior of the environment. In *step 2*, we formulated the problem by creating a function called `gridExampleEnvironment()`, which takes a state-action pair as input and generates a list of the next state and the associated reward. In *step 3*, we used the `sampleExperience()` function to generate dynamic state-action transition tuples by querying the environment we created in the preceding step. The input arguments to this function are the number of samples, the environment function, and the set of states and actions. This function returns a dataframe that contains the experienced observation sequences from the environment.

Once the observation sequence data has been generated, the agent learns an optimal policy based on this data. To achieve this, in *step 4*, we used the `ReinforcementLearning()` function. We can pass a few more arguments to this function to customize the learning behavior of the agent.

The arguments are as follows:

- `alpha`: This is the learning rate, α, which varies between 0 and 1. The higher the value of this parameter, the quicker learning is.
- `gamma`: This is the discount factor, γ, which can be set to any value between 0 and 1. It determines the importance of future rewards. Lower gamma values will make the agent short-sighted by considering only immediate rewards, whereas higher gamma values will make the agent strive for greater long-term rewards.
- `epsilon`: This parameter epsilon, ε, determines the exploration mechanism in ε-greedy action selection and can be set between 0 to 1.
- `iter`: This parameter represents the number of repeated learning iterations the agent passes through the training dataset. It is set to 1 by default.

We saw that the result of the learning process contains the state-action table; that is, the Q-value of each state-action pair and an optimal policy with the best possible action in each state. In addition, we also got the overall reward for the policy.

See also

To find out more about other RL algorithms, such as SARSA and GQ, that have been implemented on an arcade learning environment, please go to `https://arxiv.org/pdf/1410.8620.pdf`.

Cliff walking using RL

By now, you should be aware of the framework of RL. In this recipe, we will implement a real-world application of the `gridworld` environment in RL. This problem can be represented as a grid that's 4x12 in size. The episodes start in the lower-left state, with a goal state at the bottom right of the grid. Going left, right, up, and down are the only possible actions at any state. The states labeled *C* in the lower part of the grid are cliffs. Any transition into these states will incur a high negative reward of -100 and send the agent instantly back to the starting state, *S*. For the goal state, *G*, the reward is 0, while it's -1 for all the transitions except the goal state and cliff.

The following image shows the navigation matrix for the cliff walking problem:

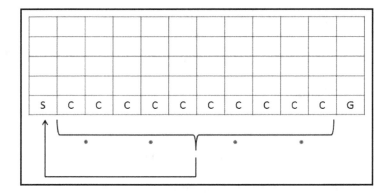

Let's proceed and solve this navigation problem using RL.

Getting ready

In this recipe, we will use the `reinforcelearn` package to get the data from the built-in environment known as **cliff walking**. This environment is inherited from the `gridworld` environment.

We will perform model-free RL using the `ReinforcementLearning` package:

```
library(reinforcelearn)
library(ReinforcementLearning)
```

In the next section, we will create an environment that represents the cliff walking problem.

How to do it...

Let's create an environment that represents our problem of cliff walking:

1. Let's start by loading the cliff walking environment using
   the makeEnvironment() function:

   ```
   env = makeEnvironment("cliff.walking")
   env
   ```

   The following screenshot shows the description of the cliff walking environment:

```
<CliffWalking>
  Inherits from: <Gridworld>
  Public:
    action.names: 0 1 2 3
    action.space: Discrete
    actions: 0 1 2 3
    clone: function (deep = FALSE)
    discount: 1
    done: FALSE
    episode: 0
    episode.return: 0
    episode.step: 0
    initial.state: 36
    initialize: function (...)
    n.actions: 4
    n.states: 48
    n.step: 0
    previous.state: NULL
    reset: function ()
    resetEverything: function ()
    reward: NULL
    rewards: -1 -1 -1 -1 -1 -1 -1 -1 -1 -1 -1 -1 -1 -1 -1 -1 -1 -1 ...
    state: 36
    state.space: Discrete
    states: 0 1 2 3 4 5 6 7 8 9 10 11 12 13 14 15 16 17 18 19 20 21  ...
    step: function (action)
    terminal.states: 47
    transitions: 1 1 0 0 0 0 0 0 0 0 0 0 0 0 0 0 0 0 0 0 0 0 0 0 0 0  ...
    visualize: function ()
  Private:
    reset_: function (env)
    step_: function (env, action)
    visualize_: function (env)
```

2. Next, we create a function that will query the environment with random actions and get the observational sequence data:

```
# Creating the function to query the environment
sequences <- function(iter,env){
 actions <- env$actions
 data <- data.frame(matrix(ncol = 4, nrow = 0))
 colnames(data) <- c("State", "Action", "Reward","NextState")
 env$reset()
 for(i in 1:iter){
 current_state <- env$state
 current_action <- floor(runif(1,0,4))
 current_reward <- env$step(current_action)$reward
 next_state_iter <- env$step(current_action)$state
 iter_data <- cbind("State" = current_state,"Action" =
current_action,"Reward"=current_reward,"NextState" =
next_state_iter)
 data <- rbind(data,iter_data)
 if(env$done == "TRUE"){
 break;
 }
 }
 return(data)
}
```

Now, let's get the data from the function we defined in the preceding code block:

```
iter <- 1000
observations = sequences(iter,env)
cols.name <- c("State","Action","NextState")
observations[cols.name] <-
 sapply(observations[cols.name],as.character)
sapply(observations, class)

# Displaying first 20 records
head(observations,20)
```

The following screenshot shows a few records from the data that was generated:

	State	'character'
	Action	'character'
	Reward	'numeric'
	NextState	'character'

State	Action	Reward	NextState
36	1	-1	36
36	3	-1	36
36	0	-1	36
36	0	-1	36
36	2	-1	12
12	3	-1	36
36	2	-1	12
12	3	-1	36
36	2	-1	12
12	1	-1	14
14	3	-1	38
38	3	-100	36
36	1	-1	36
36	1	-1	36
36	3	-1	36
36	1	-1	36

3. Using the sample observational data we generated in the previous step, we can solve our problem using the ReinforcementLearning() function. We customize the learning behavior of the agent by specifying a control object, where we set the parameter choices for the learning rate alpha, the discount factor gamma, and the exploration greediness epsilon:

```
control <- list(alpha = 0.2, gamma = 0.4, epsilon = 0.1)

# Perform RL
model <- ReinforcementLearning(data = observations, s = "State", a
= "Action", r = "Reward",
  s_new = "NextState", iter = 1, control = control)
```

Now, we print the learned state-action table, which contains the Q-value of each state-action pair:

```
print(model)
```

The following table shows the Q-value table for each state-action pair:

```
State-Action function Q
             0            1            2            3
X36 -1.5953639  -1.5952462  -1.4948993  -1.5949936
X37  0.0000000   0.0000000 -20.0000000   0.0000000
X38  0.0000000 -20.0000000 -36.1893567 -49.0059376
X24 -1.4648553  -1.3324273  -1.4812546  -1.4917518
X26 -1.3897756  -0.9741327  -1.3121494  -1.5148258
X28 -0.8636740  -0.8293248  -0.7959076  -1.3823701
X0  -1.5642927  -1.4662367  -1.5676150  -1.5102539
X2  -1.5380473  -1.2780173  -1.4251813  -1.3349818
X12 -1.4644123  -1.2590694  -1.5630369  -1.5862153
X30 -0.9595646  -0.2000000  -0.2288000  -0.5727028
X4  -1.3953639  -0.9776434  -1.3279273  -0.9610399
X14 -1.2198423  -0.8657823  -1.1166604  -0.7378560
X32  0.0000000   0.0000000   0.0000000  -0.3169141
X6  -1.0338219  -0.5904000  -0.7425920  -0.6064000
X16 -0.7560023  -0.3600000  -0.4278656   0.0000000
X8  -0.6791040   0.0000000  -0.6723200   0.0000000
X18 -0.2000000   0.0000000  -0.2288000   0.0000000

Policy
X36 X37 X38 X24 X26 X28  X0  X2 X12 X30  X4 X14 X32  X6 X16  X8 X18
"2" "0" "0" "1" "1" "2" "1" "1" "1" "1" "3" "3" "0" "1" "3" "1" "1"

Reward (last iteration)
[1] -1693
```

The optimal policy is given in the Q-value table.

How it works...

In *step 1*, we created the **cliff walking** environment using the `makeEnvironment()` function from the `reinforcelearn` library. This environment belongs to the `gridworld` class. In *step 2*, we created a customized function to query the cliff walking environment and get the sample observational data. The `step()` method of the `env()` function takes an action as the input argument and returns a list with the state, reward, and done as the output. Once the observation sequence data was generated, we used the `ReinforcementLearning()` function to make the agent learn an optimal policy based on this data in the last step.

There's more...

In many RL problems, exploring the actions to formulate an optimal policy can be costly. **Experience replay** is a technique that's used to make the agents reuse past experiences. This technique enables fast convergence by replaying already observed state transitions as new observations in the environment. Experience replay requires sample sequences comprised of states, actions, and rewards as input data. These transitions make the agent learn a state-action function and an optimal policy for all the states in the input data. This policy can also be applied for validation purposes or to improve the current policy iteratively. To implement experience replay in R, you need to pass an existing RL model as an argument to the `ReinforcementLearning()` function.

Let's get 100 new data samples from the cliff walking environment:

```
new_observations = sequences(100,env)
cols.name <- c("State","Action","NextState")
new_observations[cols.name] <-
sapply(new_observations[cols.name],as.character)
sapply(new_observations, class)
head(new_observations)
```

The following screenshot shows a few records from the new observational data:

State	'character'
Action	'character'
Reward	'numeric'
NextState	'character'

State	Action	Reward	NextState
36	2	-1	12
12	2	-1	0
0	1	-1	2
2	2	-1	2
2	0	-1	0
0	2	-1	0

Now, we provide our existing RL model, which we created in the *How to do it...* section of this recipe, as an argument to update the existing policy.

The following screenshot shows the Q-value table for each state-action pair, after implementing experience replay:

```
State-Action function Q
            X0          X1          X2          X3
24   -1.1096681   -1.0985934   -1.1113893  -1.1124119
26   -1.0924338   -1.0325305   -1.1120072  -1.1123957
28   -0.9840692   -0.7796008   -1.1051685  -1.0663833
29    0.0000000    0.0000000    0.0000000  -0.7325490
30   -0.5651880   -0.8773772    0.0000000  -1.0066913
0    -1.1109654   -1.1101782   -1.1109736  -1.1097649
32   -0.8393290   -0.5748472   -0.8657922  -0.6671089
2    -1.1129358   -1.1059532   -1.1101509  -1.1022497
10   -0.2995810   -0.2972000    0.0000000  -0.6556262
33    0.0000000   -0.6556262    0.0000000   0.0000000
11   -0.6556262   -1.0067198   -1.0423613  -0.7520509
34   -0.5449394   -0.6900636    0.0000000   0.0000000
4    -1.1084350   -1.0618690   -1.1059733  -1.0732534
12   -1.1073482   -1.0750293   -1.1110217  -1.1108705
35   -0.6556262    0.0000000   -0.9214708  -0.3520000
5     0.0000000   -0.6556262    0.0000000  -0.6556262
6    -1.0792958   -0.9430099   -0.9793951  -0.6938900
14   -1.1012670   -1.0530209   -1.1042439  -0.7551120
36   -1.1107382   -1.1107402   -1.1074477  -1.1107363
37    0.0000000  -77.6845798  -66.1043617   0.0000000
7    -0.8814067    0.0000000    0.0000000   0.0000000
38  -28.1128567    0.0000000  -66.0891457   0.0000000
8    -0.3107360   -0.8214766   -0.7964146  -0.9617286
16   -0.8003083   -0.6900636   -0.9445578  -0.8828708
9    -0.6556262    0.0000000    0.0000000   0.0000000
18   -0.6850296    0.0000000   -0.1065988   0.0000000
40  -65.6268120  -65.9877760    0.0000000   0.0000000

Policy
    24    26    28    29    30     0    32     2    10    33    11    34     4    12    35     5
  "X1"  "X1"  "X1"  "X0"  "X2"  "X3"  "X1"  "X3"  "X2"  "X0"  "X0"  "X2"  "X1"  "X1"  "X1"  "X0"
     6    14    36    37     7    38     8    16     9    18    40
  "X3"  "X3"  "X2"  "X0"  "X1"  "X1"  "X0"  "X1"  "X1"  "X1"  "X2"

Reward (last iteration)
[1] -95
```

In the preceding screenshot, we can see that the updated policy yielded a higher overall reward compared to the previous policy.

Other Books You May Enjoy

If you enjoyed this book, you may be interested in these other books by Packt:

Advanced Deep Learning with R
Bharatendra Rai

ISBN: 978-1-78953-877-9

- Learn how to create binary and multi-class deep neural network models
- Implement GANs for generating new images
- Create autoencoder neural networks for image dimension reduction, image denoising and image correction
- Implement deep neural networks for performing efficient text classification
- Learn to define a recurrent convolutional network model for classification in Keras
- Explore best practices and tips for performance optimization of various deep learning models

R Deep Learning Essentials - Second Edition
Mark Hodnett, Joshua F. Wiley

ISBN: 978-1-78899-289-3

- Build shallow neural network prediction models
- Prevent models from overfitting the data to improve generalizability
- Explore techniques for finding the best hyperparameters for deep learning models
- Create NLP models using Keras and TensorFlow in R
- Use deep learning for computer vision tasks
- Implement deep learning tasks, such as NLP, recommendation systems, and autoencoders

Leave a review - let other readers know what you think

Please share your thoughts on this book with others by leaving a review on the site that you bought it from. If you purchased the book from Amazon, please leave us an honest review on this book's Amazon page. This is vital so that other potential readers can see and use your unbiased opinion to make purchasing decisions, we can understand what our customers think about our products, and our authors can see your feedback on the title that they have worked with Packt to create. It will only take a few minutes of your time, but is valuable to other potential customers, our authors, and Packt. Thank you!

Index

R

www.ingramcontent.com/pod-product-compliance
Lightning Source LLC
Chambersburg PA
CBHW080622060326
40690CB00021B/4788